THE PATH BEYOND SORROW

SWAMI CHIDANANDA

Published By
THE DIVINE LIFE SOCIETY
P.O. SHIVANANDANAGAR—249 192
Distt. Tehri-Garhwal, U.P., Himalayas, India

Price]   1991   [Rs. 40/-

Third Edition: 1991
(5,000 Copies)

Printed out of the magnanimous donation of L.H. Varma
Public Charitable Trust, Annapurna Farms,
Powai, Bombay—400 076
(1000 Copies)

ISBN 81-7052-078-9

Published by Swami Krishnananda for The Divine Life Society,
Shivanandanagar, and printed by him at the Yoga-Vedanta Forest
Academy Press, P.O. Shivanandanagar, Distt. Tehri-Garhwal,
U.P., India

PUBLISHERS' NOTE

We have great pleasure in releasing this beautiful volume of sixteen lectures by Sri Swami Chidanandaji Maharaj, our revered President, on the eve of his 75th Birthday, which falls on the 24th September, 1991.

In a way, these lectures are the outcome of the holy Satsankalpa of His Holiness Sri Swami Sivanandaji Maharaj, who deputed his foremost disciple Swami Chidananda to the West, to convey personally his message of Divine Life to aspiring seekers.

Thirty years have passed since these talks were delivered, but their meaning and relevance are as valid today as they were at the time they were delivered. Also, the teachings and guidance contained in these lectures are universal in scope and intensely practical in their approach. It is our earnest hope that this small volume will help in its own way to further the right understanding of the timeless message of spiritual life.

—THE DIVINE LIFE SOCIETY

पूज्य श्री स्वामी चिदानन्द जी महाराज

स्वामी श्री सहजानन्द सरस्वती

AUTHOR'S PREFACE

Beloved Immortal Self! Rays of the Eternal Light Divine! It gives me great happiness to write this little preface to the series of lectures included in this volume. All these lectures, with the exception of the talk "Worship of God as Mother Divine", were delivered by me in the year 1960 in Canada where I went as a pesonal representative of my holy Master Sri Swami Sivananda to carry India's message of Yoga and Vedanta to the West.

Gurudev Swami Sivananda was revered all over India as one of its foremost spiritual leaders and was known in most of the world as a spiritual awakener *par excellence* and a friend of all mankind who tirelessly broadcast for more than thirty years the·universal truth of ethical and spiritual idealism.

In the West, there are many misconceptions about Yoga. They know not what is real Yoga. Most of them think that assuming certain physical postures is Yoga. Though there are many books on Yoga, yet there is a great urge in the West to know more about the inner aspect of Yoga. In these talks, I have made an attempt to put before the spiritual seekers (especially those in the West) the truth about Yoga as understood by me in the light of my holy Master's teachings and in the light of my own experience. I do hope that this small attempt on my part will help to dispel many popular misconceptions about Yoga and put the whole subject in the proper perspective.

Yoga is an exact science. If you define Yoga in the simplest term, it is the steady movement of the individual

v

sout towards the Supreme Soul. Yoga is a steady ascent to the Divine. Yoga transforms one's lower nature into the Divine Nature. The practice of Yoga confers upon one radiant health, happiness, peace and tranquillity of mind.

Humanity is one great family. The different races and nations have all made valid contributions to the progress of humanity. Success achieved in different countries in various fields ultimately serve the progress of all mankind.

The glory of India is its Yoga and Vedanta. India's contribution to the world is its spiritual idealism. Yoga and Vedanta are universal in their scope. They are the property of all mankind. All humanity, now and in the years to come, may usefully draw inspiration from the wisdom of the ancient seers.

It is by bringing about a greater exchange of ideas between nations that we shall be able to reach a deeper understanding of the overall problem of human suffering and misery. Under harmonious conditions, the state of man will be characterised by peace and brotherhood rather than by hatred and bloodshed. Unity of God-head in all creation is the fact of life. It is my earnest hope that this book entitled *The Path Beyond Sorrow* will show the seekers the spiritual path and take them beyond sorrow and bestow upon them true peace and happiness in life.

In closing, I wish to record my deep appreciation and thanks for the loving services rendered by my good friends, Bill Eilers, Carol Sheldan, Rosalind Dibblee and many others who organised my lectures at the beautiful Coronation Hall at the Y.M.C.A., Vancouver. B.C., Canada.

The talk on "Worship of God as Mother Divine" was delivered by me at the special request of many friends in Durban who were deeply horrified at the prevalent custom of animal sacrifices in their community.

The Vancouver talks were tape-recorded by Carol Sheldan who also transcribed them. My thanks to her for this labour of love. Also, my grateful thanks to Swami Vimalananda and Sri N. Ananthanarayanan who gave their invaluable time to go through the entire manuscript and bring it to this final shape.

May the blessings of Satgurudev Swami Sivananda be on each and every one of those who contributed in one way or the other to the publication of this volume.

Sivananda Ashram   — *Swami Chidananda*
September 24th, 1975

CONTENTS

THE PATH BEYOND
SORROW

1. BLISS IS WITHIN

Beloved Immortal Atman! I deem it a great pleasure and blessedness that God has given me this unique opportunity of being of some service to you, seeking and aspiring souls upon this earth-plane, and for this privilege I thank Him who is the Indweller of you all, the Source of our very existence, the all-pervading Presence enveloping this very universe, who is amongst us invisibly even at this moment and who blesses us.

The Path Beyond Sorrow is the title that suggested itself to me by chance, when I saw a little booklet of quotations from various sources — little sayings from different scriptures about the problem of the human being. Actually, it could very well have been worded *The Path to God*, for it does not require to be told that the ultimate cause of all sorrow is that we have forgotten our eternal link with the perennial source of infinite joy, of never-ending happiness. Cutting ourselves from one who is the granter of supreme bliss, who is more than all the happiness of the entire universe, we naturally feel that separation. We feel deprived of that experience which He is. Bliss is in the Eternal Reality, that great Truth which alone is changeless, timeless, is for ever and real. Deprived of our living contact with that Bliss, separation is experienced as sorrow. That only source of true happiness being cut out of our life in a living way, we quest after happiness.

It is a paradoxical situation — happiness being sought in all directions except in that one where it is to be found definitely and unfailingly.

Pleasure Is Not Happiness

When we observe life on the human plane, what do we see? Everyone is in constant quest of true happiness. Happiness is the quest of smiles; we have concealed sighs and sorrows, much grief and disappointment. Why? Why is this phenomenon observed everywhere in the world? This question has been pondered over, has been investigated. And we have been answered. With the dawn of discrimination, we come to realise that we have done something very foolish, because we have missed the path which leads to happiness and strayed off into the by-paths of pleasures. Happiness is one thing; mere pleasure is another. Missing the path to happiness and wandering off into the by-paths of pleasures, we are, as it were, lost beings wandering in a jungle where we do not know the correct direction to take, the correct path to pursue, to reach the destination.

Why did we miss our way? Why this wandering in search of true happiness on the part of all people and their seeming inability to find that after which they quest? It is because the great majority of them never make the right start. Before starting on the search for happiness, one never gets clear as to what is the nature of this happiness one is after and wherein does it lie. Without knowing the destination, without knowing exactly what we wish to obtain, we have started this seeking just because that has been the pattern into which we are born. We are born into a world where all beings everywhere around us are going after something, behaving in a certain way, and we think, "I am born among people living like this and I also have to live like this"; and so that pattern has become an automatic pattern with everyone. We are born into a way of life. We have entered into a current which leads us just where it has been leading the people here from time immemorial — into a whirlpool of disappointments, tears, disillusionments, pains and sufferings which are inevitable in this embodied state upon this earth-plane. Pleasures can never bring true happiness, because the very nature of pleasure is that it is an experience derived from contacts with sense-objects; and quite naturally, it partakes of the imperfections that are inherent in the sense-objects.

All objects are conditioned in space and time. They are neither permanent nor perfect. They are full of defects, they change, they pass away, and they give experiences which are mixed, which are not unalloyed. All pleasures are imperfect, because they spring out of objects which are themselves imperfect. These sense experiences are of very doubtful value and they are mixed with various side-effects. Every contact-born sense experience inevitably has bound up with it a reaction. If you are eating something very tasty beyond your limits, even as you are tasting it, there is a fear that perhaps tomorrow you will have to take a pill or a dose. Every sense experience has a reaction which brings in anxiety and lack of peace of mind. In the ultimate analysis, these sense experiences turn out to be purely negative experiences; they do not deserve the name of pleasure or happiness at all. They are not positive experiences at all.

Man's Triune Nature

Man is a being partaking of a triune nature. As an intelligent human being you have, at the same time, a part which is very base in its expression and full of gross propensities — desire, passion, sensuality, greed, anger, blindness. This is more or less on the level of the brute existence, though it is an inevitable part of the human being — a gross, sensual, animalistic nature. Man is a thinking animal, and it is said that he is essentially an animal having the same urges, the same sensual drives as the sub-human species, but endowed with the superior faculty of rationality — thought — intelligent thought, selective and discriminative thought. That is what makes you a human being, but the physical part of you is animal. Then you have within yourself your true, essential being which is totally forgotten, totally neglected, never heeded, crowded into a corner and entirely overcome by the rational human aspects and the base, gross, animalistic aspects of your being. This three-fold nature goes to make up what you yourself know as "I".

The Mental Ferment

That particular element in you which makes you human is the mind. It is a doubtful bestowal by God upon the individual soul. It is not a too happy thing to have, for, rationality and intelligence, though no doubt good, are for the most part never utilized, never properly exercised as they ought to be. In most people, intelligence is not exercised at all. And in those people who do exercise it, it is usually the co-operative partner to sensual man for devising ways and means of satisfying the senses, of feeding all the cravings of the senses. The human mind, the intellectual operation of which is a part of its function, is characterized by never-ending desires. The mind is never still, even for a single moment, except for the short time when you sink into the deep-sleep state. Except for this period, the mind is constantly active and in a state of ferment. You are not aware of this ferment, because you are constantly kept active through it. Most of it is concerned with the immediate fulfilment of desires and, therefore, you are not aware of it. If you try to check the outgoing activities of your mind for a time and try to watch your mind, then the terrible nature of its constant activity—constant irritation and restlessness due to desire—becomes apparent and you know what a thing you have in the mind. This desire-filled and ever fluctuating mind is the root cause for going outward in search of impermanent sense pleasures.

The Mechanics of Sense Satisfaction

What happens is this. There arises a desire, a craving is created, and then you are urged to go after some sense-object in order to satisfy the craving and you feel that it has been enjoyable. You tell yourself: "I have felt pleasure. I have enjoyed the sense-object". Actually, this so-called experience which you have undergone is not a positive experience of enjoyment at all. It is just an illusion. The actual experience, in fact, if you examine it, is this—the experience you get at the end of an activity to obtain a sense-object is but the momentary quiescence that ensues in the mind as a result of the corresponding desire-urge having subsided for the time being. When desire arose and craving filled the mind, the mind was thrown into a violent state of restlessness; it lost its peace, its serenity and calmness. As long as the craving was there, the mind was restless, was agitated, and when that object was obtained, the sense took it in. It may have been the sense of taste or the sense of sight or hearing or touch or smell—the sense took it in. And the craving having been satisfied, the agitation or restlessness in the mind, which this craving originally caused, subsided for the time being. And you think, when you vicariously superimpose this fine feeling (this momentary restfulness due to the subsiding of the sense-craving) upon your sense-contact with the object, that you have derived this fine feeling from the object. The fact is that this experience of sense-satisfaction has not been derived from the object. The experience you have derived is the negative phenomenon of having got rid of an agitation in the mind. So, when you get rid of an agitation in the mind, you think you have enjoyed a positive experience, but it is just the negative experience of getting rid of a certain fire within, namely, the agitation of a craving.

Actually, it is a peaceful mind, an unagitated mind, that is the condition of true happiness. And an unagitated mind is never in one's possession, unless one realizes that all experiences born out of the contact of objects outside of ourselves are negative, having no positive value. The reflected experience they give to the mind is only a cessation of the mental craving and agitation for the time being; and because there is a close tie-in, a coincidence, between the sense contacting the sense-object and the immediate sense of satisfaction, we think that these two have a connection. Actually, it is because the mind has now once again obtained its calmness that you are immediately put into a state of satisfaction.

Supposing you have been exposed on an ice-cold winter's day, immediately, you come into a room and warm yourself before a fire, take a warm drink, cover yourself with a hot blanket, and say, "Oh, such wonderful pleasure now!" Actually, what has happened is that the discomfort, the painful experience of cold, has been removed by these three things—warming yourself, covering yourself, and taking a cup of something hot—and you think this is a pleasure. But for someone who is already in the room and has not had the negative experience of the cold, these things would not hold the special value which they held for you, because in your case the cessation of pain was taken to be pleasure. If you use your intellect and analyse all the contact-born experiences a human being goes through, you will find that they are all just the removal of some painful experience or other, though man deludes himself into thinking that they are of a positive nature. When you feel very hot, to take a plunge seems a refreshing experience; or to go to a soda fountain and take a cold milk-shake or Coca Cola seems wonderful. It is because you have come out of a very hot place where you have been uncomfortable and perhaps perspiring. When you take the cold drink, it seems wonderful; but what has actually happened is that for the time being you have removed the painful experience of heat and perspiration. Every experience obtained from contact with objects outside of ourselves partakes of this nature and, together with the momentary removal of the painful experience immediately preceding it, it also contains within itself the power to give you certain positive reactions. You may sit down to a fine dinner and enjoy it. What has actually happened is: it was preceded by the painful experience of hunger, and by eating the dinner, you have satisfied your hunger and you think that your sense of fulfilment has actually come from the food which you have eaten at the table. While the dinner appealed to you because you were hungry, to another person who was not hungry and felt no desire for food, it would not have given pleasure. He would have turned away from it saying, "No, thank you. I don't want anything". For him there is no pleasure, as he has not come with that painful experience called 'hunger' with which you drew near to the table. If that painful experience had been in him also, he would have enjoyed the dinner equally. So, the so-called pleasurable experiences of this world are nothing but the removal of painful experiences immediately preceding them.

This is the very nature of contact-born pleasure. Lord Krishna, who is one of the Great Messengers and who graced this earth, says in His universal gospel, the *Gita*, "All pleasures, O man, contact-born, are the source of pain". And, what are our pleasures if not contact-born? Contact of the tongue with a tasty dish, contact of the hand with some object pleasant to touch, contact of our eyes with something beautiful to look at, contact of our ears with sweet, melodious and endearing things to hear, contact of our nose with nice and fragrant things — these are our pleasurable experiences. If unpleasant things are given to us, we are immediately thrown into a state of sorrow. With pleasant objects contacted by the senses, once we become attached to them, the removal or separation of those objects (which have become dear to us due to our becoming attached to them) brings misery, pain. Also, sometimes, the very object which attracted us in one state, when it changes its condition, becomes an object of pain. Thus, to be brought into contact with things which are not pleasing—that is sorrow; to be separated from things which are pleasant and pleasing— that is sorrow. And, if a thing which was pleasant changes its nature, that also becomes sorrow. So, all contacts with outside objects have within themselves the seeds of sorrow. They are the potent source of latent sorrow, and also, they have a beginning and an end. Therefore, the man of wisdom is never happy with them. He does not take pleasure in these outside things, because he has analysed and known the nature of these things; and he says, "No, all contact-born experiences are negative. They are not positive experiences at all. Also, they are accompanied by reaction. They have a beginning and an end". Objects themselves are imperfect; therefore, the experience gained from these objects is also imperfect, because you cannot have a perfect experience from a thing which is not perfect. Therefore, a wise one does not take delight in these things.

Instances of Irrational Rationality

How many are wise? How many use the intellect rationally? We have to analyse the objects of this universe. We have to see them, not as they appear to be, but as they truly are and analyse the experiences from the objects as they really are and not as we perceive them in a state of non-discrimination. We have to enquire. This intelligence which God has given us we must use; and use rationally, not with bias.

If you use this intellect with bias, since it is already in league with the senses, is already a slave to the sensual urges, it will give you wrong conclusions only. It cannot give you the right conclusions. Your rationality may be real and correct, but at the same time, it can be a very 'irrational rationality'—a sort of pseudo-rationality. It seems paradoxical, but there are very funny stories told in the ancient Indian *Puranas* to bring out how a person can use his intelligence, yet use it foolishly. They give the example of a very typical being—a young man—who had this type of intellect. He went to cut wood and climbed a tree and went out on a large branch and started cutting the branch. He observed it and said, "The branch is thickest where it is nearest to the main trunk of the tree; and it tapers off toward the end and that part is thinner than the part on which I am sitting. So, I shall get more wood if I cut it off nearest to the trunk of the tree". He turned 'around to sit on the thinner portion in order to get more wood by cutting more closely to the trunk of the tree. Someone came by and called to the man, saying, "What are you doing? It is foolish the way you are cutting that branch". But the man replied, "It is no business of yours. I know what I am doing. I have given it careful thought and calculation. I don't want to be fooled by this tree. I want to take as much wood as possible". So he hacked on and on until the branch came down and he with it. He was a person who did use his intelligence. He figured it out and he thought that he would get more wood this way and he was quite correct, but there seems to have been something that was not at all rational. This characterises a great many types of intelligence.

At another time, a man was asked to look after his very old and senile grandmother. India, like all tropics, is a land of mosquitoes and flies, and the man was diligently fanning his grandmother. But many flies persisted in sitting upon her, even though the man fanned vigorously. He finally said, "Look here, do not bother my grandmother," and continued fanning her vigorously. Eventually he became extremely annoyed with the per-

sistence of the flies and said, "Look here, if you are not
going to obey me, I am going to teach you a lesson"; and
after a few more moments of vigorous fanning and the
equally vigorous persistence of the flies, he looked over
and saw a wooden club and he picked up this club and
said, "Do you flies think you are more intelligent than
I?" So saying, and carefully aiming the club at one fly,
he smacked the fly and brained his old grandmother in
the process! Most of us are clever, very clever, but we
start with fundamental errors. The man should have
known whether the life of his grandmother was more important or the killing of the fly. But he did not, and we
laugh at him. At the same time, we make the same error
of judgement.

The Tumult of the Senses Vs. The Music of the Soul

It is peace of mind which is the condition prerequisite for the experience of true happiness. Is that not
more important than the removal of a little restlessness
and craving, a little agitation caused by desire? Which is
the more important? You may say: "If desires come, we
have to satisfy them. That is the way to remove them and
that is the way to get pleasures". So saying, you remove
the 'fly' of desire rather than protect the 'grandmother'
of true peace of mind by which alone you can find happiness. Real happiness comes out of peace. When the
mind is tranquil and serene, peace, bliss wells up from
within you. You do not have to manufacture happiness,
for it does not lie outside of you. Happiness is not in
changeful, perishable objects which are merely material.
True happiness is right here where you are sitting. You
are yourself happiness. Happiness is your essential nature. That aspect of your being which completely
transcends your sense nature and your mental desire-na-
ture—that third aspect of your true being, your real nature, is, in one word, bliss—pure bliss. If you want me
to define what you are, I say you are pure, unalloyed, ab-

solute bliss. That is the stuff of the soul. The soul is bliss; it is ecstasy, peerless joy. Even as this table is made of wood, even as your very clothes are made of wool or cotton, even as the very stuff of candy is sugar—the very stuff and fabric of your true nature, the true "I" deep within you, in the very centre of your consciousness, that is bliss. You are your Self, the Atma. You are Spirit, a never-ending, perennial fountain of spontaneous, self-existent joy and happiness. You are not this body and mind and intellect.

The East views the individual being in a totally different light from the West. The West says, "Man is an animal endowed with a superior faculty called intelligence". The East says, "Man is a glorious, ever-perfect spiritual entity, full of light, full of bliss, and possessing an inferior faculty called intelligence or mind which is his servant, which is his instrument". Mind is but the medium that God has given you so that the joy, the beauty and perfection of your Self may be expressed, unfolded, made manifest upon this earth-plane, but you have made a travesty of your life. The normal human being lives a life of prostitution, by which I mean, he totally forgets and neglects his glorious spiritual nature and prostitutes all his energies in satisfying the animal within him. The pattern of his whole life is just a constant effort to satisfy the sensual urges of the animal within him. Nice things to collect, nice things to wear, nice things to see, nice things to enjoy—pleasure, pleasure, pleasure—and happiness is destroyed, as it were, in a constant round of pleasures. There is so much noise through the tumult of the senses that the music of the soul, though it is always there, just gets killed completely.

The great joy of my message to you is: nothing can destroy this happiness, because it is imperishable. In your true nature you are indestructible, you are imperishable. So, the joy that you are is also imperishable, indestructible; nothing can touch it. No sorrow can penetrate that exalted realm where you dwell as pure bliss, right within the very centre of your being, the innermost core of your consciousness where dwells the true "I".

Bliss Is Thy Nature: Bliss Is Thy Heritage

This name and form, this Mr. So-and-So, this Mrs. So-and-So, this is not the true 'you'. It is just a personality superimposed upon your true being by your parents. They gave you a name. They called you 'this' and they called you 'that', but this name-form personality is not the true you. Changeless from childhood, into youth, into adulthood, into middle age, into old age is that "I" which is within you. It was within you when you were an infant; it was within you when you were a child running here and there; it was within you when you began to grow. It was within you when you were an adult and lost your peace of mind by going after pleasurable objects; it was within you when you became weighed down with the responsibility of a householder's life; and it will be within you when you come to experience old age. This unchanging "I" within—try to find out what it is. Give yourself a chance of turning within, a chance of stilling the mind and not allowing it to go externally towards objects. And then look within and try to find in silence, in a little peace, the "I", and you will find that the real "I" within is peace, bliss, all-light, all-fullness. There, there is no need, no want. You do not feel any lack of sufficiency there. It is all-full and no desire permeates that sacred realm, for it is an experience of all-fullness. Every one of you can possess this supreme experience of all-fullness, all-joy and peace right now, right here; it does not have to be manufactured. You do not have to go out of yourself somewhere in order to reach that blessed state. It is your birthright. It is your privilege and prerogative to claim. Stop being a slave to the senses and stop this ceaseless running outside towards petty and imperfect objects and be silent with your Self and know that you are bliss, know that you are fullness. Rise above desire and be aware of your true nature which is incomparable bliss, which is indescribable happiness.

This incomparable bliss is within the reach of every single human being, from the very fact of your being a human being. It is your claim. It is your heritage from your Divine origin. You are all from that perennial source of Infinite Bliss which people call "God", which people call "The Supreme", "The Reality", "The Truth", "The Spirit". Call It what you may; approach It however you will; worship It in whatever way you want to—it does not matter. But, know that It is right here within you: that perennial and changeless source of ineffable and indescribable bliss and joy. It requires nothing to attain, only willingness on your part to give away that which is petty, that which is paltry, and to aspire for and seek that which is incomparable, which is peerless—the "I" within you which is your true essential nature.

The first condition is to make use of your intelligence and try not to be deluded by the attractive objects of the senses. They will lead you on a merry-go-round, a wild goose chase which never ends, for pleasures, you see, can never be subdued by satisfaction. The enjoyment of sense pleasures tends only to accentuate the desire for them. Enjoyment intensifies craving. You cannot put an end to desires that way. You can put an end to them only by awakening to a higher sense of discrimination and knowing the sense-objects for what they are worth, saying, "I, who have been made in the spiritual image of my Divine Parent, will disdain to go after these paltry things which are like bones thrown before a dog. I am the son of the Emperor of emperors and I shall claim my priceless heritage and not go after paltry things". And, if you do that, if you discriminate and reject that which is paltry, you become heir to that which is of supreme splendour.

Inner renunciation implies discrimination between what is really happiness and what is merely an appearance, and rejection of that which is not of the essential nature of happiness and turning away from it mentally. Mental renunciation born of discrimination—that is the secret of this spiritual quest. That is the starting point of the path beyond sorrow. In one of the greatest *Upanishads*, the teaching comes to us: "O man, before each human being there always present themselves two paths—one which is merely attractive and seemingly pleasant and the other which leads towards the good, towards your true welfare". The unthinking one easily succumbs to the route of that which is pleasant and seemingly attractive; and thus he misses his own welfare, his own good. Whereas, the one who is wise, with discrimination awakened within him, examines the two paths and finds out the true nature of the apparently attractive and pleasant and rejects it and always takes the other path which takes him towards the good and there he finds his welfare. There he finds true happiness. This choice of paths presents itself to everyone of you, every day, always, all through your life, from the very beginning. And upon you alone will depend what path you take—whether you are lured away by that which is pleasant and apparently attractive or whether you have within you the light of discrimination which irresistibly takes you towards that which is good, which leads towards your welfare.

Your Unhappiness Is Your Own Creation

This unhappiness is your own creation. It is self-created. It is due to non-discrimination and due to your having become the slave of your own senses. And therefore, what you have yourself caused, you have it within your own power to cast aside. So, even as your sorrow has been self-caused, your happiness too can be self-obtained through your own efforts. It does not have to be self-created, because it is there already. It has only to be grasped and this is in your own hands. You are the one who has to move towards that which is awaiting you to experience it.

Develop Virtue: You Develop Happiness

How can you set about doing it? The basic thing is that happiness springs out of a life of virtue. That is what the great science of Yoga tells you. There cannot be happiness without virtue. Here I wish to make it quite plain that I am not sermonizing. Someone told me, "In the West, people do not like sermonizing. Don't sermonize". Well, I cannot completely fulfil that wish, for to some extent, this humble servant who stands before you and speaks to you at this moment does sermonize, but then, this sermonizing is of a different variety. He does not sermonize from a pedestal, but rather as someone humbler than yourself, but who has been given a message to convey and, as your servant, he presents it to you. Also, if I do sermonize, it is not that I say, "Oh, you are all sinners. You have all gone to a degenerate state". Rather I say, "Look at the glory that is already in your possession. Why don't you claim it?" I am telling you what a wonderful thing you are missing. Do not miss it! Now is the time! This unique opportunity of a human birth has been given to you to obtain something which is grand and which is glorious. Delay not! Why should you prolong your bondage because of desires? Why not assert your essential master-nature and claim that glory which is already there? This I would not call sermonizing. And when I say that virtue is the essential condition for obtaining this happiness, I just acquaint you with a great law. It is not merely a psychological law, but also a spiritual law, for virtue refines your nature. Your nature always manifests itself, expresses itself, upon a threefold plane—the plane of body, an interior plane about which you do not know (there is a plane of psychic energy within, which makes this body active, dynamic, and function), and the third plane of your mind where thoughts, ideas and desires constantly keep operating. And virtue is that factor, that force in your life, which refines your entire being on all the three planes. It refines the physical, it refines the psychic within, and it refines your mind; and it is only in a mind thus refined and made pure that steadiness, balance and absence of desire become possible.

You may try your hardest, but from a mind that is not pure, you cannot drive out desires, because mental impurity and desire are synonymous terms. Passion and impurity tend to put your entire being into a state of agitation on the three levels upon which I have commented. It is the nature of passion to agitate. Likewise, it is the very nature of purity to steady, to sustain, to strengthen and to make inward.

Therefore, it is a deep psycho-spiritual truth that the practice of virtues like purity, simplicity, truth, compassion, selflessness humility, removal of greed, and removal of envy and jealousy and prejudice brings about a slow transformation in all your nature and makes it refined, subtle and pure; and with the advent of purity, the condition of the mind undergoes a change. That mind which was restlessly plunging outward towards objects of the senses, begins to go inward, begins to develop calmness. I do not want to use the term "introverted"; actually the mind becomes inward, it is no longer filled with the tendency to become externalized. With the mind thus collected within through purity, you slowly begin to have little glimpses of the true happiness that springs from your own inner Self.

These are old-fashioned recipes, but they are the only effective recipes. One cannot be impure and hope to have happiness. One cannot cling to objects in blind delusion and attachment and yet hope to have happiness. You cannot, out of your selfishness and hardness, cause pain and sorrow to others and at the same time hope to have happiness for yourself. The more you give happiness to others, the more you get happiness. This is the law. The refinement of one's nature, the culture and purity of one's whole personality—that is the indispensable prerequisite for the dawn of happiness in one's life.

Thus, happiness is the product of selflessness, the product of negating the constant pull of the senses, the product of virtue actively practised in your everyday life. This law has always been there and it will continue to operate in human nature as long as humanity exists, and this is the only effective recipe. If you are pure, all the unhappiness that comes out of the guilt of impure living is gone. If you are simple, all the complications and frustrations arising out of a desire-ridden personality are gone. A simple life immediately relieves you from the strain of constant desires. If you are truthful, you can yourself know that the whole world of constant fear and anxiety which follows untruth is immediately gone. One untruth, and to protect it you have to repeat a dozen untruths, and then your mind is in a constant state of fear and anxiety: "If found out, what will be the result?" By sticking to truth, you totally eliminate all the fear and anxiety and unhappiness which untruth or falsehood puts you into.

Then, contentment. When you are contented, you are the richest person in the whole world. You do not have any jealousy. When you are fully contented with what you have, you do not envy others who have more than what you have. Rather, you rejoice in the good fortune of others.

The Higher Happiness of Your True Being

Thus, developing virtues is the direct way to experience happiness on the lower psychological level. But on a higher level, this is not enough. You should not be satisfied with the happiness that you get on the mental level, though even that experience you will find most exhilarating. That itself is a great gain, but still greater is the happiness that you should aim at. That greater happiness is the happiness of your true being, of your real nature, of the Spirit within, and that comes by constantly being above body, above senses, above mind and intellect. Beyond all these is the eternal, changeless, silent Witness (Consciousness) of all the changeful modes of these lower aspects of your being.

You are not the mind; the mind is your instrument. You are not the body and the senses; the body and the senses are but your external apparel. They are just your covering, your material sheath. More glorious than all, supremely transcending all, You are there within as an untouched spiritual personality which is Divinity Itself. Infinite Bliss is Its very nature. No sorrow, no fear, no desire, can ever touch It. Therefore, try to go into a little calm, silent, inward meditation every day. Feel yourself as you really are. Once you get even a moment of that experience, once you get even a little glimpse of that experience, you will never give up meditation. You may give up your eating and drinking, but you will not lose this opportunity of being silent, going inward and knowing yourself as you really are.

Inward, within yourself, lies the Path Beyond Sorrow, the path to perennial joy, the path to the real happiness in the truest sense of the term. It is an unalloyed experience of joy totally devoid of any painful reaction, of any imperfection, of even the least vestige of any material earthly blemish. It is a perfect condition of joy, full of peace, full of ineffable light and satisfaction within. And it is within the power of every one of you to tread this Path Beyond Sorrow. It does not require special qualifications. You do not have to be an aristocrat. You do not have to be a man with a fat bank balance. You do not have to have an M.A. or a doctorate degree. God, as He has made you a human being, has given you all the faculties necessary for this inward practice, for this wonderful gain of true happiness. The only condition is that the paltry has to be rejected and the glorious has to be accepted as your ideal, as the object of your quest in life, as the central seeking. Make that your goal. Make the realization of the Truth within, the God within you, your True Nature, the central goal of your life. Let all other things be secondary to it; let this quest be the main thing. You will begin to experience it, begin to get a glimpse of that joy right from the first day you start this inward quest through discrimination, through inquiry into the real nature of things, through mental renunciation of that which is paltry, and through deep faith in yourself, in your own powers to ascend unto this experience, and deep devotion to this quest, to this ideal, and daily effort through calm contemplation and meditation. This is the supreme panacea. This is the destroyer of all sorrow, all pain. This will give you the great experience here and now, not in some other state after you have passed the barrier of death. This experience has to be right here and now, in this life, so that you go out of this life gloriously, triumphantly, as a Master, laughing with joy. That should be your destiny. That should be the great purpose of your life. No fear of death. No fear of anything at all, for you are deathless by your very nature.

We have to reject only those which destroy our happiness, and when we reject these little sense pleasures and objects, we are not rejecting anything at all. On the contrary, we are doing the wisest thing, for we know them to be those factors that rob us of our happiness and, therefore, we reject them. We do not reject things of worth, but we reject only those factors that are the real enemies of true happiness, factors that stand in the way of our getting the Supreme Experience, factors that destroy the real happiness by a spurious substitute in the nature of some sense experience which is not at all genuine and which is not a positive experience at all. Establish your life, therefore, upon intelligence, common sense, true discrimination. Use intelligence in a true and rational way and know that objects do not give the Supreme Experience. So, build your life upon discrimination, constantly inquiring into what is real, what is unreal, what is perishable, what is imperishable, what is paltry and changeful and evanescent and what is true, everlasting and changeless. Thus discriminating, always move towards that which is eternal, that which is perfect, that which is enduring and real, and reject all that is of a contrary nature. That is the heroic life.

God bless you. May the Eternal Indweller shower upon you His divine grace and may all the great saints and sages of East and West, bygone as well as present, shower their blessings upon you and give you inspiration, the strength to tread this path that leads to the Supreme Blessedness, Supreme Joy, and put you in possession of this great joy right here and now in this very life. That is the sincerest wish and heart's prayer of this most humble servant of yours, a brother-seeker on the path that leads beyond sorrow to the supreme Atmic experience, to the Truth experience, to the realization of the Bliss within. May God bless you all.

2. OCCULT PHENOMENA—THEIR PLACE IN YOGA

The term "Yoga", unfortunately, has been connected with notions of strange and extraordinary experiences, mysterious occurrences and mystical powers. The term "Yogi" is popularly understood to mean not an adept in Yoga, but one capable of doing certain things which ordinary people are not able to do. In a way this is true, as a Yogi *is* capable of doing certain things which are not possible for many persons, but a Yogi should not be conceived of *merely* as one who is capable of flying through the air, going without food for months and being buried alive underground for several weeks, or of such other feats as are considered spectacular, extraordinary and unbelievable unless seen.

These notions have arisen more due to distance than anything else, for anything that is far away often seems mysterious. Also they are perhaps due to the ridiculous stories that have been spread about such feats.

The popular conception of a Yogi, though very wrong and very mistaken, is not totally without basis, but that basis has been exaggerated, exploited, magnified, taken out of its context, and given a twist which makes it appear completely different from what it is.

There is an element of phenomena in Yoga, and undeniably, there are elements of mystical experiences too; but these are not what they have been built up to be. What are the bases and what are the explanations of these phenomena? What is the attitude of Masters towards these phenomena? These are points which are not only interesting to consider; these are also important

for you, since you are all seekers, and at least one aspect
of it all is something very personal to you.

In the title of today's lecture, the subject is not just
"Occult Phenomena", but "Occult Phenomena in Yoga".
An occult phenomenon, we are told, is anything that is
hidden, not easy to observe, something secret or mystic.
And today we are concerned with a reference to these
phenomena as occurring in Yoga, to teachers and seekers
on the path of Yoga, during the practice of Yoga. Therefore, we shall try to consider this subject of occult
phenomena as related to the Yogic way of life.

Yoga Is Conscious Hastening of the Process of Evolution

First of all, it is necessary for us to have a clear conception of what the Yogic way of life is. The destiny of
the human being is evolution and we are all progressing
towards ultimate perfection, since we are all meant to
realize once again our innate divinity. However, the normal course of human evolution is very, very slow — perhaps spread over countless years and requiring many
lives, taking only a few progressive steps in each life. In
this process of taking a few forward steps in each body,
one undergoes untold suffering, untold sorrow, so much
of pain, so much of misery due to the bondage of the
body and the interplay of currents of like and dislike, of
attachment and repulsion; one undergoes all the different
experiences which this physical frame has to go
through — growth, change, decay and death. To be
brought into contact with anything that is unpleasant is
sorrow; to be removed from the contact of anything that
is pleasant is sorrow; to be deprived of that which we
want is sorrow; not to get what we desire is sorrow; and
to get that which we do not desire is sorrow; and ultimately, to part from all, that is sorrow.

The great ones pondered over this life with its
bondages and imperfections, its restlessness and peace-

lessness, its pain, suffering and sorrow. They ruminated over the various miseries characterising this earth-life and said, "No! We should not thus drag on through this earth-plane, life after life! There must be some method by which we can complete our great destined journey more quickly and find ourselves in that ultimate state of supreme blessedness and perfection".

The technique evolved to rapidly go through this process of achieving fulfilment and perfection is named "Yoga". The Yogic way of life is one that implies a great intensification of the process of evolution, since the Yogi does not want a slow, dragging process. In India, the achieving of "at-one-ment" with that wonderful Perfection (Divinity) is known as "Yoga". This then implies that if you take to this life of Yoga, you are trying to do within the short span of a given incarnation, a given embodiment, what perhaps would have taken you a thousand years or two thousand years, spread over several successive incarnations, to achieve. Therefore, Yoga means an intensification of evolution within a single life-span, or perhaps even within just a few years of a single life-span. If you look at the Yogic way of life from this angle then you will begin to understand many things which may be puzzling to you.

If a Botanist were to evolve some method in his floral laboratory whereby he could sow a seed of some fruit, have the tree growing in three months and yielding fruit in six months, it would be considered that he had accomplished a miraculous and extraordinary thing. He would doubtless become a man of the day with the whole world agog at such an accomplishment, with publications full of articles on his research and pictures of the product, and the radio and the TV carrying the story of his miracle, of what formerly took a much longer time having been accomplished, through intensification, in a relatively short period.

Yoga is intensification. During this intensified effort to pack into a short span all the experiences that the evolving individual would otherwise have had to go through over a much longer period of time, very unusual appearances, unusual phenomena, are frequently brought about. To one who does not realize what is taking place within the consciousness of the concerned individual, these things appear as extraordinary, but one who understands knows exactly why they have come about.

It is not in the lives of all seekers or all practitioners of Yoga that one comes across these phenomena, but only in the lives of those who go all out for Yoga with every cell and nerve fibre, with all their heart, mind and might, with an all-soul dedication to the life of Yoga.

Changes Upon Five Levels of the Yogi's Being

During the process of this evolution, this unfoldment, various transformations arise in the individual upon five different levels of his being. On the physical level, various changes and experiences are seen. Upon the psycho-mental level (the mind and the Prana), certain changes take place, certain abilities come in the natural course, and certain phenomena are witnessed, subjectively by some, and objectively by others. Thirdly, certain phenomena occur at the level of the astral plane which is even more interior than the psycho-mental level. Fourth, you have your spiritual level, and with spiritual unfoldment, you begin to experience many inner experiences. Here it is more subjective, and it is the seeker who is aware of what is going on, and not other people who are not able to know, for it is a still finer realm, still deeper, in the depths of his being. The fifth is the highest level of super-Consciousness. It is universal consciousness—God Consciousness—and upon this level, the phenomena that are witnessed are the true miracles as we know them. Christ operated upon this level and whatever was witnessed in His life was the manifestation of the glory and the power of this supreme level of cosmic consciousness, of Divine Consciousness. He performed the miracles not as an individual, but as a Divine Being.

So, upon all five levels of the Yogi's being, occult phenomena are witnessed. When the practice of Yoga is started in earnest, even the physical processes like the Yogic postures and breathing exercises, or a little concentrated attention on the breath in Pranayama, may bring various mystical experiences.

If one honestly tries to practise the Yogasanas (Yogic postures) and keeps on with this practice until one acquires what is known as Asanajaya or "Victory over posture", extraordinary sensations may be experienced from time to time. You may feel that you weigh a ton, that you are pressing into the earth and the earth itself is being depressed with your weight, that you are so heavy that nothing can move you from that place. At times you may feel the very opposite of this and feel feather-light (absolutely weightless) and you may not even be aware that you are sitting. Both of these experiences come when one attains Asanajaya, but they are subjective experiences. At other times, when sitting in one of the meditative poses, one may get 'jerks'; and it is not uncommon, when one of these poses is held for quite some time, for the aspirant to find himself seated several feet away from where he was at first seated. This is not actual levitation, there is no injury to the aspirant, nor is the aspirant aware of the movement. This is something that anyone who has been doing Asanas for a long time may experience in the course of a year or two. This is why many Masters ask aspirants not to sit in any high place, on boulders, etc. Rather, the aspirants are asked to sit in a room with something covering the floor.

How does this come about? In Hatha Yoga, much insistence has been placed upon purification. Yoga means "the ascending into purity". When this purification process is at work, there come about changes in the body cells, and also changes in the psychic energy through the various inner currents or channels ("Nadis" as they are called). When this happens, a new nerve current, which hitherto has been inactive, is set into motion by the prevalence of an excess of Sattva in the body, and the body reacts, and sometimes these 'jerks' are experienced.

Some Psychic Powers

On the psycho-mental level it is the very common experience of those who have done a little sincere seeking (whether they have known it by the name of "Yoga" or just been seeking and practising certain physical exercises) to find that they have developed certain abilities. The most common of these abilities or inner occult experiences is thought-reading. You may be talking to someone, and before the other person speaks, you know what that person will say. You may pick up a telephone and say something and it happens to be exactly what the person at the other end is thinking; and when talking, you anticipate the other person's conversation. You may begin to repeat what is in that person's mind. It is telepathy, but it is spontaneous rather than developed telepathy. Even when you are exercising it, you are not aware of so doing. This spontaneous telepathy just happens and it is the first and the most common of occult phenomena and is on the mental level.

The second is clairvoyance, which is also common. Many people are able to see things that are far away. In clairaudience, you may suddenly be put into a state where you are able to hear someone who is talking two hundred miles away.

The three occult phenomena of telepathy, clairvoyance and clairaudience are all upon the lowest level. When one's Prana becomes refined and one's mind becomes purified, these phenomena come naturally and often one is not aware of them, and some, even though aware of them, do not know they are extraordinary and take these powers for granted. When a thing grows very slowly and gradually in a person, that person is not conscious that it is unusual and thus takes it for granted. These three powers are the primary powers in Yoga—the primary occult phenomena in the path of Yoga—and they come much more rapidly in Yoga than in other methods.

Personal magnetism comes when your evolution goes still further and when, from the psycho-mental level, a little unfoldment of the astral level also is started; and the development of other powers begins. One may lay hands upon someone who is ill and the person becomes well. One may enter a room wherein is a person in a terrible mood, and the person gets rid of that mood. The seeker may encounter someone who is violently angry with him, about to give him abuse, and upon nearing the seeker, that person is unable to say a word and just walks away. These things that begin to develop in one—the power of healing and the power of instantly subduing a person—are on the astral level. They are powers which are not exactly on the spiritual level and they begin to develop even when you are progressing very little.

Pure Occultism Which Is Not Yoga

Here I have to tell you a fact of which you had better take serious note. The first three powers upon the mental level, the psycho-mental level, and the astral level—all these powers one can have by sheer effort. If the necessary effort, with determination, is made, one can develop them. In Yoga they come through purification, and in the second case, which I have just mentioned, they come through will-power, practice and unceasing efforts. Telepathy, clairvoyance, clairaudience, etc., are found to be actively present in certain hypnotists, practitioners of mesmerism, etc., and in some people whose lives are in no way ethical, who are not seekers and who are in no way the followers of the principles of Yoga, which principles are purity, self-control, devotion to God, faith, etc. Certain persons possessing powers such as hypnotism and mesmerism are plain and pure occultists who have made occultism their main vocation. The powers they have developed in this way do not indicate the evolution of their nature or any progress upon the spiritual line; for, if the powers are not acquired through an aspiration to realise the Truth based upon a deep and abiding faith in God as the only Reality, and as the goal and destination in life, then it is not Yoga.

Everyone of us has contact with the Cosmic Mind, for we all belong to the Cosmic Mind. Our consciousness is a part of the Cosmic Consciousness and our mind is a part of the Cosmic Mind, but the link is not there. It is broken. Why? Because we are bound up with our own ego-personality. But when we try to rise above it, the channel which connects us with the Cosmic Mind and which connects our consciousness with the Cosmic Consciousness becomes clearer and we are able to feel our oneness. When this happens, knowledge hidden from ordinary minds comes into our possession — knowledge of distant events and objects and, sometimes, even the knowledge of the future. This is due to expansion of consciousness when a certain level of development is reached and the spiritual being within is activated and the spiritual nature is awakened.

This whole projected universe has come out of the subtle elements which were the first evolutes from God. The subtle elements are Fire, Earth, Air, Water and Ether — Ether being the most subtle. These subtle elements should not be mistaken for the gross elements — fire, earth, air, water and ether as we know them — for they are the most subtle principles or the basic supraphysical primal stuff out of which the gross elements have evolved. It is not this earthly fire or earthly air or earthly water or earthly ether of which I speak, but the subtlest essence out of which these grosser manifestations have developed to make up the visible universe. The source of these gross and material elements is invisible, purely subtle, cosmic. During the course of the practice of Raja Yoga, when the Yogi reaches the stage where he is able to concentrate, meditate, and go into trance meditation all at once upon one or more of these subtle elements, then he gains mastery over these elements. He is able to travel in space at lightning speed. He is able to withstand fire or water, because he has complete mastery over these elements at their very source. This is the extraordinary phenomenon that explains the immutability of certain Yogis. Even when passing through fire and water, they seem to come through unscathed, and this is on account of the Samyama which they did upon these elements.

Playing With Kundalini Is Playing With Fire

When your spiritual practice takes the form of Kundalini Yoga and you begin the inner occult process of Hatha Yoga, then, with the rise of the power of the Kundalini from the lower mystical centres (Chakras) into the higher mystical centres, which are in the occult body of each being, there arise various extraordinary powers and experiences. Why? There are mystical spheres in the inner realm of the universe and each Chakra governs certain mystical spheres and all the phenomena of those spheres become the experience of the seeker when he ascends upon this path of Kundalini Yoga and operates upon that particular Chakra. Kundalini Yoga is something which I always condemn. In this Twentieth Century, to the vast majority of modern persons, Kundalini Yoga is unsuited. And unless one has the extraordinary good fortune of coming across a perfect Guru who has achieved his Illumination through Kundalini Yoga, I

would not advise one to go near this science at all. When
people question me about these inner centres, I invariably tell them, "It does not hurt you not to know". Some
knowledge is better left to itself and it is better not to
know. Kundalini Yoga is a violent method, a forceful
method, a method to try to force into awakening certain
dormant powers. Yoga is a method of intensified evolution; and Kundalini Yoga is a still greater intensification
of this method, and therefore, it is dangerous. It is playing with fire.

In all paths of Yoga—whether in the Yoga of pure
love for God (through prayer, through faith, through
worship, through the Divine Name, devotion and surrender) or in the Yoga of the intellect (the philosophical
Yoga of rationality, of hearing and reflecting over the
words of the Guru and deep meditation upon the great
Truth) or in Raja Yoga (the Eight-fold Ascent of a virtuous life, daily religious observances, steadiness of pose,
control of breath, withdrawal of mind, concentration,
meditation and superconsciousness) or in the Yoga of
cosmic service (serving all with absolute humility, egolessness and total self-surrender unto the Divine Power,
considering yourself as an instrument of God; selflessly
serving God in and through man in this universe and
worshipfully dedicating all your service at the feet of
God)—the awakening of Kundalini and its ascent from
Chakra to Chakra takes place spontaneously, until Kundalini reaches the highest occult centre. In the Jnani, in
the Raja Yogi, in the Bhakta and in the Karma Yogi, in
all of them, this activation and awakening of the Kundalini power and its gradual ascent from the lowest
centre to the highest centre takes place within the hidden
occult personality of the seeker; so it is something which
comes about as a matter of course. But, if you
deliberately try to bring this about by specific forceful
techniques, there is always—and I say *always*—the danger

of arousing powers when your personality is not pure
enough to assimilate and absorb them, is not ready to
withstand them. Whereas in the other paths of Yoga, as
you progress, you bring about a total change and perfection in all your personality, in this forceful Kundalini
Yoga, what happens many times is one goes all out for
the technique and neglects the prime preliminaries,
neglects the essential preparations, and then, before the
seeker is ready, these powers unfold. Kundalini Yoga is
an exact science, and its techniques are unfailing if
properly followed. Thus the seeker finds himself in a
position with an excess of power and not able to manage
it, not able even to bear it and then all Yogic life comes
to an end for him.

It is in Kundalini Yoga that extraordinary powers,
occult phenomena and all these occult experiences
manifest most intensely, because it is the scientific technique of awakening the greatest power that is within you.
In the other paths, through purity, the dormant powers
in the various spiritual centres of your being
manifest...right up to the end when through Cosmic
Consciousness, you are endowed with all the divine
powers, and then there is nothing which you cannot do!
Through perfection, when you get to the end of Yoga,
you are endowed with the eight major Siddhis such as
"Anima" (i.e., the ability to reduce yourself to micro-
scopic proportions), "Mahima" (the ability to expand to
gigantic proportions), "Laghima" (i.e., weightlessness),
"Garima" (i.e., extraordinary increase in weight), etc. For
instance, Laghima. If one who has gained this Siddhi is
taken to the top of the Eiffel Tower or the Empire State
Building and dropped, he would not fall, but would just
float to the ground like a wisp of feather-down. These
powers have been demonstrated by Yogis under observation. I have heard that excessive heaviness was
demonstrated by a Yogic Master in the West during the

early years of his stay in the United States in order to
make the people understand that he was not just 'talking
through his hat', and that the subject of his talk was
something which was based upon experience and upon
fact. In public lectures, he sometimes used to
demonstrate (as a token) the truth about Yogic power.
He would, for instance, sit there and call upon anyone
from the audience to try to lift him and there were in-
stances when not one, but several together, tried unsuc-
cessfully to lift him. Once a police constable, a very big
and powerful man, tried to shake this young Yogi, who
was not very big at that time, and the constable could not
even budge him, not even by a hair's breadth, and this
was demonstrated before an audience of five to six
hundred people in the city of New York. These
phenomena are all a part of the Yogic ascent.

Persons Blessed with Mystic Powers

There is a totally different type of mystic
phenomena and powers that come through the Grace of
God and a person who has not practised any of the
Yogic techniques may just obtain all of these powers
spontaneously. This happens only when God wants to
make use of a person for some Divine purpose and He
has found a person who, through absolute life-long moral
perfection, is found fit as a perfect channel, as an instrument which is fit and worthy. In such cases, the person
is always characterized by an extraordinary humility and
self-effacement and he never makes use of these powers
of his own volition. The "I" (ego) always stands aside and
this person is just used as a willing and egoless instrument. Such an individual is always absolutely desireless
and does not go after anything which this world has to
offer, but lives a life of the utmost simplicity, almost of
poverty. Utmost humility and desirelessness become the
chief characteristics of such a person. Such individuals
are very rare, but I mention it just to let you know that

such cases are not impossible. Such cases have been witnessed in India as well as outside of India, the powers
coming spontaneously and being due to the fitness of the
person and through Divine Grace.

Occult Powers and the Spiritual Seeker

What is the place of these various inner powers in
Yoga? What are their uses and abuses? What is the attitude of the true seeker to these powers? What are the
attitudes of Masters towards these powers? What is the
place of these powers and the various experiences in the
life of the Yogi?

In the first place, one of the most important things
you have to know about them is that they are byproducts. They are not the quest of the Yogi. They are
not the thing for which the seeker has taken to the path.
For him, they are just something to pass by on the way.
Just as, when you are on a journey to the city, you arrive
at and pass, for instance, the Eldorado Motel, and
Simpsons-Sears, and then a bridge — all of which have to
be *passed by* since none of them is your destination, the
destination for which you started. You may ask, "Why
do these things come?" Well, because you are progressing, because you are moving onward, you must pass by
these things that are on the way — *by the side of the highway* — and they are a sure sign that you are progressing,
that you are moving along.

Secondly, they serve as encouragement. After all, a
human being likes to know whether he is accomplishing
something or whether all his efforts are just turning
futile — whether they are proper and right or misdirected
and useless.

These powers come as temptations to test your
moral worth and they are the greatest barrier to Self-
knowledge. These powers gain entry into you so subtly,
so insidiously, that unless you are extraordinarily intro-
spective, extraordinarily watchful and extremely careful,

even without your knowledge you may succumb to them and become vain. Then one begins to have a superior type of pride which is much worse than any gross pride, such as pride of position, pride of wealth, of youth, prestige and power; it is the pride of being high and above the rest of mankind.

"All the rest of mankind does not possess that which I have. I possess something which no one else has,"—this type of subtle vanity and egoism is the greatest obstacle. It is the greatest danger to the seeker, for it goes to nourish the ego which is his deadliest enemy. It is this "I" which has to die in order to get God, and anything which fattens this "I" is the very antithesis of God. You may conclude that the Devil or Satan enters you and gives you these powers, that Satan takes possession of you when you get these powers. To use a spiritual metaphor, the throne which you have prepared for God is then occupied by Satan. So these powers divert you from God, taking you away from the straight path and inflating your false ego.

The seeker has to be very careful that he does not encourage these powers at all, that he does not have any thought about them, and that he brushes them aside.

What is the attitude of Masters to these powers? All Yogic Masters—The greatest Master, my Master, Swami Sivananda, one of the greatest saints that India has produced in recent times, and Sri Ramakrishna, the great Master of Sri Swami Vivekananda who came and gave Yoga and Vedanta to the West in 1893, and many other saints—have been absolutely at one in their opinion regarding this matter. "Right from the beginning of the spiritual path," they say, "beware of psychic powers. Beware of occult powers." If you get caught in their fascination, you are lost. Your spiritual life is destroyed and all of your Yoga will simply go away. And once you lose Yoga, it becomes very, very difficult to regain it. It is almost impossible to regain it. Once you fall from Yoga, then you have indeed to work very hard to regain the lost status. The Masters are very strong in their terms of condemnation. They say, "Shun occult powers as you shun poison", and they are indeed poison to spiritual unfoldment. Kick them aside.

Sri Ramakrishna had this actual experience: he said that once these powers were brought to him in a basket. This was an inner mystical experience in which he -was offered them, in which he was pressed to take them. At first glance they appeared as truths and he was about to look at them, when suddenly the whole thing became real to him, and in this reality he found them to be occult powers, mystic powers, lordship of the whole earth, and he immediately spat upon them. Spitting is the worst form of insult in India and he spat upon them and began to shout, "Take them away! Take them away at once!" People who were near came running and asked, "What is it? What has happened?" and then he kept quiet and controlled himself. Later on he told his disciples that the power of the whole universe was offered to him and for a moment or a split second, the mind almost looked at it, "but my Mother came to my rescue and I was able to shove it aside completely". So, the teaching of the Masters, from the very beginning, is: "If you want God, shun ruthlessly all powers, all occult phenomena, as poison". Do not be fascinated by occult phenomena and do not be diverted by them. Or, before you know it, you will be caught in their coils. If you want God, do not want anything else but God, for if you have God, you have everything. Take it from me: if you have God, you have everything. There is nothing in this universe that you lack, and all things but God will appear to you like ashes, as they are not essentially anything.

If you want God, you go on to the greatest, the highest, the sweetest and the ultimate. Do not have the

least desire for anything else, and if these occult powers
come in the way, then just ignore them. One should not
be diverted, for the Yogic ascent is something which has
to be done with your whole being, with your entire personality. The whole heart, mind and personality has to go
into it one hundred per cent and any distraction in which
you become lost causes your whole progress to be
delayed.

Now I come to the last portion: what are the uses
and abuses of occult phenomena? Its abuses have been
made very clear. To use them, to get caught in them—
this in itself is an abuse, because they are not meant to
be used at all. A great danger is that what has been built
up as moral structure, as humility, as goodness, as truth,
as kindness, as love, as mercy, may be directly affected
by these powers if one does not become absolutely based
in moral perfection, and does not surrender totally to the
Lord and look to Him for guidance at every step, and
does not sustain the spiritual life with constant prayer
and constant recollection of Him. If one is still weak and
in the making and these powers come, they corrupt the
mind and one may begin to make use of them for obtaining those very things which had been renounced at
the start of the spiritual life. One may become a slave
to money, to sensual indulgence, to passion and to all
that is base and animalistic in the human being if these
powers are used. It is said that a person may remain virtuous in the absence of temptation, but when temptation
comes, then virtue flies. So, in the beginning, one has to
be very careful, for these occult phenomena have the
power to corrupt.

Uses of Occult Phenomena

To seekers, to aspirants, to those who want God and
are trying to make use of their life to attain God, there
is no question of the uses of these powers, for the true
seeker just ignores them, and for him they have no con-

tent or value, but are things which he passes by on the way. However, if I may speak of these powers independently of the seeker, then there are uses to which these powers can be put, in a limited way. Supposing a person is not in any way a seeker of God, and especially if these powers are in the nature of healing, or magnetism or of prophetic vision (where one is able to know of certain things before they happen, due to clairaudience or clairvoyance), then use may be made of them, but it has been observed that in such situations when these powers are made use of, after some time, they leave the individual.

Magnetism is something by which one heals and cures people, and prophetic vision is something which can be made use of to help people. Supposing one has come to know something about some person, some danger that is in the offing, then that person may be warned of such danger and thus helped. In these entirely limited ways, the person, who is not a true seeker in the real sense of the term, may use these occult powers selflessly—unselfishly—out of compassion, out of love, out of a desire to help others. Some persons have a sense of mission: "I have come here. God wants me to do such and such a thing. This has to be done by me". And if one endowed with this sense of a mission is also endowed with useful occult powers, it means that the powers have been given to him for a purpose, and so, such powers may be used for the purpose given, but such a person will not attain God. For that, one has to work.

And then, there is a use for these occult powers on a very superior level. These powers have their place in Masters who have the special task of guiding spiritual seekers and bringing people to God—bringing people to the path. Sometimes the Masters make use of these powers to induce faith in a seeker who is ready for the path, but whom a lack of faith is holding back. And

sometimes Masters help even common people. They help
them overcome the suffering of Karma. They cannot help
them to overcome Karma, but they help them to overcome the sufferings of Karma by these powers. Upon a
very high level, sometimes, these powers are used by
Masters on a large scale, to help not just one individual,
but a whole area with many people. There have been
cases where Masters have used these powers to help
areas stricken with famine, drought, etc., but we are not
directly concerned with these, for such Masters are on a
level by themselves. They know what is to be, and in the
fulfilment of the Divine Will, they make use of these
powers.

Avoid All Occult Phenomena

On the lower level, these occult powers can become
the greatest of corrupters, the greatest of obstacles for all
true seekers. Ultimately, seekers have to realise God and
once one has realised through his own discrimination that
everything except God is just transitory, evanescent, just
a shadow-play, a momentary thing with which one has no
lasting connection, once one knows this, then everything
except He, from the little speck of dust to the highest
power, all occult phenomena, mystical experiences, become devoid of substance. They all partake of the same
nature of this passing, transitory, evanescent world. They
are not real. They are not true and they have no ultimate
value, no inherent worth.

Therefore, do not run after shadows; hold on only
to the substance. Do not go after the chaff; go only after
the grain that nourishes and gives life. Do not be
diverted from the path of truth by all that belongs to the
realm of untruth. See only the real and do not be
deluded by the unreal. All of these things except God —
the highest, the greatest, the innermost centre of your
being — are in the realm of unreality. Therefore, the only
thing the true aspirant should do is to completely be-

come blind to all these phenomena and think only of the Lord. Live only for the Lord. Love only God. And seek and be questing with absolute one-pointedness and whole-heartedness for the Great Reality—God and God alone. That is the message of the Masters—to avoid all powers.

Seek God alone and never allow yourself to be diverted even one whit towards anything other than God.

May the grace of the Divine illumine your intellect. May the love of the Divine fill your heart. May the blessings of all great Masters ever keep the light of discrimination and true awareness in your heart. May the Masters guide you on the path. May they give you the true understanding. May they give you the inner spiritual strength to resist all temptations and to overcome the lure of all occult powers, petty powers, that seek to divert you from the path. May they inspire you, strengthen you and lead you on to the goal of supreme blessedness and crown your life with the highest attainment of divine realisation, infinite bliss, eternal wisdom and light and the immeasurable divine peace that passeth all understanding. God bless you.

3. MEDITATION

Glorious Immortal Atman! Blessed Children of Light and Immortality! Beloved Seekers on the Pathway to the Divine! How privileged we are to be able to gather here in this holy morning hour to bathe ourselves in the glorious stream of meditation and the Divine Name! Such an hour is a gift from God. It is a bestowal of love from One who is ever eternal, from One who is our source, One in whom we eternally abide, and in whom we are all one. Such a gift should be accepted with love, received reverentially, and with devotion utilised by us all. Indeed, the token of our true recognition of God's continuous compassion and grace upon us would be to ever try to make ourselves worthy of such marks of His grace and to that extent we would be drawing nearer and nearer to Him. We should ourselves live our lives in such a way that, seeing one of us, He, the indweller (who knows our true aspirations, our innermost desires) would tell Himself: "Here is a child that has wearied of the toys of this mortal earth-plane, that has wearied of the worthless, passing and perishable objects, that has wearied of the appearance, the names and forms, of this great game of Mine, this drama of life, and now wishes to turn to Me and, therefore, I should not tarry". Thus recognising, He brings into the life of one who is truly in need of Him, who truly desires Him and Him alone, who is earnest in his quest, all that is needed for his spiritual unfoldment and the attainment of the highest. The yearning, the strong aspiration, therefore, is our part. That is the step the finite takes, and that being sincere and earnest, the fulfilment of it becomes His task. Thus it is that the great Master Jesus said, "Ask and

it shall be given". The asking of it is the task of each
individual soul and the giving of it is verily the Father's
task through wise love. And, as sure as the glorious dawn
and the radiant sun do follow the darkness of the night,
so sure and certain is the fulfilment of the true aspiration
of the sincere soul in earnest quest of the Supreme. Such
occasions as this—of prayer, of worshipfulness, of meditation—are not only proofs of the tangible presence of
Grace in our life, but from our part is proof of our sincere desire for Him. Every time we turn away from
earthly pursuits, every time we set aside mere things of
this world and collect ourselves in the stillness of our
inner being, and sit to worship Him and a call goes out
to the Infinite, "Here I am. I need You. Be Thou gracious. Reveal Thyself unto me. I turn away from the
passing and seek the Eternal", it becomes as it were, a
true token of the sincerity and earnestness of the soul,
of the innermost being's sincere desire.

The Nature of Meditation and Its Place in Yoga

Meditation, therefore, is the exercise of the deepest
part of your being. It is, in truth, the highest and the
noblest exercise of the supreme prerogative, the supreme
blessedness of human birth. There is no exercise loftier
than worship upon this earth-plane. Let us be thankful,
therefore, for this beautiful morning, for this solemn
hour and for the privilege of sitting at the altar of the
Divine Presence, entering into the silence and bathing
ourselves in the glorious radiance of His presence. Let
us be thankful for this privilege of trying to purify ourselves of all that is earthly within us, trying to fill ourselves with the Divine. Such acts of meditation form but
a variation of the process which our entire life is meant
to be. Our life is meant to be a constant opening of ourselves unto the Divine—a process of stilling our nature,
a constant process of turning away from the perception
of the non-self, a continuous process of rejecting the call

of the non-eternal upon our being and a resolute, a persistent, and an insistent opening of ourselves to the
Atman, to the Imperishable, to the Eternal. Our entire
life is meant to be an attempt to turn away from the unreal and move towards the real, an attempt to reject the
pull of darkness and seek light and light alone, a resolute
rising up from this plane of mortality to the recognition
of the immortal nature of the Self within. And meditation is the same process intensified in a systematic and
deliberate way, canalised at a specific time. Meditation is
intensified living in the Spirit, and our entire life (and its
movements) is a diffused flow of the spirit of meditation,
of the spirit of our spiritual quest. These two processes,
therefore, should have no specific break or barrier
separating them. Meditation should supply the dynamism
for our living. Meditation should be the re-charging of
our life battery in an intense manner. Meditation should
be the spiritualising force for all our life — for all our
thoughts, feelings, ideas, sentiments and aspirations — for
all our dealings with the world. Our perception of the
whole world and of all life should be a movement fully
bearing out the inner spirit of meditation. These two,
viz., life and meditation, are contiguous and continuous
processes. They are not two processes with a clear-cut
separating barrier.

Meditation is not some isolated act that you do in
life and which has no bearing on life, which is entirely
of a different nature altogether, and something which
goes against the normal current of your life. Yet, it may
be going in a direction opposite to the normal current
of your lower self, of the desire nature of the mind, of
the object-ward movement of the senses. Such outward
movements are the inherent tendencies of the mind and
meditation may go in opposition to these, but these outward movements do not constitute your Self; the senses
do not constitute your Self; the mind and the desire na-

ture do not constitute your Self. Your true being is as a
river rushing towards the ocean. Thus, in that being,
there should be no separation between your meditation
and your living. If this point is not borne in mind, you
will find that between meditation and the rest of your
day-to-day life there is a sharp divergence, and meditation becomes, as it were, a tug-of-war with the impulses
generated by your day-to-day life. It becomes a hard
process — one part of the mind contradicting the other,
opposed to the other, with much waste of essential energy. There is much conflict within, in the self of the being.
The harmony, the peace and the joy with which meditation can flood your being and fill your countenance, that
is lacking in your expression; even though you meditate,
there is not the calmness in the eye. But where this inner
secret has been recognised and life and meditation go
hand-in-hand, are fully in sympathy and rhythm, one
finds that in such a meditator the calmness of meditation
flows through his life; the peace of meditation shines
through his eyes; the joy of meditation pulsates and
radiates through his entire being. Such, indeed, is the
place of meditation in your life. Such, indeed, is the role
of meditation in the day-to-day living of your entire
being.

How to Start the Current of Meditation —
The Technique

We being embodied beings and our mind being
what it is, our everyday life does have a certain impact
upon our soul consciousness, the innermost awareness,
and the senses again and again cloud the radiance of the
inner consciousness. Therefore, when you sit for meditation, instead of starting the process immediately, you
should allow a certain time for the movement or the
momentum of the external life to calm down. Give a little time. Let the thoughts subside, and then, after the
mind has ceased its whirl of objectification, and is settling

down, then gently lift it up out of the self-awareness, out of the consciousness of its union with its immediate surroundings and with the body. And to that end, the chanting of the Divine Name, of Divine Mantras, produce wonderful spiritual vibrations, divine in their potency, which help to lift the mind up into a state of subtle awareness of the Divine. In the state of calmness and upliftment generated by the quietness in the withdrawal of the mind, the Divine Name evokes your concept of the Supreme, your idea of the Great Reality. The whole body, the entire mind and the senses quieten; and the mind is elevated. It is ready to contemplate upon the higher ideas. Gently, the clinging of the mind to lower ideas gets loosened. You should, therefore, prepare your mind for meditation by filling it with Divine Bhav—a feeling or attitude of spiritual affection—spiritual Bhav. It is somewhat like this: after having travelled through a vast area of mountains and valleys and jungles and variegated scenery, you suddenly come to the ocean-shore and all these multifarious names and forms and ever-changing objects cease and you see just a vast expanse. Your gaze is absolutely undisturbed by any object. You gaze only upon vastness, only upon stillness. From the many, you arrive at the vision of the One.

These processes of stilling the mind, of withdrawing yourself, of calming yourself, of lifting up your consciousness through Mantras, through chants, brings you to a state where the mind is rid of all multifarious objects and is just centred on the God within—on Brahman or the Atman or the Reality, the one Absolute Truth, the Supreme Being, the Changeless Infinite. And even as from the far horizon of the eastern ocean the orb of the sun rises up into that indescribable vastness, your concept of that Being rises in the vastness of the ocean of Pure Being. It may be in the nature of a sound, a Divine Personality, a formless concept, a special idea or a set of ideas you have of the Divine. And, as though the ocean itself has turned into a wave, no different from itself, not separate from it, being the same, and yet appearing for the time being as a wave pattern, you invoke upon this ocean of Pure Being, gently, the appearance of your particular concept of God in the form of your idea or set of ideas and then slowly, gently, flow forth to that idea, that set of ideas or that personality. Let your entire being melt and flow in a continuous stream of love and adoration, reverence, worshipfulness, prayerfulness and faith until your entire being just seems to be a continuous stream of such divine sentiments calmly flowing towards your concept of God.

This pattern should be kept up — a continuous and unbroken flow of loving God-thought. This is the very essence of meditation. It is a state of mind when the entire mind is filled with God and God alone, nothing else besides God. It is very necessary to recognize the process of meditation as such, for there are various wrong conceptions, wrong ideas about meditation, one of them being that it is an attempt to make the mind empty. When this concept is presented to me, I always remember the good old saying that an empty mind is the devil's workshop. Anything can come into the mind when it is empty. It is a very difficult concept to break away from the minds of people, because it contains a grain of truth. If there is a complete falsehood, you can contradict it, but if there is a part that has a grain of truth, it becomes very difficult to contradict. Uttering a half-truth is more dangerous than a hundred percent falsehood. So, to these people who seem to have grasped the meaning of a part of the process of meditation and who completely ignore the true process, I repeat: "Meditation is filling the mind with God-thought" and, therefore, it means emptying the mind of all thought other than that of God. This emptying the mind of all that is non-Atman or non-Self or non-Divine is only a part of the process; it is only a thing that is implied by the true process. The actual process is to fill the mind with God. The awareness is always there. If you empty the mind, a blank is not created, a void is not created, but God fills it. The Supreme, the Ideal, the Truth, the Reality, the Light of Pure Being—That floods the entire field of your consciousness. God fills it, and where He is, the world cannot be. It is said, "Where there is the Supreme, there is no desire for the world". So, where God is to come, there should be no desire for the world; for, where the world is, He cannot be. God says, "I am a jealous Master. I will not tolerate the presence of anyone else in that place which is meant for Me. It is Mine". The heart of the individual is the royal throne of God, and if there are other things there, He looks in and says, "No, it is not ready for Me to come".

So, meditation is emptying ourselves of all that is not-God and filling the mind with God. The particular conception of God or the Divine does not at all matter, and the greatest curse are those who advocate and inflict upon the human race one certain religion and one certain concept of the Divine and insist that God or the Divine is such-and-such and only such-and-such and insist that all think of Him only in a particular way, with a particular book. For, that is the very destruction of the pure idea of God, the destruction of the very spiritual core within. God cannot be defined. He cannot be comprehended. We cannot conceive of Him, but He is everything which one can conceive of in love. He allows Himself to be known in any way. Just as, when a child pulls the hair of the mother, twists her nose, slaps her, twists and pushes her face, or sticks its finger into her eye, or does anything, the mother loves the child and bends when it pulls her hair, and allows her face to be pushed whichever way the child wishes. Why? On account of love—love of the mother for the child, and love of the child for the mother, also. In the same way, if the loving heart conceives of God in whatever way it can, then that is God. Lord Krishna said, "In whatever way the sincere one seeketh Me, I reveal Myself to the seeking soul in that very way". And if you try to confine Him rigidly to your set conception, you destroy the very conception of God as the Infinite, as the Omnipresent, as the Omnipotent. What can He not do? What is He not? He is everything. There is nothing which He is not. Therefore, even though we know that He is absolute, that He is transcendent, that He is beyond all name and form, beyond the reach of mind and thought, yet He is everything. He is all.

The Vedanta is the grand culmination of all the attempts at giving the Supreme some sort of recognizable form. It says, "You, of countless names and countless forms, are infinite. You are everything". So, conceive of Him in any way. Do not be disturbed. Do not have any anxiety, for He knows when you are sitting for meditation. He knows. He can see even where you are sitting. When you start the thought in meditation, He knows even the thought.

Take, for instance, the father of a family, a good man, loved by all, and just imagine how differently he is conceived of by everyone in the family. The son and the daughter look upon him as the father, someone gracious, someone elderly, protecting them, looking after them, an ideal to follow. His brother looks upon him, not as a father, but as a gracious brother. The wife looks upon him as her master and lord and loving husband. And his own parents look upon him as a son, the father of their grandchildren. And his neighbour will think of him in a way entirely different from all these. These conceptions — in the parents' minds, in the children's minds, in the brother's mind, in the wife's mind, and in the neighbour's mind — all differ. So they all have different conceptions in their minds of this one being and all these are valid and right.

Saturate the Mind with God-thought

In the same way, you should think of God in whatever way your heart conceives of Him, and you should start the day with a prayer: "O Lord, I come with love before Thee to the altar. I seek to humbly offer myself to Thee. I come to Thee with love. Raise my consciousness to the realm of Thy great divine nature. May You be pleased to lift me up unto yourself. The clamour of the senses, of the mind—may they be stilled. I pray that they may not intrude upon this solemn moment. I want to think of You and You alone. I want to be completely absorbed in Thee". Say this prayer and then begin to meditate on God. If other thoughts arise in the mind, do not be concerned. Just ignore the mind. Just say, "Do what you wish, but I shall think of the Lord. I shall think of my Beloved, no matter what you do".

Do not try to subdue the mind. Do not try to forcefully evict the thoughts. Do not use force, for then you will hamper the very object of your meditation which is to think of God; and instead you will be thinking of the mind. Your attention, instead of being focussed on Him, will be diverted and misapplied and misused in a negative process. You should not waste your energy in a negative process. Do not think of the thoughts, do not think of the mind—ignore these and just hold tight to the Divine. If the mind begins to fall away from the Divine idea, chant "Om Om Om Om...", with thoughts of the Limitless, the Eternal, the Infinite, the Transcendental, filling the mind. Or chant the Name of your Ishta, and in this way, wipe clean the mind of all earth-thoughts and think only of God. And now and again repeat the Name of God and start conversing with God and offer a prayer: "My God, Thou art all-in-all. I offer up unto Thee this entire love of my heart, of my whole being".

The idea is just to saturate yourself with God-thought, with the beauty, the radiance, the light, the divine idea, forgetting all other things and trying to get the feeling of being in the presence of God—of just being there with Him. Every moment that you do this, a transforming process takes place in the depth of your own consciousness. More and more the Light of the Soul begins to fill your entire being. For the moment that you are thinking thus, completely absorbed in God, you are actually transformed into the realm of God. For that moment, your entire being becomes transformed into the God-nature, and when you come out of meditation, this impress of the God-nature which you created in meditation persists. And if you do this again and again, daily, without a single break, what happens is that this impression of the Divine Nature gets to be part and parcel of your consciousness and you feel always one with the Divine. You feel, "I am not this body. I am not this mind. I am not the senses, not the intellect. I am a part of the eternal Sun of God, made in His image, one with Him, a resplendent ray of the Great Radiant Light within". The mind takes up the form of that idea upon which it dwells with much reverence, love and in-gathered attention and concentration.

I pray to the Divine that He may bless you all with wonderful concentration of mind and success in deep meditation.

4. REAL RENUNCIATION

Blessed children of the Lord! Radiant rays of the eternal Light Divine! Salutations to you all. With great joy I once again speak to you to give you a little message from the Master Sivananda and from the cultural treasure-house of the Sacred Land of the Himalayas, the Land of the Holy Ganges, the Land of the *Upanishads* and the *Vedas*.

Mother India has ever been the great torch-bearer of spiritual light to people of all parts of the world, at all times and in all climes. She has held aloft the great ideal of Self-realization, of God-realization. The attainment of God has ever been the great hunger of the children of India. More than all the other things of this external, visible universe, they have cherished the supreme attainment of Moksha or liberation in Divine Realization.

Renunciation Should Be Based upon Right Understanding

Renunciation has been the key-note of the teachings of the Great Masters of India. Renunciation is the very essence of spirituality and the secret of God-realization. Renunciation is not lethargy, escapism or irresponsibility. It is the great strength that the aspirant has in his onward march to the Kingdom of Heaven. It is the strength of renunciation that truly sustains the aspirant in his arduous journey to the Supreme.

Renunciation of cravings for sense pleasures is the gateway to permanent happiness. Of all qualifications that are laid down for students of Yoga, for aspirants on the spiritual path, renunciation comes foremost. Renunciation alone can make you fearless and happy. It is the bestower of peace and, ultimately, the bestower of immortality.

One should become disgusted with the world through right understanding, through discrimination and inquiry—getting into the very heart of the nature of this universe and by realizing how all things, all names and forms, are full of defects, are passing, are changeful and perishable. Thus, by looking into the defects of sensual life, one gets true renunciation.

Disgust with the world implies disgust with worldliness. We should not get disgusted with things as such, but rather with our desire to possess things, to attain things. Reason should strengthen our renunciation. Logic should back up our renunciation. This renunciation is lasting, is well-founded. It is not merely the outcome of a little emotional upheaval. The renunciation that comes momentarily through the loss of wife, position, friend, son or property—this will not help you much, for it is a momentary flash in the pan, as it were. It is not real sustaining renunciation born of inquiry and discrimination and constant reflection.

Conviction about the necessity of renunciation will not arise without reasoning, without inquiry and discrimination. Just reflect for a while on the fate of the human being. As a child, the human being in the womb is covered with urine, pus and dirt and scorched by the fire of hunger. As an adult, one is puffed up with enjoyment of sense-objects and indulgences. And as a senile old person, one becomes extremely weak in body and mind and becomes an object of scorn, even of relatives. No one wants to have anything to do with such a person.

Worthlessness of Worldly Life

A life of delusion amidst sensuality, money and sense-objects is the pitiful lot of the normal human being. Life is transitory; death is silently staring at you like a venomous serpent with expanded hood, ever ready to strike. Various dire diseases cause much havoc to the body. Youth abandons the body quickly and old age grips it. He alone is saved who makes haste to utilise this precious life in striving to obtain the *summum bonum* of life through renunciation, discrimination and inquiry. Maya, the great illusory power of the Supreme, is a very great jeweller. She prepares a skeleton, covers it with flesh and muscles, and hides the various impurities within with a very shining skin. Oh, immediately, a human being is absolutely deluded with this appearance—with this doll prepared by Maya. How long are you going to call this body your self? Develop an undeluded imagination and identify yourself with your real nature, Satchidananda (Existence-Consciousness-Bliss) which is your true Self.

Are you not tired of saying, "*My* son is ill with typhoid. *My* second daughter is getting married. *My* wife is worrying me to purchase a new dress. *My* husband is going after drink and gambling. *My* son-in-law died recently"? Indeed, such miseries should open your eyes to the great goal of life. Human love is hollow. It is animalistic attraction. It is passion only. It is carnal love. It is a love that is pure selfishness, for one loves another for the pleasure that the other person is able to give one. At the bottom of it, it is selfish, and also, it is ever changing. The love of one person for another depends upon so many external factors which are changing, and when they change, the emotional attitude of a person also changes. To a great extent, it is mere show. Beloved friend, you can find real lasting love only in God, only in saints. God alone knows how to love and His love knows no change, knows no lessening.

Tell me, beloved friend, how long do you wish to be a slave to these fleeting things of this world? How long are you going to repeat the same monotonous round of sensual enjoyment, day after day, morning, afternoon, evening and night? How long do you wish to worship this body, these sense pleasures? When will you find time to break the bondage of your attachment to these fleeting things, these passing things and, renouncing all desire and craving and passion, meditate on the Lord and do virtuous deeds in life? Think and reflect! Is there really any pleasure or happiness in this world? Think! Think and reflect daily. Analyse the nature of the objects of the world. Try to inquire into their nature and the nature of the experiences you derive from them. See how incomplete they are and how imperfect they are, how mixed-up they are with a lot of exertion and restlessness and desire and craving and disappointment, and how much wrong thought and wrong action are necessary to obtain sense pleasures! Why does man still stroll about here and there—like a street dog in search of bones—in search of little petty pleasures from the perishable objects of this earth-plane? Break your bond of attachment to these things. Search within. Look within and introspect and realize the supreme abode of peace and immortality.

One should not delay. One should renounce. One should understand the glory of renunciation. One should understand the magnitude of human suffering, the absolute worthlessness of all sense pleasures, and the wonderful glory of the Supreme Attainment and the great necessity of renunciation for this attainment.

Turn your back on the maddening crowds of worldly-minded persons, anchor your faith in the Lord and live the life of pure thought, high ideals and supreme wisdom. Adopt universal love, truth and purity as your guiding stars in life. Renounce untruth, renounce harsh nature, and renounce impurity. Refuse to swerve from the path or to look back and, in due course, you will surely attain Realization.

Prepare for this renunciation by the necessary Sadhana practices. All these are designed to subdue and control the mind and make you established in renunciation. The vagaries of the mind should be controlled; the heart should be cultured towards the ultimate ideal of universal Light and Love. Put into daily practice, with humility and faith, as many of the *Twenty Instructions* of Swami Sivananda as possible. The more you succeed in doing so, the more of mental strength and peace you will have. This will react on your physical life conditions for the better and you will gradually grow more and more in strength and renunciation.

There are three elements in the mind which obstruct the vision of the Supreme Reality within. One is the external impurity of your own nature—various desires, passions, cravings, likes and dislikes. The other is the uncontrollable restlessness of the mind. A steady mind will not be worried. It is only the wavering nature of the mind that brings in untold worry and restlessness and this restlessness is on account of desires and cravings. The impurities of hidden past impressions imbedded in the mind on account of past enjoyments, past experiences and deeds, are responsible for your restlessness and worry. This is the third element of obstruction. Excitement and anger come out of desire and you are not able to discriminate when you are angry, when you are excited, when the mind is restless. To overcome desire is to establish peace in the mind.

These impurities of the physical and the mental aspects of the personality should be removed by the study of scriptural books, by developing selflessness and the active spirit of service, by charity, by devotion to the Lord in the form of prayer and worship, and in the form of devout remembrance of God at all times through the repetition of various chants or the repetition of the Divine Name. The Lord's Divine Name is a powerful specific for all these imperfections of your external personality. Lead the Divine Life; then and then alone will you be able to overcome the imperfections of your physical and mental natures and become established in desirelessness and renunciation.

The Riddle of Life

Try to understand the riddle of life and the riddle of this universe. Acquire discrimination. Take recourse to the company of seekers like yourself, getting together now and then with those of your own nature, those who are spiritually inclined. Even this will quicken your discrimination and give you the spirit of renunciation. Inquire into the nature of the Great Reality. Study books like the *Gita* and the *Upanishads* and then you will have a comprehensive understanding of the innumerable problems of life. There is not an iota of happiness in this world. Seek the happiness that is within.

In this world, people run after pleasures. Is not great wealth valuable to be owned? Is not a beautiful summer resort somewhere in Switzerland, with a pleasant garden and beautiful smelling flowers and wonderful scenery, pleasant to live in? Is not the company of beautiful people very desirable, very pleasing? Yet, in spite of the desirability of beautiful company, wealth and wonderful health resorts and modern amenities and a great deal of pleasure, gay society, you see young people, intelligent people, people having great prospects for their future, with a wonderful career ahead, kick aside all these things which the world holds dear and take to a life of seclusion, of silence, of renunciation, of dispassion, of inward meditation. Why? Why do they kick aside all these things like worthless straw and retire into seclusion and meditate on the Lord? If there were real pleasure in these things, these people of understanding and intelligence would not do such a foolish thing. So, try to think out the reasoning behind this. Think out what exactly has been their process of reasoning to come to such a conclusion, to take such a step and to adopt such a way of life.

Even now, thousands of young graduates, young doctors and lawyers in India, come to Rishikesh in the Himalayas and wish to be initiated into Sannyas. They then go away higher up into the Himalayas and live there in silence and seclusion, practising deep meditation and Pranayama. Why? You have to reflect and find out for yourself what these young people, these intelligent people, these highly educated people, these people with powers of reasoning, found out for themselves within their hearts, through reflection, through inquiry and discrimination. They were able to get the strength to make God the very centre of their lives and just push aside all things which they knew to be secondary and unimportant.

Amidst the din and boisterous bustle of worldly activities, there do come some moments of tranquillity and peace for everyone when the mind, for the time being, however short it may be, soars above the filthy things of this world and reflects on the higher problems of life, the why and the wherefore of this life, the riddle of the universe. You begin to inquire, "Who am I?" The sincere inquirer becomes serious and becomes absorbed in reflection. He begins to search and understand the truth and discrimination dawns in him. He seeks renunciation and dispassion, concentration and meditation, purification of the body and the mind, eventually to reach the highest knowledge of the Self and become eternally free. But the person whose mind is saturated with worldly emotions and materialistic thoughts is quite heedless of these tranquil moments and does not make use of them and is inevitably carried away by the dual current of attraction and repulsion, like and dislike, love and hatred, and is tossed about helplessly on the tumultuous sea of worldly concerns. How uncertain is sensual life in this world! If you constantly think of the transitory nature of sensory

pleasures and their concomitant evils—miseries, worries,
troubles, tribulations, anxieties, decay, premature death—
then you will slowly develop renunciation within.

Sensual Pleasures Opposed to Spiritual Bliss

In the presence of continual sensual pleasures,
spiritual bliss cannot exist, just as darkness and light cannot co-exist. If one should come, the other must go.
Therefore, show extreme contempt for worldly objects.
Destroy all desire from within. Turn the mind away from
sensual objects. Give up cravings. Give up deluded attachment and you will develop real renunciation. You
yourself have made your life complex and intricate. You
have entangled yourself in this quagmire of Samsara by
increasing your own desires, your own wants. By making
life luxurious and complex, you have multiplied your
wants and desires. Every day you are forging additional
links to this chain of bondage by creating fresher and
fresher wants, newer and newer wants. Simplicity has
vanished. Luxurious habits and ways of living are
embraced. No wonder there are all sorts of problems in
human society. Unemployment everywhere, a sense of inadequacy and want everywhere, discontent everywhere,
dissatisfaction everywhere. There is depression in trade
and there is unrest everywhere. It is created by man's
own folly.

Due to these uncontrolled desires, persons are always dissatisfied. There is no end to their desires. One
nation is dissatisfied with other nations. Some nations are
preparing for war. Life has thus become a matter of uncertainty due to the increase of desire and, due to the
heedlessness of the human being to this great message of
renunciation, this message of simplicity of life, this message of renouncing inordinate desire, there is only movement towards more confusion, more chaos and
bewilderment. Life has become stormy and boisterous
everywhere. It is full of under-currents and cross-cur-

rents. Is there no escape from these troubles and difficulties? There is one supreme way. It is the development of intense dispassion. It is a life of dispassion. It is a life of simplicity, of self-control, of purity, of selfless service, of shedding all selfish nature, of cosmic love.

Develop the habit of taking the right point of view— the habit of thinking rightly, feeling rightly, acting rightly. Practise devotion and meditation. Then alone is it possible for you to have happiness and perfect peace—not somewhere, in some other realm, in some distant future, but right here in the midst of all these external distractions, this external restlessness and boisterousness of life. If you are grounded in dispassion, you will taste of the supreme fruit of such dispassion in the form of absolute tranquillity and peace and in the form of a bliss that springs out of such detachment and peace.

The Indispensability of Renunciation

At this point, we may try to consider one or two modern trends which have a direct bearing upon the vital subject of renunciation. Is renunciation really necessary? Many people in these modern days fight shy of renunciation. They put forward various ingenious arguments to prove that it is not necessary and that it is even useless. In fact, they go a step further and say that renunciation is harmful.

I have clearly shown that renunciation is the very basis of spirituality. You cannot have God unless you empty your heart of desires. When desires fill your heart, how can you seek immortality? How can you have the necessary aspiration for the Supreme? Without this aspiration, the Great Attainment is just a dream.

Renunciation is necessary for progress in spiritual life. All religions and genuine religious teachers are at one upon this point and agree without any difference that mental renunciation is absolutely essential and imperative to attain God-realization and Divine Love—all are certain and emphatic upon this point. Now-a-days we hear certain well-known leaders carrying on crusades against renunciation, but if you try and look below the surface of these so-called intellectual philosophers, you will find that there is an element of pseudo-sensuality in them. They may be very great, no doubt, towering intellectual giants, people of wonderful attainments, people of great organizing ability, but true greatness lies elsewhere. It is not in these exceptional traits and the development of some distinct talents that true greatness lies. We forget that persons may be very great in one respect, but they may be just as absolutely unlettered as regards the true implications of religion. Intellectualism alone does not imply the religious spirit. Religion is something serious, something earnest. It means strenuous practice and ceaseless endeavour, endless quest after Realization—strenuous practice based upon renunciation and ceaseless quest enlivened by renunciation.

There are many modern people posing as Masters and teachers who are inclined to belittle renunciation. Why? Perhaps they themselves are still in the grip of desire. All true teachers, whether of the East or of the West, whether of the present day or of the bygone past, are quite unanimous with regard to the need for absolute inner renunciation. The outward form of it is a different question, but true inner renunciation, the total renunciation of all desires for worldly things, the burning up of all cravings and sense urges, is absolutely essential—that is the essence of renunciation. All true teachers are agreed that knowledge of the Eternal is not compatible with attachment to the non-eternal. The attachment to the very antithesis of Divine Love cannot co-exist side by side with true love for the Divine. These two are not on the same plane and the one excludes the other.

We must give up all consciousness of, and desire for,

earthly things in order to know God and attain Him. As long as we have the slightest desire for things other than God, we cannot have Him. It is therefore that Christ was so very uncompromising in His teachings to those whom He wanted to become His intimate disciples. He said, "Leave everything and follow me. Don't turn, don't even hesitate for a single moment to attend to other things. Renounce and follow me". That means we should be prepared to generate in our hearts this element of total renunciation; then alone true aspiration for God can fill our hearts and goad us onward towards earnest and true spiritual life, true spiritual effort.

Sri Ramakrishna, one of the greatest teachers of modern times, used to say that as long as even a little fibre was sticking out of the end of a thread, that thread could not be passed through the eye of a needle. Even if it is only a single cotton fibre sticking outside, unless and until the entire tip of the thread is absolutely pointed, it may not be made to pass through the eye of a needle. Unless absolute concentration of your entire being is directed towards the purpose of your life, the attainment of God, there cannot be success in spiritual realization. We have to be on guard, therefore, against these dubious, compromising sort of doctrines. Apart from the danger of being deluded, there are also other dangers from these false philosophies.

False Prophets of the Modern Age

The modern age is materialistic. The dominant note in the era of today is the materialistic sense of values. Materialism also has many forms. There is a materialism which says that this world alone is everything, that this world alone is worth having. Then there is the other kind of materialism—a subtle materialism which says that God alone is not enough, that there must be the universe also besides Him and that you cannot totally ignore or neglect this universe. To know God alone, according to the votaries of this subtle doctrine, is imperfection; and perfection is to know the ultimate Reality of God as well as this world. They say that you must know God and you must know this universe also in the true sense.

What is knowing the universe? Those who have known the universe have all been deluded by their own knowledge. If you know the universe, in its true sense, that it is absolutely transitory, evanescent, passing, perishable, changeful, worthless, then you will no longer entertain any value for it. But these subtle philosophers say that knowledge should not be one-sided and, according to them, the knowledge of God alone is lop-sided, is one-sided, for it is not powered by a knowledge of the universe also. They do not seem to realize that when God is known, everything is known. This universe is just a shadow-play upon the Permanent Reality which is God, and when the Reality is known (It is infinite, all-pervading, one without a second), everything becomes known. But these people have a peculiar slant upon the subject of Self-realization and the great spiritual goal of life, and they say that you have to know both God and the universe and then only your knowledge is perfect.

What a conception of knowledge these people have! It is like saying that you must have nectar as well as poison. What do they mean: experience both? When you experience God, the experience of the universe vanishes. When you experience the wakeful state, then you cannot have the experience of the dream state. This false philosophy is just like clinging to dreams and those who advocate this philosophy may advance many subtle arguments in support of their thesis. If reason and the teachings of other great teachers do not support them, they have no hesitation in accusing the other teachers of being lopsided, or ignorant, or dogmatic. Even the great Shankara, who has expounded the theory of Maya, comes in for criticism at the hands of these false teachers. They

say that Shankara is not right in emphasising the doctrine
of Maya. To me, at least, there seems to be no doubt
why such people are so ever eager to link God with the
world. It is probably because they have a secret (or even
perhaps an unconscious) desire for the world. So, in their
conscious thought, the world has a hidden validity, a certain value, a certain meaning. Therefore, they still want
to hold on to this world and do not like the idea of
renouncing it completely from their hearts and minds.
Their renunciation, therefore, is not complete. And partial renunciation cannot be. You cannot jump over a
chasm between two cliffs in two jumps. There is only one
complete jump or no jump at all. You cannot have a sort
of half-jump when you want to leap across this chasm
dividing the relative existence and the absolute, untrammelled, limitless Cosmic Existence.

The minds of these false prophets are not fully ready
for God. This is plain. Hence there is a sort of veiled
attempt at refuting the need of renunciation and the
doctrine of Maya, and at trying to prove that the world
is also important and that one should not completely
reject it. I do not agree with this double-think at all. The
world has to be rejected. It does not mean running away
into the Himalayan caves. It does not mean giving up all
the objects of this world. It does not mean that you
should throw off your shirt, that you should give up
eating normal food, that you should start eating leaves or
start living upon water or air. It does not mean any such
eccentric and extreme action.

Inner Renunciation Is Real Renunciation

After all, where can you go to get away from the
world? Even if you go to the Himalayan caves, you are
still *in* the world. What really is needed is not so much
the renunciation of the outward form of this world, is not
so much the giving up of all outward desires. Renunciation does not mean renouncing merely a house, a beach,

a garden or a piece of ground, or a mode of eating. Renunciation means completely renouncing worldliness. This is the secret of true renunciation.

You may renounce the objects of this world; you may renounce all your wealth, your property, everything; but your heart may be attached to them still. You may still have inner desire for all these things. Such renunciation cannot give happiness. Outward renunciation alone is not true renunciation, unless it is accompanied by inner renunciation. And if you are established absolutely in full inner renunciation, then outward renunciation becomes superfluous. Whether you renounce outwardly or not, it does not seriously matter. The great thing is to be not *of* the world even when you are *in* the world. The thing is to see that the desire for objects does not enter into your being even when you are in the midst of objects.

What is the root cause of such desire? It is the very antithesis of renunciation. The root cause of desire is the feeling of your individual personality—"I". It is this "I" that wants, it is this "I" that desires, it is this "I" that craves. And therefore, real renunciation is not so much in the abandonment of all things and all actions. It is not eccentric diet alone. It is not to be without any possession, without even a cloth, without even shoes. This is not the essence of renunciation. It is not in shaving the head and wearing monk's robes. True renunciation is the renunciation of desires and cravings, of the possessing nature and passions; and these are rooted upon the ego sense—the "I" and the "mine". Therefore, the secret of real renunciation lies in the complete renunciation of egoism and mineness. The heart should be devoid of the "I" consciousness, the "I" sense and all idea of "mine". The secret of real renunciation is the eradication of attachment and the ego.

Real renunciation is renunciation of all cravings and

the subtle mental impressions that fill your mind—mental impressions of previous enjoyments. To get rid of all mental impressions through Sadhana is real renunciation. Real renunciation is the eradication of attachment to all passing things of this world. Real renunciation is freedom from the idea of "I am the doer; I am the enjoyer; I see through the eyes; I smell through the nose; I hear through the ears". This identification with the senses and the body has to be renounced. This is the bondage.

Identification with the body, with the mind and its desires—this has to be renounced and you have to just centre yourself for ever in the consciousness of your own nature, your true nature—totally transcending body, senses, Prana, mind, intellect and thought attachments. Beyond all these You are—the absolute, unaffected, changeless, Witness Consciousness, the Supreme that knows no birth, no death, no suffering, that has neither want nor desire (for It is ever full and ever content).

A deep perennial satisfaction characterizes your true being. Nothing is lacked, for It is all-full and perfect. Plenitude is your true nature. To be established in the awareness of this plenitude is the greatest secret of real renunciation. Abandon ruthlessly the present wrong identification with the body-mind personality. Live in your Self within. That is true renunciation. To be rooted in your splendid Atmic Consciousness, splendid Spiritual Nature, your splendid Divine Essence—this is the secret of real renunciation. Freedom from all the bonds of attachment—that constitutes the glory of real renunciation.

5. KNOW THYSELF

If, for a moment, we cast our eyes upon the vibrant and dynamic life upon the surface of the globe today, immediately we see that tremendous advances have been made in the past couple of centuries. Man has progressed, tapped new resources, discovered more about things than ever was known before. By his ingenuity and scientific acumen, he has evolved such instruments that things which could not even be perceived are now laid bare before the gaze of the human eye—instruments of such magnifying power that nearly invisible phenomena and cosmic phenomena alike are revealed to the penetrating eye of the scientist. So great are the achievements that have been made in the field of the physical sciences—in physics, chemistry, mechanics, engineering, electronics, etc.—and so much greater is the control that man holds over external forces that life is now filled with innumerable comforts and conveniences for enjoyment. Such advances, such improvements, such wonderful progress has been made that this modern life might have been thought impossible, fantastic, sheerly fanciful even a hundred years ago. What might have been considered a dream creation then has, nevertheless, become a fact now.

However, let us take a second glance and observe mankind itself. We see vast masses of people in different parts of the globe, with an improved material lot, but without a corresponding improvement in inner satisfaction and peace, which improvement ought to have been the result of the progress in the external sciences. If man is to improve and advance, he must do so on all levels and in all spheres of life and activity.

There is no doubt that efficiency has been raised and organisation has been widened. But, why is increased happiness in the life of the individual not apparent? There are strange imbalances existing between groups which enjoy great prosperity and groups which suffer in abject poverty. In one area there is tremendous wealth and affluence; in another there is impoverishment and starvation. Even in the life of the average man, there is prosperity together with sorrow, convenience together with discontent, both at the same time. Man's possessions have been increased, but his joy—his essential joy of living—has clearly not been increased. If a census were taken, no one could honestly say, "Yes, I think that all these material improvements have put us into a state of perennial joy and unalloyed happiness."

Even in the physical welfare of human beings, real progress is dubious. The number of hospitals has increased beyond compare; doctors, medicines, chemical factories, the manufacture of drugs and various methods of surgery have all increased tenfold; but diseases have multiplied by leaps and bounds. The farther mankind progresses in science, the more prevalent become the new kinds of diseases and sufferings which afflict man on earth. Could there be any reason for this?

The Basic Neglect of the Study of Man

There is a simple reason. Man is, ultimately, the most important unit in this universe. In his hands lies the key to the direction to be taken by human affairs. Over storms, tides, earthquakes, drought, whirlwinds, cyclones—over the universal elements—man has no control; but in so far as the life of the individual is concerned—be it in the family, in the community, in the civic centre, in the capital, in the nation, or in the world—in so far as this life, in all its various and ever-widening aspects is concerned—the control does lie in the hands of man. Man is the director of these affairs.

He can say, "Yes, let us continue in this direction" or "No, now let us change from this direction and take that direction instead". With this most important unit of life, namely man, not everything is all right. While advances are being made in all the fields of external nature, man's own nature is being neglected.

"The greatest study of mankind is man." The human being has to understand himself. He has to understand his own nature. It is in the knowledge of oneself that the laws that govern life are discovered and the factors that determine human behaviour are revealed. With a knowledge of the forces within, one learns to apply the laws that govern those forces and thus properly direct one's own behaviour. If this essential knowledge is not made the object of one's serious study and seeking, if the basic knowledge of oneself is overlooked, then not all the knowledge of external things — no matter how vast or impressive this latter may be — can bring about a real state of progress in man's world.

At present, there is a total eclipse of this knowledge of one's own nature. With this inadequacy in human knowledge, basic degeneracy in human nature is the natural result. Power makes the human being selfish, ego-centred and greedy. The phenomenon of power-grabbing is so common that it is to be seen in all parts of the globe today. Each confined community is protecting its own interests, wishing to acquire all knowledge and power for itself and is, therefore, setting itself in opposition to all the rest of humanity. Also, each community is afflicted with the dangerous urge to make use of the power thus acquired for the destruction of all those except the few with whom it identifies itself.

This is the picture of the precarious state of affairs at this turn of the first half of the twentieth century. We see that real progress has been vitiated, that progress has been perverted, due to a lack of refinement in the nature of the human being. If, as man had progressed in controlling external nature, he had also gained the knowledge of himself; if, as he had refined the code of etiquette, he had also improved the quality of his being by increasing its capacity for love, its capacity for compassion, its capacity for putting service before self, its capacity for sacrifice; if progress such as this had kept pace with the progress arising out of man's mastery over external forces, then the whole picture today would be one of balance and well-being in all the communities of the world. There would be more happiness. There would be more brotherhood and friendship. There would be more mutual co-operation.

The imbalance between the outward advances made by human society and the basic degeneracy undergone by the human individual is the root cause of the unhappy state in which humanity finds itself today—a state fraught with fear, uncertainty, and a sense of insecurity. The question is: when so much knowledge has been acquired and so much power has been obtained during the past century, knowledge and power hitherto beyond the reach of man, why is there such a deep feeling in all human hearts that this is hardly a period worth living? People do not want to think about the present. Either they project themselves into a future Utopia where man perhaps would have solved all his present problems or they think wistfully of the past "when things were better". The present seems to be a present full of unrest. This attitude is due to the one basic error of the human being. The entire power of his mind, his perceptions and his senses has been totally externalised. He has not tried, first of all, to start from the proper starting point.

If man does not know himself, how can his life be lived successfully? It is like a person who is familiar only with the art of driving a car upon a long and hazardous journey, perhaps for thousands of miles, without knowing one bit of the mechanism of the vehicle which is to carry him all the way to his destination. He is actually in a precarious position at every moment, for if the mechanism goes out of order, he will not know how to assess its condition or make the necessary repairs. That is the position of those in the present day who recognize that things have gone wrong, but who do not know exactly how to make corrections. Not all the psychiatrists and psychologists can convince people that they have unearthed the basic knowledge that is required for this repair work.

Who Am I? – The Great Enquiry

The knowledge of oneself is the required knowledge. And the education in this knowledge has to start right from childhood. It is only when the art of right thinking is taught in childhood that true progress ensues in the life of the individual. We have, first of all, to understand what we are, and what are those factors in our personality that will increase its beauty, and what are those factors that will mar that beauty. How many people take time to think about themselves? Throughout our lives, we think about our engagements, our week-end plans, our pleasures and our pets. We think about what type of dress we shall have, what new model of car we shall buy, what type of house painting we shall afford. At every moment, things which are outside of ourselves occupy our attention. Who spends half an hour every day in calmness and silence? Who asks, "Who am I? How I came here? What is this world in which I am living where a little while ago I was not and a little while from now I will not be? What is the connection between me and this universe, between me and those around me with whom I have a temporary relationship? In this temporary everchanging set-up, what is my duty?" These questions you do not take time to ponder over. Unless and until you find the answer to them and obtain the essential knowledge of what you really are, whence you have come and where abides your ultimate destiny, effective and purposeful living will lie far off in the future for you. You will be no happier while departing from this world than when you were coming into it; and you will not leave this earth a better and improved place (by virtue of its receiving greater light and joy) for your having been here.

You Are Not the Body

These have ever been the central questions of Hindu philosophy. Both the ancient sages and the modern Masters have ever tried to bring about an awakening in man so that this earth-life might be properly used to get an essential knowledge of the Self. The ignorant, the idiotic, the stupid or the foolish think that the body is one's own self. Man's idea of himself is: "I am five feet, nine inches tall; I weigh so many pounds; I am so many years old, etc." What greater folly, what greater ignorance, what greater blindness or stupidity could there be than to identify oneself with this perishable cage of bones, this gross composition of flesh and muscles and skin! After all, what is this physical sheath if it is not wholly dependent upon perishable food? When food is administered to it, the body grows, but when it is withdrawn, the body is finished. Are you this—this absolutely abject thing—dependent so entirely upon materials which are themselves subject to decay? But that is what the majority of people say.

This body is not yourself. This body came into being only a little while ago. Its fate is to become disintegrated and dissolved soon. You—you cannot be this body. You can never feel that you will cease to exist. The idea that you have ceased to exist is unthinkable for you. By your very nature, such a thought is absolutely inconceivable and impossible. The consciousness will never permit you to do so, for even as you postulate, "I do not exist", you feel yourself to be the maker of this statement. You feel yourself to be beyond the very idea.

It is in folly, in blindness, in sheer thoughtlessness that one considers the body to be oneself. The body is merely the object of your perception. You can look at it and speak about it as you would refer to a desk or a chair. It cannot, therefore, be the subject, the seer or the perceiver. After all, you are able to say, "My body, my hands, my feet, my head"; and even if you were to lose your limbs, you would not feel that you had been lost. No aspect of your personality would have been reduced by the loss of your limbs. You would still feel that you were all right, unharmed and intact. You conclude that you are the perceiver of the body which is merely an object of your perception.

You Are Not the Mind

Consciousness cannot be dependent upon the senses. Could the aggregate of the senses be yourself—the sense of sight, smell, taste, touch and hearing together with the sense-centres in the brain which make them work? If you do not hear, the loss of hearing does not make you lose your individuality; similarly, the loss of sight or smell does not make you lose your personality. And when you go into the deep-sleep state where all the ten senses are totally inoperative, and as it were dead, You are still there. You are able to posit your continuous existence. When you get up, you say, "I am the one who went to sleep, and now, I am the awakener. I am able to say that I have enjoyed my sleep".

What is this "I" which continues to exist even in the depths of deep, dreamless sleep, when the consciousness of the body and the external world are absent and the functions of the mind are discontinued? *You* are in existence during deep sleep when the body is totally inert, when the senses and the mind do not function and when the intellect is no longer active. Immediately upon awakening, *You* take up the thread of your personality-consciousness as though it had never been absent, and you say, "I went to sleep and I enjoyed a good rest. Now I have awakened refreshed". What is this mysterious factor independent of the activity of the senses and the functions of the mind and intellect which enables you to feel continued consciousness of "being"? Even if you were affected by amnesia and suffered a total loss of memory, so that all things constituting your previous personality were totally wiped out and effaced from your consciousness (even as something written on the blackboard is erased by a duster), you would say, "*I* don't know" or "*I* don't remember". This I-awareness is never lost. What is this I-awareness which is independent of all phases of personality including even the all-important memory?

The Universal Factors: "I" and "I Am"

When you go deep within yourself, it becomes apparent that this *I*, your very Self, is something that links you so very close to all humanity and to all life upon earth, that it is universal. Consider a vast group of people of different nationalities, races, religions, beliefs and castes — everyone totally different from everyone else in name and form, in language, in thought pattern, in colour, in creed, in dress, in manner of eating, drinking and sleeping, in short, in everything. You will find to your amazement that every one of these totally different beings says "I", "I", "I" and, also, says "I am". He may be an African Hottentot, he may be an Eskimo of Alaska, he may be a Malaysian, an Arab, a European, a Canadian, a Hindu or a Buddhist, but he invariably says "I". This feeling of *I* and *I am,* therefore, is unlike those factors that split people apart and make them remarkably different. This is definitely a common universal factor. This is the factor that knits humanity into subtle oneness.

Wrong Identifications Destroy Universality

We have seen that everyone says "I" and "I am", and thus far everyone is perfectly all right, everyone is in accord with all other beings upon earth. But then, from this second word onwards, man voices his ignorance. He proceeds with "I am an American", "I am a Canadian", "I am a Hindu", "I am a Republican". Whatever he adds to "*I am*", immediately limits his consciousness. It at once vitiates the consciousness of oneness. Thus when you say "I am", you are at one with all mankind; but when you say "I am So-and-so", you separate yourself and create a barrier between yourself and every human being contrary to you. You immediately cut yourself off from the rest of the world and regard others as inimical to yourself, opposed to yourself, and what is worse, harmful to yourself. Herein lies colossal ignorance. Herein lies the necessity for the utmost clarity of thought. Here it is that you have to make use of your intelligence.

If your intellect is to be your friend and ally in this life, it is here that it may be used to render you a very great service—used in its highly purified form and not blinded by delusion or by personal like and dislike which involve and enmesh it in the appetites and attachments of the lower sense and desire nature. If your intellect, your pure reason and understanding, is entangled in the lower nature, if it is thus deprived of its freedom, then the pure consciousness of *I am*-ness becomes vitiated. The feeling of universal oneness with all life gets lost. The intellect starts chaining you to misery by binding you to attachment, selfishness, passion, hatred, anger, jealousy, envy, pettiness, meanness, hardness, harshness to others. Due to the perverted work of the intellect, these impure tendencies spring up and produce a separatist mentality and a confined consciousness of the individual personality.

Again, *I am*-ness makes you feel at one with the entire universe, but saying "I am a human being" at once circumscribes you into a particular species—the human species. You feel, "I am not that creature". You say, "Kick that dog", "Kill that rat", "Crush that bug", "Shoot that rabbit". You thus separate yourself from all other species. And then, after saying, "I am a human being", you say, "I am white", and the whole world of the non-white races becomes something outside of you. You create a barrier and it does not end even there. You narrow your consciousness still further by saying, "I am a Frenchman" or "I am an American", and then "I am a Parisian" or "I am a New Yorker", until you are made less and less, so confined indeed that your heart, instead of expanding, becomes narrow and constricted. It means that you are in the process of stifling your spirit and choking up the universality of your true being, your pure consciousness and your natural spiritual essence. That is death. Confining your spirit into smaller and smaller rings is the same as going to the very root of life or the Fount of Life and there trying to choke it. The Fount of Life overflows and pervades the entire universe, but by confining yourself, you are withholding that fluent inner expression of peace, thwarting its natural and spontaneous outflow. By identifying yourself with passing aspects of your being such as the pigment of skin, faith, class or creed, etc., you are losing all the vastness and elation of the universal consciousness which is yours. You deprive yourself of the true and exalted experience of your Self. You no longer know your Self. You know but a pale, insufficient, false shadow of your true Self. You then weep, because you go against the very law of life.

Expansion is joy. Oneness is joy. Coming out of your little self is becoming fearless. The more you confine yourself to a narrow conception of individuality, the greater the limitation that results. There is bound to arise fear, differences, enmity and hatred; and peace, which is the essential nature of the being, is lost. When love is thus contradicted by the confinement of consciousness, how can there be happiness? It is love that brings light and happiness into the life of the human being. Love is the essential stuff of your being.

You Are Existence-Consciousness-Bliss

Now, this much becomes clear. When you say "I *am*", you assert your Existence. This Existence is your true nature, and this Existence is for ever. This Existence is indestructible, because it is not a created thing like the body of the five elements and because it is not identical with any of those non-essential factors of your being like the body, etc.; it is independent of them all. It is changeless. Mind constantly changes, takes on new ideas and sheds old ideas. There is constant flux in your mind. This mind, which is ever in a state of change and movement and flux, cannot be the eternal factor in you. The eternal factor is Existence. You are indestructible, imperishable Existence. Everlasting Life is your true and essential being. That is your nature.

You are also Consciousness or Awareness. You are not inert or insentient, and since you *know* that you exist, therefore, there is Knowledge in you. It is also a part of your essential nature. Thus, you exist; and you are conscious of your Existence, you have knowledge of your Existence. You are Self-aware.

You are Existence, Consciousness and Bliss. When you know that you are that pure Existence-Consciousness and also when you know simultaneously that you are not that which is constantly agitating you, then you become totally devoid of all the defects and imperfections of the lower perishable aspects of your being. All pain, all sorrow, all fear, all grief, all suffering is for the body. To suffer pain is the fate of the body. To experience grief, delusion, jealousy, passion, desire, joy and sorrow, fear and affection, is the fate of the mind. When you know yourself as independent of the body, independent of the mind—distinct and different from these two—then how can you allow these facts that characterise the two lower aspects of your being to affect you or even touch you? You are without pain, without suffering, without sorrow, without delusion, without like and dislike, without all those blemishes which characterise the mind and intellect. Thus you are essentially full of joy. Your true nature is Bliss. You are Existence-Consciousness-Bliss.

This *I am* is distinct from the body-mind part of your being and devoid of all its blemishes and defects. You are of the nature of bliss and that Bliss can never be touched no matter what afflictions, what changes and vicissitudes you, as a human being, have to experience on the lower levels of your being. Such experiences go only as far as the mind, and if you allow it, as far as the intellect, but beyond that they cannot go. They cannot touch You. They cannot approach You even remotely, for You are truly Existence-Consciousness-Bliss, eternal and absolute, incorruptible and changeless. Know Thyself as such. The true nature of the individual is verily this.

You Are God Even Now

This is the nature of the highest illumined soul who knows this. It is the nature of the intelligent, thinking man who is often puzzled, who sometimes seems to know this and again seems not to know this. It is also the nature of the ignorant man who is unlettered and does not even know how to think. It is the nature of the fool and the idiot. No matter what state of evolution or what state of unfoldment or manifestation of the inner spiritual consciousness you find yourself in, essentially, inwardly, in truth and in fact, you are Existence-Consciousness-Bliss. Even at this moment. Nothing can rob you of that.

This knowledge is your greatest wealth. This is the wealth of all wealth. This is what you have to unfold.

You have come here only in order to realise this. You have come here to know Thyself. This Truth shall make you free. You are, in fact, ever free, even now free, for this Truth abides aside from the fact that you are unaware of it. This Truth cannot be taken away. It is ever-existent. Your not knowing It does not affect the fullness of your Existence one whit.

This Truth of your being is the one subject upon which you should ponder and reflect, upon which you should meditate. This Truth you should try to realise. Above all, your life should be an expression of this inner Truth. Your life should be a spontaneous demonstration of this, your true Bliss-nature within, and not an expression merely of that nature which does not belong to you, even though as a human being, you have both these parts. You cannot run away from the part which is not really you, which is false, which has a beginning and an end, which is corruptible and perishable.

Your true and essential nature is one with the Universal Consciousness which people call God, which people worship as the Supreme Being but by different names: Allah and Jehovah and Ishvara and Brahman and Almighty Father. It does not matter what name you give It—It is God. He is the supreme, infinite, eternal Existence Absolute. He is the Universal Being, the One Common Consciousness (underlying all humanity) which knits and unites mankind and fills the entire universe with happiness. He is that great, unfailing, perennial Fountain of Joy.

In your essential nature, you are That. You are eternally linked with that Infinite Ocean of Joy and Bliss and Wisdom. If you realise that, your whole life blossoms forth into a radiance of love, into a radiance of bliss, into a radiance of happiness and peace and serenity. Every day try to make a point of being conscious of what you really are. Make yourself God-centred. Become one with the Existence Principle which is even in a blade of grass, a speck of dust, a wisp of cloud, and in every mode and expression of life. Feeling yourself one with all, how could you hurt others? How could you bring yourself to be false or cruel? How could you bring yourself to deceive others or to play them false? How could you bring yourself to hate or to be angry?

Walk with God: Talk with God

This is the view and the vision that man, both as an individual and as collective humanity, needs today. When Professor Einstein once was asked in a certain interview, "What shall we do, Professor, in order to improve the world?", he said, "We must have improved people". That means we must live in the consciousness of our true nature. Even if a few people, a handful of people, make it their firm resolution, their greatest aim and aspiration in life, not to live any longer as mere mundane creatures, but to feel themselves divine, to be always at one with the Divine Essence, then real progress will have been made. Live in this way every day.

Make this your aspiration: "I will not feel myself as the body or as the senses. I will not feel myself as the imperfect intellect full of desire and delusion. I will always feel myself as I really and truly am". If you make this your determination, Light will enter your whole life. It will fill your home. Wherever you go, people will see that you bring brightness with you. Sick people will begin to feel well. You will become a centre for the radiation of Truth.

You have come here to live like gods, walk like gods, talk like gods, act like gods and feel like gods, for verily you are all children of the Divine. You are eternally one with Him who is all-perfect, all-pure, all-conscious and all-wise. This great fact is the central fact of your life. It is the most precious treasure of every human heart. You must always feel yourself radiating the Divine

Essence within. You must look with the Eyes of God; you must touch with the Feeling of God; your heart must throb with the Nature of God. It must be full of love for all humanity.

To know Yourself is to feel yourself connected to the Perennial Fount of Joy. In silence, know that you are Divine. Then live in that Silence. Grow day by day into a greater realization of that Joyful Awareness. Such a life ultimately expands your consciousness into the Universal. The attainment of Cosmic Consciousness is knowing that you are part and parcel of the Divine Essence. Every other task in life has only a relative significance. Perhaps, being caught in this framework as we are, we may not reject other things completely, but they are only secondary. If you fulfil all the so-called tasks of this life without knowing *Yourself*, your life would be wasted. But if, in your own humble measure, this one Truth has been pursued, attained and felt within as your own personal experience, then no matter how you may have fulfilled the other tasks, you will have lived your life fully, gloriously and successfully. Out of you, untold blessings will come to those who accompany you in this life.

This Divine Life is the sole task of your mortal existence. From Divinity has your being been brought. In Divinity let your life be led—even while in this embodied condition. Eternal Divinity is your ultimate destination. As life leads to Glory, let it be lived in Glory. Let your life be crowned with Supreme Fulfilment. Let Bliss and Truth be your only experience, and let Peace, Serenity and Love be your only bestowal upon this world in which we live. Know Thyself and be Divine—and be Divinely Blissful!

6. YOUR TRUE PURPOSE IN LIFE

Glorious Immortal Self! There is a permanent Reality behind this entire universe that lies before you. There is a vital living Truth behind the names and forms that constitute the world we have come to know. That great Reality, that living Truth is of the nature of bliss and blessedness. It is a state of untrammelled freedom, limitless peace, boundless wisdom and indescribable bliss. It is a joy which nothing upon the surface of the earth can even remotely equal. And that bliss, freedom, peace, wisdom and joy is your essential and eternal state. That is your real abode. That is your ultimate destiny. Your life has, as its purpose, the attainment of that state. This life is given to you in order to realize that Reality. It is this realization that ultimately gives you the power of totally transcending all sorrows and miseries and limitations which this earth-life imposes upon you. In one word, the goal of your life is the realization of the Supreme Reality. It is this achievement, and this achievement alone, which is the central purpose of your life. This is the fact which is the one redeeming feature of human life upon this earth despite all its sordidness, all its wretchedness and misery. The fact is that life is a glorious means of attaining the Supreme State in which real and unalloyed happiness can be experienced.

The Great Search for Happiness

Let us make an observation of life. What significant point emerges out of our observation? It is that wherever man exists, activity is also evident. People are running about, everyone bursting with activity! There never seems to be a moment just to pause and reflect. And what is this activity? Let us try to analyse it. Most of this activity is a furious search for happiness, for enjoyment, for pleasure, of different degrees and shades of experience. Simultaneously, man is ceaselessly trying to rid himself of sorrow, pain and suffering. He is trying to avoid all that is unpleasant, painful, sorrowful and grievous, and to attain all that is joyous, pleasant, happy and enjoyable. It may be argued that man willingly endures much hardship and discomfort, and even makes a great deal of effort to work hard during all the five days of the business week. He accomplishes many difficult tasks, so how could it be right to say that he was trying to avoid unpleasant and painful experience? But then, go deeper and discover the motive of his voluntary struggle! Through all this effort and exertion, man aims to take it easy later on, to cushion himself with comforts and to pension his life with pleasures. All these efforts are directed at the earning of money, for money enables one to obtain greater pleasures.

This should give us an inkling that the true nature of the human soul is bliss. In the state of embodied existence, this true nature of bliss is hampered. There are limitations of the body, limitations of the senses. There are defects imposed upon us, such as heat and cold, hunger and thirst, discomfort and disease. There are mental afflictions such as sorrow, bereavement and dejection, separation from those whom we love, contact of those whom we dislike or fear, anxiety, disillusionment, jealousy, frustration, etc. All these factors in this embodied state veil our true nature—we are ourselves all-bliss. But, despite all this, we ever seek unconsciously to assert our true hidden higher nature. Thus, the individual exercises his faculties in order to obtain things which are calculated to promote the experience of happiness. Unfortunately he does not get happiness. Why? For a very simple reason. He is searching for something where it is not. He is looking for happiness amidst objects of this universe which are imperfect, changeful and impermanent. Since imperfection and changeability are the very nature of external objects, they cause in the mind mixed experiences to ensue from their contact. This is the reason why man's efforts invariably end in disillusionment, disappointment and total dissatisfaction. Whenever one object fails to satisfy, man will try another and then another and yet another. Thus, during an entire life, man ceaselessly searches to find happiness in objects, changing from one to another in quick succession in order to find the experience of happiness which will put an end to all sorrow. His life is wasted away. All too soon, he finds that his temporary existence has come to an end. The true purpose of his life has been missed.

The Great Ones who have pondered over life and who have delved right into the very depths of outer as well as inner nature have realized through their intense inner effort the nature of the Ultimate Reality—God, that Essence out of which all life has come forth. They have stated in clear and unmistakable terms, "Oh mortals, you cannot find unalloyed perfect happiness and bliss in this imperfect and limited phenomenal universe. By its very nature it cannot contain that ultimate, transcendental experience. The ultimate state of joy and bliss can be had only within your own self which has as its source the permanent and eternal Self. All the bliss and joy lies within you". Even this statement could be corrected. Let us say, "This is your very *nature*". This does not lie "within you"; but, you are yourself that bliss. Your innermost being, your true self, is essentially ineffable bliss and peace. The rediscovery of that living awareness of bliss is life's great task. It is the great purpose of your life. This is the goal of life for which we have taken birth on this earth-plane.

Right Education as to the True Meaning of Life

It is the duty of every parent, educator and elder to give to growing souls (young people) the sense of life's wondrous purpose. If from the very beginning of one's life this were inculcated in every soul, a great deal of searching and struggling and sorrow would be obviated. Right from the very start, life would be meaningful. Life is not just a haphazard flight from one object to another. Life is a quest full of significance and meaning. But, all too often, this purpose is lacking and man merely conforms to the pattern of his grandsires mechanically and blindly. "My great-grandfather did it like this. Therefore, I will do likewise. Why, everyone is doing it like this!" — this is the sheep mentality that characterizes the lives of a great many people. The experience of the rest of the world will be the experience of these people also. Sorrow and disappointment is the ultimate harvest of those whose lives are devoid of discernment and discrimination.

Therefore, the sooner the eyes are opened to the great meaning of life, the greater the degree of perfection that will be attained right from the very start. Otherwise, life would be like setting upon a journey without direction, or like getting out onto a highway without a knowledge of destination or route. If someone then asks you where you are going, you will not be able to say. Without knowing the destination, you will be merely moving like an aimless loiterer along the highway called life. That is not real living.

Living Is Not Life

Thus you are caught up in this whirl called life, and so closely gripped by it, so deeply entangled in its meshes, that the mere process of living rather than the true life engrosses you entirely. *Living* takes the place of *life*. And naturally, with the true purpose missing, there lies an essential emptiness within, and this emptiness you try to fill by ever exerting to obtain external objects. But objects cannot bring the experience of happiness within; they foment anxiety and bring the experience of unrest and turbulence. Happiness is a state of the inner life of the individual. It is a state of the mind and the intellect. It is therefore a condition of the inner being. It is not in any way related to the external state of opulence, for here the peace of mind is easily disturbed by anxiety, insecurity and fear; there is actually a spiritual bankruptcy within. Whatever progress has been made towards the true attainment, that is the real wealth. All the objects which you may have gathered during an entire life-time will be left behind. They pass away. Not all the objects of this world put together can give you real satisfaction, for, by their very nature, they are powerless to do so.

The necessity of filling your life with objects is an implication of want. One accumulates objects to fulfil this want. One feels that without this fulfilment real joy and bliss cannot be obtained. But as long as one is a slave to wants, he cannot be really happy. Slavery and happiness are incompatible. It is freedom that makes you happy. While you are bound to want, you are merely a fettered creature. How can you enjoy the happiness which is to be found only in freedom? Happiness is the all-fullness of the blessed experience of that Reality which is beyond all want. Know that you are beyond all want.

The state of unmanifest splendour is your true state. All-fullness is your nature. When you realize that Fullness, you will transcend all sense of want. Then you will not merely be getting rid of wants, but getting rid of the very element of want from your nature. You will feel, "I am all-full. No wants have I. No desires have I". This feeling of plentitude within you is veritable bliss. If this sense of plentitude arises in your heart, then you are the master. There is no bondage. Nothing in this world can attract you or enslave you. Know yourself for what you really are and fill yourself with that bliss and that supreme plenitude. This is the glorious task before you. This is the central meaning of life.

The Goal of Life According to Indian Philosophy

You know that changeful, imperfect objects cannot give you the changeless perfect experience. Now try to make your life a quest after That which is changeless, which is all-full and, therefore, perfect and blissful. You are at once confronted with the fact that as embodied beings, you cannot entirely dispense with the performance of your day-to-day duties as members of a family or as citizens of a society. Whether you like it or not, for the time being, we have to fulfil these duties. How should they be co-ordinated with the exercise of our highest duty in life — the attainment of Bliss?

Those who have only a nodding acquaintance with Indian philosophy have acquired a strange and rather confused conception of the Buddha, Nirvana, the theory of Maya, the theory of Karma, etc. There is a nebulous haze in their minds out of which has emerged the idea that India professes a philosophy of fatalism, as though everything were pre-destined and there were no need for doing anything. Indeed, one could not do anything because the ultimate goal would be a nullity, according to this way of thinking. In this conception, man himself would be a cipher, because Nirvana means nothingness. This is the inference which has been drawn by some people from the message of Patanjali. There could be no greater mistake than this. Indian philosophy declares in bold and unmistakable terms that the great aim of human life is to attain supreme bliss. It asserts: "All beings in this universe have come forth from Bliss. In Bliss they have their being, in Bliss they are sustained, and to attain Bliss they are destined. Therefore, it is perennial Bliss indeed which is the great and the ultimate Truth and Reality".

This is obviously not a philosophy of fatalism. This is not an advocacy of do-nothingness. When it is said that the supreme state is Nothing (No-thing), the meaning is that it is nothing which could be described by articulate utterance. Utterance is too weak and inadequate to do so. It is also nothing that the individual human soul, in its state of relativity, in its state of duality, has either known or ever experienced. So it is a totally new and novel experience from the point of view of the experiences which the human being, in his state of finitude, has ever known. Silence is the only way in which one can express That which is beyond all speech and thought.

The great goal of life, according to Indian philosophy, is the attainment of Bliss. Whatever we do, we must not forget this goal. Attaining this goal, we are not deprived of anything. Rather we are filled with something — something which the whole world can never give, which all the objects of the universe are powerless to give. Our outer lives are characterised by the very antithesis of that blissful, peaceful experience. But if one is to start in quest of that great attainment, is he to cancel completely the course he has already adopted? Is this life to be set aside? *Can* it be set aside?

Spiritual Life and Life in this World — A Reconciliation

Both the ancient and the modern Indian sages are idealists, but their idealism is practical; it is combined with a very sane and sensible realism. In the quest for bliss and peace, the other life has to be reconciled with the striving for perfection. The physical and intellectual aspects of the being which operate upon this relative plane have to be reconciled with the great urge of the truly spiritual being. This reconciliation is one of the tasks of the spiritual life.

With this reconciliation in view, two things must be understood. One is that the body and the mind and all the intellectual faculties have been given to us as instruments, whereas in ordinary life, man is at the beck and call of the physical body and the senses. He does not know himself to be apart from them. That is the first thing to be understood. And the other is that man finds himself totally entangled also in the desires and cravings of the mind. But to consider yourself the servant of the senses and the slave to the cravings and desires of the mind is a woeful misconception. To regard the senses and the mind as instruments given solely for indulging in an endless round of sense pleasures and objective enjoyments is a deplorable perversion. These instruments have been given in order to bring you closer to the attainment of the great goal. The mind, the body and the intellect should be recognised as such, treated as such, and nobly utilized to this end. In the great teachings of the sages we find that man as a social being, and as a member of the community, is advised to live a life of honest labour. This labour may take the additional form of selfless service to all.

Experience shows that every great benefit conferred upon others by the exercise of man's faculties comes from this highest form of labour. In his practical affairs, man should continue to care for, and look after, his family, his immediate relations and his friends. In his personal affairs, he should take due and proper care of his own body and mind. Thus living a life of usefulness and service unto others, you maintain your integrity. In doing thus, you are not taken out of the spiritual life. When your life is based on the principles of truth and honesty, your exertion for the means of maintaining a livelihood is in no way an obstacle or a bar to your advancement in the interior life of spiritual unfoldment.

As right action must be followed in the external life, so right thinking must prevail in the mental life. Thoughts that trail after the pull of the senses are wrong. Thoughts that follow the principles of righteousness are right. Therefore, think thoughts of goodness. Think thoughts of purity. Think thoughts of selflessness. Forget about "What shall I get? What shall I obtain? What pleasures and enjoyments shall I find to fill my life?" Think instead, "Out of me, what good could come to all people? In what way could I add to the happiness of others? In what way could I lessen the sorrow of others? How could the intellect be used to obtain the true knowledge of this universe? What is real? What is unreal? What is permanent and what is transitory? What is the ultimate goal and what belongs to the temporary life?" Thus let the intellect ever discriminate between the truly good and the merely pleasant, between the real and the unreal, between the permanent and the passing. To get an insight into this world, into the nature of things here, and into your own nature is the proper use of your intellect. Thus you may find out how thoughts operate, how desires operate, how the senses try to deceive you, how the thoughts and the senses may be controlled. Awaken discrimination and let it serve as the guide. Most important of all, let the spiritual life lead you towards the attainment of the goal.

Whenever problems present themselves to you in life, put to yourself this question: "Is this going to take me nearer to that ultimate attainment, or is it going to slow me down in my progress towards the noble fulfilment of life?" This must be the criterion. If a thing or an action tends to bind you more to the sensual life, then reject it, but if it tends to hasten you towards the ultimate attainment, then adopt it. Thus the mind and the body may be made to serve their proper functions in life, and the physical, the mental and the intellectual aspects of the personality trained in a practical way to advance you in your all-important spiritual life.

When all aspects are harmonized, the form or pattern of your exterior life is not of prime account. If you are a doctor, you may continue to be a doctor. A teacher may continue to teach. A businessman may continue to be a businessman. But he must be an honest businessman! And a doctor has to be a kind-hearted doctor and not merely a fee-extractionist! When the principles of righteousness are practised, even a soldier may continue to be a soldier, fulfilling his duty at the command of his superiors, and yet be truly spiritual. If he is detached, his life will take him closer to the goal. Therefore, let the principle of righteousness be your guide.

Practice of Virtues

Of what does righteousness consist? The answer is to be found in the very structure of truth. If one is fulfilling the truth, one is drawing nearer to the realization of God. But if one's life is characterized by falsehood, one cannot have God, one cannot have happiness; for one is cutting himself away from the Source of all blessedness. If one is cut away from Him, then not even the whole of the earth can give him happiness. Peace and happiness cannot, by their very nature, come into the life of the individual who contradicts truth. Righteousness is, therefore, the fulfilment of the principles of truth in life. It consists in being true to your inner real nature which is Divine.

Compassion, love of all, and kindness to all creatures is the practice of truth. These constitute your real nature. These constitute the higher spiritual part of you. Have, therefore, compassionate regard for your kith and kin, parents and children, brothers and sisters, friends and neighbours. Without this practice in your life, spiritual blessedness cannot come. Harsh speech, a sharp tongue, flashes of anger and annoyance that wound the feelings of others should never be allowed. Happiness comes by increasing the joy in the lives of others. It comes to those who are centres of love, centres of kindness and compassion, and who never entertain even remotely the thought of hurting the least of God's creatures.

Behind all action should be a perfectly pure motive. Both the thoughts and the motives should always be noble, sublime and pure. The person respecting the standard of absolute purity partakes of pure speech and action. Impure thought or motive, characterized by greed, lust or anger, instantaneously discredits any action. Greed is a fire which blazes more and more fiercely if it is fed. The contented person is always alert and recognizes the greedy thought which he thereupon stamps out of his mind.

Happiness comes only to the one who is contented. If such a contented person receives objects which are interesting, he is happy; if he does not receive any, he is happy; or if he is deprived of objects, still he is happy. He is not deluded by the notion that objects bring happiness. How could you describe as happy any experience which depends for its fulfilment upon objects? For, as soon as the objects are removed, such an experience comes to an end. Also, even as the object is changed, so does the experience, too, change. All objects are changeful and your residence here is only temporary; your connection with all the objects in the universe is, therefore, transient.

My Master says in a humorous way, "Amidst all the uncertainties and insecurities of this world one thing alone is certain—you have to pass. You cannot remain here. This is only a drama you are enacting. You have come from an unmanifest state into an embodied, manifest state. Every second shortens the period allotted to you here. What that period is, no one knows. Every birthday which you celebrate with so much happiness, with birthday cards, cakes and candles, takes one year away from the period allotted to you. Soon the allotted period has to come to an end. Once again you will have to go back into that unmanifest state where you will be disembodied, where you will have no personality, no name. You have to pass".

What greater thoughtlessness, what greater folly could there be than to depend upon objects of a changeful and perishable nature to give us happiness! Happiness does not come from outside. He who knows that happiness comes from within holds on to the "old-fashioned"rule of contentment. It is a golden rule. Do not covet that which does not rightfully belong to you. He who has not been naturally endowed with beauty of features need not cast jealous looks at the beauty of another person's features. God has given him those particular features. When this thought is in the mind, "Why should I not be like that person? Why should I not have what that person has?", there is no peace in the mind. And without peace of mind, how can happiness be found?

If, in the daily lives of all people, this rule against covetousness were applied, then all strife, all war, all hatred and all violence would come to an end. Even on a national scale, agitation is due to the breaking of this one rule. Every man wants to put his hand into the chest of his neighbour. If individuals are thus indiscriminate, how can we expect great nations to abjure violence? Governments which have at their service the highest intellects, the foremost scientists upon earth, have also been ensnared by these foibles.

The principle of righteousness takes you to the root

of the happiness of all people. Therefore, let your life be guided by the highest ethical principles—the principles of truth, purity and universal love. It is not necessary to leave one's family and go to live in a cave or in the Himalayas or in the forest or in a monastery to observe these principles. Your own house, wherever it is, will be a heaven of blessedness if you practise these principles. It will be made into more than a monastery or a cloister. Within its very doors, your life, based upon compassion and kindness, will rise to the highest standards of the moral and ethical ideal.

This regular observance will sustain you in your constant quest after the Truth within. Every day that passes will bring a deeper inner awareness of the supreme purpose of life.

Life is very precious. Say, "I have come here to realize the supreme state of blessedness and to experience the highest bliss. I have been given this unique opportunity of a human birth and a human life in order to attain that Ultimate Goal".

The chance is now given. Who knows if the keen state of aspiration and receptivity to the highest principle will last? Who knows if the keen state of devotion to the ideal will continue? Therefore, now is the time to make a supreme effort to realize the true purpose of life. Now is the time to make an earnest effort to attain the highest blessedness and the wondrous bliss of Realization.

7. LAWS OF HEALTH AND PROSPERITY

Beloved Immortal Self! Glorious Rays of the Eternal Light Divine! Salutations to you and crores of adorations to the Supreme!

Today I speak to you a few words from the wisdom of the ancients—the great seers of India—on a subject which, though of that part of your being which is perishable, which is unreal, which is not the Ultimate Truth of your being, is important in its own way in as much as it is a means to the realization of your True Self, and in as much as the body, its well-being and health in this life, and the happiness and prosperity in this life, both become helps and instrumental factors to you in fulfilling the true and only lasting purpose in your life, which is to know who you are.

Knowing the truth of who you are, you become free, free for ever from the bondage of this terrestrial existence, free for ever from the vexing limitations of this body-mind bondage, free for ever from all the fetters of desires, cravings, fears, and the basic ignorance which has made you forget your true Self and dream of yourself as something which you are not. For ever immortal you are, unborn, birthless, deathless, unchanging and undecaying. Immortal you will always be, for this is the eternal Truth, the Reality of your existence, and even at this moment, this is the splendid Truth of your being. You are Immortal, even now. You are the very essence of Bliss Infinite and Peace Immeasurable—right now, at this moment in time. You are That in all Its fullness, in all Its perfection, in all Its unblemished, untarnished splendour. To realize this is the great meaning of life on earth.

The great ancients, though illumined with this vision

of man's glorious inner nature and fully filled with the
great spirit of this unfoldment, were in their own way,
realists regarding man's body-bound condition. Thus we
have, side by side with those four great repositories of
ancient wisdom which contain declarations of eternal
truths—the Four *Vedas*—, a fifth scripture which in India
is called "The Fifth *Veda*" and which is known by the
name of "Ayurveda". This is a very significant word.
"Ayuh" means the span of your life here and "Veda"
means knowledge or science. Thus, "Ayurveda" means
the science of life or the science of living.

That secret, the science of human life, of how to
preserve this life, of how to keep in comfort, of how to
live in well-being, is the significance of the Ayurveda.
And that secret has been given to the Indian system of
health and well-being (both physical and mental) from
the great bosom of spiritual wisdom reposing in the other
Vedas. Thus the Ayurveda tends to base itself upon the
fundamental truths that have their residence in the four
great *Vedas*.

The Human Being as Viewed by the Indian Masters

Indian thought evolves from within outward so that
the first task and the most important thing is to know
yourself, for you are the prime factor of all knowledge.
There must first be a seer to see things, and there must
first be a thinker to ponder over matters, to ponder over
all things seen. There must first be a knower if any
knowledge is to be at all. Therefore, the knowledge
about the knower, the science of your own Self who
forms the pivot of this universe, who is the basic factor
in all knowledge, was placed first. Know Yourself—and
then start knowing all else that is other than yourself.

The great knowledge which the ancient seers of
India arrived at about the truth of the individual was that
he was no material being, that he was no being of this
earth, and those parts of his personality which were

material and partook of the nature of the material universe, viz., mutability, change, destruction and decay were but appendages or sheaths or coverings which enfolded and held in bondage, as it were, the true splendour of his essential Self and, as such, they were outside of him and not essential to him, and the essential being was the spiritual Consciousness within.

Nearest to this spiritual Consciousness is the mind, and to the Indian Masters, the mind is as much matter as the physical body. They do not give a higher place to the mind than to the body in as far as the mind's relationship to the soul is concerned. In relation to your true Self, mind is no better than a clod of earth or this flesh-and-bones body. Mind also is matter, but it is matter in a very fine state. It is subtle material. It is only the spiritual Consciousness that is truly of the Divine Nature, and compared to it, mind is matter, the body is grosser matter, and the external stuff is the grossest of all.

The entire view of the human being, as held by the Indian masters, is that the conditions of the body depend upon the interplay between the innermost Self of man and the various sheaths covering it. If full and unhampered play of the soul-force is allowed through the mind, through the intellect, through the feelings, through sentimental thought, through the vital energy within, and through every cell and nerve fibre of the body, then the body would be in a perfect state of health. If this free play of the soul-force is blocked, is vitiated, then a condition of sickness arises in all the enfolding sheaths.

How does this blockage come about? In two ways. If your consciousness becomes so clouded that you totally forget your eternal link with the spiritual source of your life, which is God, and you become totally engrossed, enmeshed and entangled in the desire-personality of the mind and the intellect, and in the passion-personality of

the senses of the body, then your link, your channel, with
the Supreme Being is "cut off" and you cannot have fullness of life and abundance of well-being, for all well-
being, all abundance, stems from the Eternal Source of
your life. It is from God that we get all well-being in all
the different aspects of our nature, and in all the different levels of our nature, and if we cut ourselves off
from this source, then, like unto a branch that has been
cut off and hanging loose from the parent tree, we tend
to wither. The very source of our life being cut off from
us, our life tends to partake of illness, disease, weakness,
imperfection, sorrow, suffering and misery.

In the same way, if through the misuse of our body
and its physical energy, of the inner vital power that is
expressed through the form of subtle Prana within the
physical body, and of our own thoughts and emotions, we
make them so gross and totally unsuited to the expression of our essential Divine Nature, then these levels,
being deprived of the benign and beneficial influence of
our own soul-force, tend to become sick. Therefore, the
whole of Ayurveda is built upon this theory, viz., that instrument which is pure and perfect, which is in a state
of fineness and thus permits the true Divine Nature full
and unhampered scope for expression through itself,
tends to progress in health. And so, where this free play
is vitiated by our misuse of the various forces at the different levels of our being, our entire being tends to get
into a state of ill-health and suffering. The theory of
Ayurveda also says that even the suffering is just a
reminder to the individual to correct himself and once
again regain a clean and fine state, a refined state; and
if he learns the lesson of the disease and ill-health immediately and changes his habits and sets right the error
in living, both physically and mentally, then that health
which is the inherent state of the human body, which is

the natural state of the human body, will prevail once again.

You are now familiar with the four levels of your being. There is your true being, your true nature within, and YOU are seated at the centre of this body chariot— existence, consciousness, bliss, peace and purity, of the nature of perfection. Secondly, around YOU is the mind-matter, the mental sheath, where all intellectual activity, mental activity, emotional activity takes place. And still further outside, there is the vital sheath holding the energy that animates the body and makes it live. And you then have the external form which is made up of gross flesh, bones, muscles, tendons and the various organs which make up the physical body. In the three levels of the mind, the Prana and the body, one has to maintain a certain standard of purity and a certain standard of refinement.

How to Eat to Keep Fit

The refinement of the body, the purity of the body, is ensured mainly through diet, through food. If the proper food is taken and it is properly taken, and taken at the proper time, then the health of the body is ensured. One of the great sages, Athreya, said: "Proper food taken in moderation, at the proper time, in the proper manner, goes to ensure one's good health". What did he mean by 'proper food'? Sattwic food, fine food, in a pure condition. Taken at the proper time? Well, all health authorities will tell you that at certain periods of the day our body powers are on the ascent and food taken during those periods becomes beneficial, and when the body powers begin to ebb, food is not to be taken. Food is not to be taken when one is in a state of agitation or when one is emotionally disturbed.

Properly taken? Properly taken means taken with a devout attitude, with mind attuned to God, taken unhurriedly, without too much haste, and taken with calmness

and chewed thoroughly and, above all, taken in moderation. If all these conditions are fulfilled, then food goes
to purify the body, increase its powers and keep it in a
refined state, for food has a very unique definition according to this science of Ayurveda in India.

Food is called "Annam". Anything that is eaten is
called "Annam". Annam has a two-fold meaning. One
meaning of this word is 'eat or consume'; and another
equally valid meaning is 'that which consumes'. This latter meaning is very deeply significant in Ayurveda. Diet
is consumed; diet is also that which consumes. If you will
reflect upon it, you will see how true this two-fold definition of the word diet is. Food, if it is taken in moderation, becomes the giver of life; if it is taken in
immoderation, it becomes the destroyer of health and the
destroyer of life, ultimately.

Even if taken according to law and rule, food is the
greatest devourer of the energies of the human individual, because a great deal of the energies of each individual each day, and day after day until the very last
day when he enters the grave, is just devoured or consumed by food for its digestion, assimilation and excre-
tion. More than eighty-five to ninety per cent of the
energy that is produced in the body each day is consumed for the processes of digestion, assimilation and
elimination. So, you can see how food consumes your
vital energy, how it consumes your very life-energy.

When food is eaten, the entire blood supply is taken
to the stomach and the entire system has to go all out
and work to digest and to assimilate this food. As the
system goes on doing this day after day through
childhood and youthhood, middle age and old age, a time
comes when food can no longer be taken, because the
body has not the energy to deal with this consumer of
energies, and one may find he has spent all his life's
energies in digesting tons of food. Perhaps, the food

taken since childhood, if it were heaped, would cover a big barn or a large storage tank. Thus it is that food is both what is eaten and also what eats through your life and consumes it.

I have given these broad views to commend moderation, the root principle of health, according to the science of Ayurveda. The proper type of food, when it is taken at the proper time and in the proper way induces good health. This food, which is converted into energy, pervades the entire body in the form of the physical force, the inner Prana; and if Prana is misused, then life is destroyed, health is shattered. In what form is this Prana present in the human being? It is present in the human being as sex energy, as the vital power, as the life-force; and the misuse and waste of this life-force is the greatest destroyer of health, of well-being, and of life itself. We have the great declaration: "Life is the preservation of one's vital energy; and the loss of one's vital energy is destruction".

Self-control and Preservation of the Life-Force

Indian doctors lay the utmost emphasis upon the preservation of one's life-force. Great moderation in one's sexual life is the one note upon which they perennially harp. A physician, after examining a patient and enquiring and advising about his diet, will then stress the fact that while the patient is under his care, his treatment, he must live as a single being, and it is only when the patient is completely well that the physician will consider advising him that he may live a normal physical life; and a normal physical life, according to Ayurveda, is not indulgence. It is taken for granted that normal physical life is characterized by two factors: restraint and moderation. The entire Ayurvedic science of health rests upon this basic principle of conserving one's life-force, one's vital energy. Without this, there can be no health. If you neglect this factor, not all the drug factories in this world can bring you any health; not all the doctors and physicians of this world can bring you any well-being, any strength, any vitality. It is something which is within you and which you have to preserve, and if you are a profligate, others cannot give it to you, because it is something which is not given from outside. It cannot be obtained from bottles, from pills, powders or potions. It is impossible. It is something which is a part of yourself and it is to be increased only by conservation and moderation in living.

The science of Ayurveda rests upon this one principle, and to this end, from the very beginning of life, the student is taught the importance of self-control and the importance of the conservation of one's vital energy. If that is lost, if that is vitiated, then the Pranic sheath is thrown out of balance. Just as an error in food vitiates your body and makes it impure and gross, so an error in this life-energy vitiates your Pranic sheath. The vital energy is the very quintessence of the energy the body assimilates from food. If that energy is not conserved, the Pranic sheath is thrown out of harmony and the Prana begins to vibrate in a discordant manner. And all disease springs from the discordant state of the Prana within.

And if the mind, instead of becoming a field of expression for your inner perfection, becomes a field for the play of thoughts, emotions and sentiments which are totally unspiritual, which are totally animalistic and gross, which are full of lust, anger, passion, greed, hatred, jealousy and envy, and if these thoughts begin to flood the mental level, then health cannot be achieved by the body.

The Mind and the Body—Vyadhi and Adivyadhi

You cannot have a diseased and unhealthy mind and have health of the body at the same time. The blood which the food forms in the body will become poisoned. The body will not be able to assimilate the maximum

energy from the food taken if the emotions that fill the
mind are destructive and impure and gross, if they are
not of the soul-nature, not of the spiritual nature, but
partake of the body-nature, the gross, flesh-nature. Carnal passions and animalistic emotions like hatred and
jealousy and violence make the mind totally unfit as an
instrument for the expression of your true being, since
such a mind becomes the hotbed of disease seeds. The
inner state of such a mind becomes the fertile source,
the prolific ground for the springing up of disease conditions. The Ayurvedic Masters gave out this truth more
than three thousand years ago; and now, during the past
hundred years, the Western psychologists have "suddenly" begun to find that more than fifty to eighty per cent
of actual physical ills in hospitals have their cause in the
mind and only manifest in the body.

That physical illness stems from the mind has been
realized only very recently in the West through the work
of a few European psychologists, but this knowledge
made up the very foundation of Ayurvedic science. The
Ayurvedic Masters said that unless the moods of the
mind were serene, full of calmness, full of love, characterized by love and purity, disease could not be cured.
The physician would also tell the patient to observe
silence to conserve energy.

Jesus gave to one who wanted to approach Him the
advice: "If you want to draw near to the altar of God
and if you bear ill-will, if you have not forgiven your
brother, first of all go and forgive him and then draw
near to God's altar in worship". Likewise, the physicians
of ancient India said: "If you have hatred, if you have
envy, if you have hostility towards anyone, I cannot treat
you; I cannot give you this medicine, for my medicine is
something spiritual, my medicine is something sacred and
holy. First of all, you must make your mind free from all

undivine thoughts, and then come to me and I shall treat you".

The theory of Ayurveda is that the root of disease is not in the body, but in the mind. This disease in the mind is the cause for the outward physical disease. The disease of the body they called "Vyadhi"; and the mental cause, the root of the physical disease they called "Adivyadhi". "Adhi" means prime or the first or the beginning; and the inner emotional state is referred to as "Adhivyadhi", meaning first disease. A first disease comes and from that springs a second disease; thus, the actual effect of the wrong moods, the wrong passions of the mind, and the misuse and abuse of one's own vital energy, the vital life-force, bring about certain conditions in the body which cause disease.

The Ayurvedic Theory of the Tridoshas

The ancient seers of India interpreted these body conditions in a very unique way, and not in the Western way. They had the theory of "Tridoshas". The Ayurvedic science of diagnosis of the disease conditions (which manifest as a result of malaise in your mind and in your vitality) was based upon the "three humours" of the body. The Ayurvedic scientists said that such upsetting of the purity of the mind and the fineness of the vital energy brought about a state of disturbance in the balance between the three humours that characterize the normal condition of each human being. The theory of the three humours was not entirely unknown to mediaeval medicine in Europe and in England. In Europe, I do believe, they had something similar to Ayurveda, and perhaps, it had come through Arabia and Greece.

The three humours are the "phlegmatic humour", the "bilious humour" and the "windy humour". These humours are found in a certain proportion in a healthy body, and when there is an upset in the vital force due to abuse and misuse, due to over-indulgence, and there is an upset in the mind due to wrong thoughts and emotions, there comes about an imbalance in the three humours (wind, bile and phlegm), and then disease conditions begin to manifest. If due to this imbalance, there is a predominance of the phlegm condition, then all sorts of phlegmatic diseases come about—bronchitis, lung trouble, coughs, colds, toxins. If this imbalance brings about an excess of wind, then rheumatic diseases manifest in the body—aches, joint pains, rheumatism, lumbago, flatulence, etc.

It is the imbalance of the three humours which is sought to be set right by the actual medicine which the Ayurvedic physician gives, but he says, "I can, with this medicine, but try to bring about once again a re-balancing of your three humours, but you have to work from the inside". So the first necessity is, of course, complete self-restraint; and secondly, come the emotions. Get rid of all bad emotions. How? Here, the Ayurvedic seers were of real help. They did not know 'psychology' as the modern psychologists know it, yet they knew what ought to be known. They said: "If you want to calm your mind and free it of all emotions, arouse in it a spiritual wave". And to this end, a physician always prescribed the uttering of such and such a Mantra, or a particular mode of worship to some particular aspect of the Deity, to be offered in a certain way, in a certain shrine.

Worship, you know, is such a powerful instrument in your life, and when you once again lift up your mind to God, when once again you attune your spirit to the Higher Being, that Source from which you have cut yourself off—which cutting off is the root cause of this great disease called worldly existence, this human birth—, the mind is completely overhauled. When once again, in worshipfulness, you attune yourself to the Divine and start repeating His Mantras, start chanting the Divine Name, then the whole of the mental stuff is put into a state of purity and fineness and the gross condition which had given rise to the disease symptoms in the physical body is corrected. So the physician on the outside and the patient from within co-operate and once again the body is restored to its healthy condition. This, in short, is the theory and system of health according to Ayurveda—the Fifth *Veda*—the Science of Life.

Based upon the first premises that man is Divine, that health is his natural condition, and that purity and fineness are the prerequisites of health, Ayurveda has a very interesting declaration to make. In the Hindu view of life, the individual is supposed to live and work for the four great attainments—Dharma, Artha, Kama and Moksha. Dharma is fulfilment of the ethical norm. Artha is the earning of wealth in order to live comfortably. (Wealth is not left out in the Hindu scheme of things; that is, the earning of wealth in an honest way in order to live comfortably.) Kama is the fulfilment of all legitimate desires that are necessary for dignified and honest living, that are necessary for one's well-being, and also, for the well-being of all others with whom one lives. Kama is the fulfilment of all legitimate desires that are not opposed to the welfare of others. Moksha is, ultimately, liberation in the Divine, eternal freedom in the Divine.

Ayurveda says that for these four attainments, our health is the supreme and excellent root or basis. Without health, none of these four can be achieved and, therefore, the proper care of the body is one of the most important duties to be attended to, and this can be done only through (i) the conservation of the vital energy through moderation and restraint, (ii) the refinement of the mind through right thinking, right feeling and worshipfulness, and (iii) the proper care of the physical condition through pure food taken moderately at the proper time and in the proper way—thoroughly chewed, taken when you are calm, with a little rest after eating.

If thus through the proper care of your health, the proper conservation of the vital energy, and the right attitude of mind you are in a state of good health, how shall you try to attain, also, a prosperous condition of living? How to have a fair level of prosperity? Which, of course, does not mean the fulfilling of cupidity, of avarice, of greed, or of inordinate desire. But which means, within legitimate bounds, to have a comfortable life permitting calmness of mind, freedom from worry, freedom from agitation and restlessness, so that you can give mind and thought to the service of your fellow-men and to the worship of God, in order to be of use on the outside and to be of the utmost use to yourself. What are the laws of prosperity? I am not telling you the *secrets* of becoming prosperous, but I am telling you the *laws* of prosperity.

How to Attain Prosperity

The secret of prosperity, of course, would be to live within your income, to spend less than what you earn. And, do not go into debt! That would be the greatest wisdom in a nutshell! How to be prosperous? If you earn a hundred and fifty dollars, spend a hundred and forty-nine; then you always have one dollar left. If you would have me comment on it, I would say: "Never get into the instalment system". If you have cash, then all right, purchase things. If you do not have cash, go without them.

Yet, there are certain laws of prosperity which also stem from eternal spiritual truths. If you begin to feel and think lack or want, you experience lack. If you assert your abundance, then, as the shadow follows a person, abundance follows you. If you begin to desire, immediately you admit poverty. Desire is poverty. Desire is a feeling of inadequacy, and when you begin to desire, you are a beggar already. The secret of the ancients of becoming prosperous was to live in conformity with this law of prosperity and also to live with common sense.

Once one unconsciously begins to affirm poverty by desiring, then poverty only becomes the law. To get free of desire is the secret of setting free the law of prosperity into motion. Why? All plenitude is within you. There is nothing that you lack, for you are of God who is all. He is all-in-all. He is the source of all. In Him there is everything, and if you know that you are in Him, you have everything; you are in everything. And to affirm this knowledge, to affirm this fact of your ever being in Him is the master-key to make prosperity follow you like a dog following its master.

After all, you are the master of the whole creation, for you are heir to the One who is the master of everything. You lack nothing. All-plenitude, all-abundance is your Self. Your true nature is plenitude. The more you begin to assert that, to affirm that, with perfect confidence, not as a thing to be, but as a fact that is — prosperity is yours.

Want, or a feeling of poverty, is an attitude of the mind. If you have so much and you feel "I have everything", then you do not want anything else; but if you have so much and yet you feel "I do not have it", then you have not anything. A millionaire, who is always wanting to make ten million or twenty million, is really a beggar. A cab driver or a porter who is getting, say three or four dollars a day, and says, "That is quite enough for me; my pocket is always full", is always greater than the millionaire. He is richer than the millionaire for he has not the nagging feeling of lack and of want and the beggarly attitude of desire.

So, the inner secret of the true law of prosperity is to affirm your plenitude, to affirm your abundance and live in that everpresent condition of lacking nothing, of having God and, therefore, of having everything. This is the only way. This is the only secret, and the moment you start affirming it, you will find conditions changing, for your conditions are the product of your own thoughts. The ultimate vital factor that goes to make up all your life is constituted by your thoughts. They are as much tangible and substantial as the bricks that pile up and become a mansion. They can build your whole life. They can create any condition in your life. They can even create the conditions of your own health if the proper thoughts are thought. Just as a human being catches hold of something and mounts it, even so, proper thought has the power to build up, and cell by cell, broken cells can be built up. Anything that has been destroyed in you can be built up by the proper thought and, in the same way, the wrong type of thought can destroy whatever is whole and make it diseased.

The power of thought is something that stems right from you, that stems right from the soul, because it is nearest to you; and the soul-force is beneath and behind all thought-force, and the affirmation of your true condition overcomes all conditions that are foreign to you, that are not natural to you.

To this end, contentment is the true secret of affirming your abundance. Whatever comes, feel full. If it is one dollar, feel as though it were a million, and if it is ten dollars, feel as though it were ten million. Once you have contentment, there is nothing that can make you unhappy; and if you do not have contentment, nothing can make you happy.

The secret of prosperity is to affirm your true, abundant nature, the true fact of your plenitude. Be contented and put a notice on your mind: "No admission for any desire". The moment a desire arises, just reject it. Say, "Desire! Get out!" And then you will begin to experience that the desired object comes by itself to you. As long as you run after a thing, you cannot get it. The moment you turn away from a thing, it follows you by itself. This is an Eternal Law. This is a law which has been proven in the lives of all those who have discovered it and applied it to themselves. The more you desire, the more your want increases. Let this theorem be in your mind; let it be in your heart.

The Spiritual Law of Prosperity

There is something a little higher than even this. The Hindu believes that whatever there is in this universe is all the Divine Essence. Everything is God. Every force is God. Every phenomenon is God. Every being is God. Every name and form is God. Everything you experience is only the Divine Essence in various manifestations, and prosperity is one of the direct manifestations of "the Divine Power as the sustaining force in this universe". The Divine Power in this cosmic process expresses Itself first as a projecting power, a power that brings into being, and then It acts here upon the threefold time continuum of past, present and future, as the sustaining power. That which has been brought forth It sustains, nourishes, protects, takes care of. You see, it is God again at the other end of the cycle. The same power once again dissolves all that has been brought forth and reabsorbs projected phenomena into their original state of non-manifestation.

It is the central portion which is the most important to us—that aspect of the Divine Force which protects, sustains, nourishes, takes care of. And this It does in various ways. The Divine Force is present as food. It is present as the seasons. It is present as the clouds and the rain. It is present as the abundance that comes out of the earth, the fertility of the earth. And It is also present within us as the gastric fire that digests the food and nourishes us. It is also present as all prosperous conditions.

In this way, food is God, everything that keeps us

going is God. Food is a manifestation of God, outwardly. Within you, the vital force is God. All things that sustain life are expressions of God. The great life-force is God, and in your innermost being, the light of intelligence, with the consciousness it is derived from, is God.

You must not insult food. You must not treat food in a contemptuous way, in an angry mood or in a mood of displeasure. No. When a Hindu takes food, first of all he takes a morsel of rice and lifts it up to his forehead reverentially, bows down, and then puts it into his mouth to eat. He first of all salutes the food, and then he eats it.

So, food should not be eaten with disregard, or in a huff, or in a criticizing manner: "What is this food you have put upon this plate?" You must not be in a temper when you eat food. Eat your food in a worshipful manner. And you must not waste food. A waste of food is another insult, is another misuse of food, and he who wastes his food will not have prosperity.

Food is assimilated into your body as energy. Therefore, the vital force of your being is also called God. It is the manifestation of Divine Power. It also has to be treated with honour, treated with respect. It should not be insulted. It should not be misused, and it should not be wasted.

To such a one, prosperity comes. In the ultimate analysis, all your thoughts and moods, they too have to be pure. Prosperity follows truth. Prosperity follows purity. Prosperity follows compassion and kindliness, and prosperity follows goodwill. If you always wish for the welfare of others, if you always wish for the prosperity of others, if you always wish for the good of others, you automatically draw to yourself prosperity. Prosperity need not necessarily mean that you will have millions, but you will never lack. You will never suffer. God will look after you and see that no want of yours is not met. At every moment, whatever want comes will be met by God.

We have to know, we have to realize, that the whole human life is being directed by God. He is the inner guardian of the whole universe. He is the inner director of the entire cosmos, and He is the one who is guiding your life too. In every moment of your life, if you fulfil the conditions of honouring the law of prosperity, of honouring the manifestations of God in various forms — in the form of food, in the form of your own energy, in the form of money, in the form of your own talent and thought, and in the form of your intelligence and put them to the highest and noblest use, and do not waste them, and make use of them respectfully, with reverence — there, prosperity is assured; there, prosperity cannot but take its place at your feet. It will fill your house. That house will always be full of radiance, cheerfulness, charity, goodwill where there is honouring of food at the table and where there is always even temper.

Some Valuable Clues to Prosperity in the House

I have four or five things which, as a Hindu, I wish to tell you. Where elders are respectfully honoured, there prosperity prevails; and where elders — father and mother, grandfather and grandmother, uncles and aunts — are treated with contempt, with harshness, with scant respect, there is no prosperity.

These things are not known. So when people are miserable, when people are unhappy, when people lack prosperity, it is not known why it comes about that way. It is brought about by oneself by a total breaking of these laws. And then you try to find out the consequences of the bad situation by looking at the diary, or statistics, or expenditure and income account. Perhaps you blame economic conditions. But, no — you create your bad conditions by breaking the spiritual laws. Where elders are treated with respect and honour, are treated with reverence, there, in that family, in that house, prosperity will abide. In the life of that person who honours his elders, prosperity will always rest.

Secondly, where the women of the house are treated with reverence, where they are put upon the pedestal which they deserve, there is prosperity. Where are we all, where is humanity if it is not for the women? It is the Supreme Mother who is the very source of the whole universe, and where the mothers, the women, are treated with the reverence that is due to them, in that house, there is prosperity. And where women are treated with disrespect, unkindness, harshness, prosperity cannot come. Prosperity does not abide in that house where the wife and the mother are made to weep, where tears of women fall. Prosperity takes wings and flies away from that house where the woman weeps.

Thirdly, for the womenfolk themselves, modesty is the magnet of prosperity. For a woman, modesty is the highest ornament. The ornament of a woman, the beauty of a lady, is not in the jewellery she wears or in the type of material or the dress she wears — no, that is not beauty. After all, what is the beauty of the body? The moment you take leave of the body, it is just a useless thing here. So the true beauty and the grace of a woman is modesty. If a woman is modest, if she is chaste, she becomes worshipful; and prosperity becomes the servant, the handmaid of that family where women are adorned by the ornaments of chastity, modesty and gracefulness.

Sometimes it is very pitiable to see women getting unsexed in some of the modern, high-born societies. They are losing their feminine quality. After all, the thing that makes a woman a woman is her feminine quality — her tenderness, her grace, her kindness, her forgiving nature, her forbearing nature. These are the things which make a goddess of a woman. If these are not there, if women are sharp-tongued, if they are caustic, if they are bitter, if they are full of hostility, there prosperity cannot come. It cannot come where a woman wants to be, in all respects, like a male. No! She can claim a certain type of equality, but not equality in all ways. If in this craze for being equal with man, woman loses her grace, her modesty and her chastity, then she has lost the most precious thing that God has given to her.

A Vedic declaration says: "Where women are worshipped, there indeed, the gods dance with joy". And where woman loses this right of worship by her own immodesty, there prosperity cannot be.

And, last but not the least, where God is worshipped every day, there the whole house becomes blessed with the highest prosperity. All joy, all blessedness, all prosperity comes to that house where God is worshipped regularly. Say thanks when you get up in the morning, for your health, for your body, for a clean mind, for energy in the body to live a life of usefulness to yourself and to all, and in the evening, thank God again for the bounty of a good day, for clear weather, fresh air, good health and energy, opportunity to serve and be useful to yourself and to others. If every day there is thanksgiving and you always worship God in your home, there is bound to be prosperity. Where there is worship, in that place, there is the tangible presence of God, and where there is this tangible presence of the Deity, what to say of prosperity? Everything that is good, everything that is blessed, will pervade that house, will fill that house.

Where God is, all auspiciousness, all blessedness, all prosperity is there as a matter of course — just as luminosity is there, radiance is there, where there is light. So, if you wish to fill yourself with prosperity, be worshipful. Do not make the church alone the place of prayer and worship. Let every house be a place of worship. Let every house be a centre of prayer. Let every house be the abode of God. And, let women be the repository of such virtues as modesty, chastity, purity and graciousness, and let the children of the family and the male members of the family give due respect to the ladies and treat them with kindness, treat them with courtesy, treat them with the dignity that is due to them, and let the children revere their elders. If these things are followed, if these things are fulfilled, prosperity will become an axiomatic condition. There can be no want, there can be no difficulty, there can be no lack in such a house.

This is the ultimate wisdom of the ancients. They say: "Prosperity is created by the behaviour of the human being". Outside factors are secondary factors only. They are not the main factors.

8. WORSHIP OF GOD AS MOTHER DIVINE

Radiant Immortal Atman! Glory be to the Divine.
May the Grace of the Lord bring peace to the whole
world and happiness and welfare unto all mankind.

The ancient Vedic way of life, termed the Sanathan
Dharma, and known generally to the Western world by
the name Hinduism, gives as the supreme objective in
life, eternal freedom from the shackles of earthly
bondage and death through Divine Experience or God-
realisation. This state of spiritual emancipation and eternal blessedness is termed Moksha or Kaivalya. This is a
state of absolute felicity and eternal satisfaction, characterized by cessation of all pain and suffering and attainment of supreme bliss. You go beyond birth and death.

Indicating also the ideal and desirable pattern of life,
favourable and conducive to the attainment of this
supreme objective, Sanathan Dharma mentions three
other objectives besides Moksha. They are, first of all,
Dharma or righteousness of conduct; secondly, the endeavour to obtain the normal necessities of life without
contravening the dictates of Dharma; and thirdly, the fulfilment of your legitimate personal (not selfish) desires in
life arising out of the various duties that confront you
and which you are called upon to fulfil. Here too, these
desires are not to be contrary to the dictates of Dharma.
Thus, it has to be noted that Dharma reigns supreme in
this earnest process of attaining Moksha. A true
Sanathani, therefore, must necessarily adhere to Dharma
under all conditions and in every circumstance. A true
Sanathani Hindu is he who never for a moment forgets
the supreme divine goal of his life, and ever remember-

ing it, bases his entire life upon the principle of Dharma or righteousness.

Now, the ultimate goal or Moksha through Divine Realization being the main objective before the true Sanathani Hindu, this ancient religion very clearly defines the practical means or methods of attaining it. Numerous means and techniques have been shown; but no matter how numerous and apparently different, they may yet be summed up by one single term, namely, "worship". God is attainable through worship which draws forth the Grace of the Divine. Worship implies drawing near to God. It covers within its range all forms and types of worship, from the crudest stone or totem worship of the forest-dwelling tribes to the highest state of deep spiritual trance or Samadhi, where in a state of superconsciousness, the seeker directly worships the Deity without the media of the mind and the senses. Worship implies duality of the worshipper and the worshipped. The concept of the personal God has a direct relevance to this approach by worship. It is precisely in this context that we perceive the genesis of Mother worship, or in other words, the worship of God as the Universal Mother Divine.

The Genesis of Mother Worship

God as the Universal Mother has a special appeal to man due to numerous reasons. Firstly, the mother is the earliest recognizable friend of the infant human being; she is the supreme wish-fulfiller of the individual and, at a certain stage, the all-in-all. Secondly, of all human relationships on earth, the sweetest and the most loving is this relationship of one with one's mother. Thirdly, the father image is always associated with sternness and discipline; whereas, the mother image is that of spontaneous love, compassion, protective tenderness and care, forbearance and forgiveness too. No wonder then that erring man is naturally drawn into this approach to the Supreme Being as the Mother Divine rather than as the Universal Father. Seeking comforts, solace and forgiveness, man turns to the Mother rather than to the Father. Stern justice is more likely to stem from the latter, whereas solicitude, forgiveness and love would be expected from the Mother. Thus, down the ages, man has evolved this approach to the Supreme Deity in Its aspect as the Cosmic Mother through the time-honoured tradition of Mother worship.

In this worship of the Mother Divine, the worshipper naturally feels himself as a child of the Mother. In this Bhav or attitude lies the very essence of this mode of approach. As a child approaches the mother confidently and with full trust in the mother's all-goodness, even so the worshipper adores the Mother, pouring forth the heart's love in surrender and sweet trust. This relationship in this worship has a profoundly transforming effect upon the worshipper's personality. Crude egoism gives place to child-like simplicity. Crookedness gives place to guilelessness. Self-assertive arrogance gives place to silent submission. Fear and awe give place to fearlessness and trust. Thus the Mother is worshipped.

Mother means love. Mother means compassion. Mother means protectiveness and tender care. This must be well borne in mind if our worship of the Mother should maintain a sublime spiritual level and be effective in taking us towards the ultimate goal of all such worship, namely, God-realization. The process of worship is aimed at bringing about a gradual divinisation of your consciousness. To experience the Divine, you must become the Divine. To invoke the love and the grace of the Mother, you must become a radiating centre of love yourself. An ascent into Divinity is from Tamas to Rajas, Rajas to Sattva, and Sattva to Suddha Sattva whence one goes beyond the three qualities and attains the Divine state. True and correct worship of the Divine Mother is therefore a lofty spiritual technique of the highest Sattvic quality. If the purely impersonal aspect of the Deity is stern and remote, this personal aspect of the Deity is tender, close, intimate and fully approachable. The Divine Mother is a love-filled Mother who awaits with outstretched arms to draw the devoted soul to Her divine bosom.

Distinctive Forms of Mother Worship

Worship of the Mother, as it presently prevails within the Hindu religious world, is to be found in three or four distinctive forms. Certain sections of the Shaktas devote themselves to the worship of the Mother according to methods laid down in the *Shakta Tantras*. This is a highly technical mode of worship entailing specific ritual into which one must be initiated as per Shakta tradition.

There are other sections of the Shaktas, as also non-Shaktas, who engage themselves in the worship through pure Bhakti, with simple ceremonials. This is far less technical than the Tantric worship and it tends to invoke Her solely as love.

Then again, Mother Divine is worshipped throughout India by all sorts of people during the nine days of the Navaratra Puja. In this countrywide annual worship, the Mother is invoked mainly as auspiciousness and blessedness and prosperity.

Here it will not be out of place to make mention of yet another form of Mother worship. It is really a degraded and impure form of worship that deserves to be renounced. It is Mother worship through fear and superstition. In this form, the Mother is regarded as a dire Deity given to anger and vengeance. She is more in a mode of punishing than loving. This is no Mother worship at all. It is a travesty of the concept of Motherhood. This is a Tamasic form of worship which evokes in the worshipper the Tamasic qualities of guilt, fear and cruelty. To appease his dire Deity, the worshipper takes recourse to the despicable means of committing violence upon other living creatures. He takes lives which he cannot give and which, therefore, he has no right to take. What such a blind worshipper fails to see is that the Mother is not the mother of man alone, but that She is the mother of the entire creation. Every fish, fowl, beast and insect is a divine child of the Divine Mother. Birds and animals too are Her children. All life is sacred. Taking of life is sin. If murder of man is a crime against the law, the murder of dumb beasts is a crime against Dharma. Their murder in Mother's Name is a crime against God Himself. Such sin cannot bring down Divine Grace. It will only bring the inevitable result in the form of much suffering. Worship should not contradict the universal Dharma of love and compassion. Cruelty cannot be condoned under any name. It may have the sanction of ignorance and superstition, but it has not the sanction of Sanathan Dharma.

Thus, the last form of Mother worship is no worship at all, because it takes the worshipper farther and farther away from God, and will ultimately lead him into hell. Such worship stands self-condemned. It should be abandoned immediately. The sooner it is abandoned the better it will be for man.

There is a deeply significant thing to be noted with reference to one aspect of Motherhood. Upon occasion, She is worshipped differently as Maha Lakshmi, Maha Sarasvati and Maha Parvathi or Durga. Worshipping Her as Durga, you invoke Her Power to destroy the evil within you in the form of egoism, anger, lust, greed, jealousy and delusion. These lower qualities of darkness constitute the animal within man. It is the impure Pashu inside the Manushya. The worshipper is expected to offer as sacrifice this inner lower self made up of egoism, lust, anger, greed, falsehood and hatred. This is true sacrifice that elevates the worshipper and takes him near to God.

Worship the Mother with the flowers of compassion, peace, mercy, forgiveness, truthfulness, simplicity. Approach Her as the Mother of love. Approach Her for the highest blessedness of Moksha. Then She is no other than the Supreme Almighty and She can give you the Kaivalya Moksha. O, Children of Sanathan Dharma! Approach Her for this highest gift and not for any petty objective here. The real glory of Mother worship is that it can bring far quicker response than approach to God as the Creator and Law-giver. Mother is especially there to forgive and save, whereas the Lord has to dispense justice. Thus the devotees of the Universal Mother laud their approach.

9. YOGA IN THE HOME

We take up now the vital subject of how, being in the midst of worldly activities one may yet fulfil the supreme purpose, the spiritual purpose of life on earth. While both the secular life and the spiritual life are a part of you, it is true that the spheres of the two are different, in the sense that the secular life has its sphere outside of yourself and the spiritual life has its sphere within yourself. But then, your spiritual life does have some expression outwardly also, and wherever you are, there your spiritual life has to be. If you are in a family set-up and living the work-a-day life in the busy field of worldly activity, then your spiritual life must be there. This interior life cannot be created by bringing about visible external changes in yourself or in your circumstances. You cannot live the spiritual life better in Rome than in Vancouver. You cannot be a better spiritual man if you are living at the top of a mountain than if you are living at the foot of it. Geography cannot change it. Mere changes of external form cannot really and truly affect your spiritual life, for it is the life of the soul, and wherever you are, the inner self can be looking towards God.

Even in the holiest of surroundings, the most sacred of places, right in the tabernacle of God, if your soul is not in Him, is not lifted up towards Him, then you are not in the spiritual realm at all.

A Story From the Life of Ramakrishna Paramahamsa

In various ways great Masters have tried to bring home this truth to seekers and an incident comes to my mind — a very familiar story and not too ancient. It was

in the life of Sri Ramakrishna, the spiritual preceptor of
the famous Swami Vivekananda. In his early life, Sri
Ramakrishna was a priest in a Hindu temple in Calcutta,
then the Capital City of India. This temple was founded
by a lady who was something of a small queen. The wife
of a native ruler and a lady of immense riches, she had
the temple built with a fabulous sum of money and endowed it with rich lands. She was a very devout lady in
spite of her great wealth and affluence. Apart from her
concern of looking after her property, her life was
spiritual. Occasionally, she would drop in at the temple
at the time of worship and sit in the sanctum. Sri
Ramakrishna was a young priest at that time, perhaps
twenty-four or twenty-five years of age, and on this occasion, this great lady having purified herself with a bath
in the Ganges, was sitting just inside the sanctum,
meditating. The worship came to a certain stage where
the Deity had to be hymned with praises and glorification
and, just before Sri Ramakrishna was about to burst into
song, this lady said, "Would you please sing this particular song?"; and he said "Yes" and started hymning
the Divine Mother. As he was singing, suddenly, he was
seen to stop, turn to this great lady and give her a
resounding slap on the back. And he just said, "What!
Here too!" That was all and he recommenced singing.
There were armed guards nearby who had followed this
lady to the temple, and some of the highest officials of
the temple, and all were simply stunned. Some started to
tremble and one or two were thinking, "Now this man's
life has come to a close. Perhaps she will order him to
be bound up immediately"; but much to their surprise,
just as though she were a daughter being chastised by her
father, she suddenly became docile and kept quiet and
began intently to attend to the song. When the song was
over, the service proceeded and, at the end of the service, she came out as if nothing had happened. The of-

ficials and the guards were just waiting and wondering, "What is going to happen now?" And the superintendent asked her, "Have you any orders? I observed what happened, but I could not step inside the sanctum, and so I could not do anything". The queen simply said, "No. There are no orders". Later on, her son-in-law, who was managing the temple on her behalf, came to hear of this incident and asked her about it. She said: "He (Ramakrishna) was perfectly right. I had asked him to hymn the Divine Mother, because it was the Mother who was enshrined there, and while he was singing, I was thinking of a law-suit coming off tomorrow at the City High Court about the estate and was worrying about it. I was not thinking of anything else—the Divine Mother or the song he was singing in Her praise. It was the law-suit which was occupying my mind, and so I had to be pulled up and he did it...It was not really he who did it, but it was the Divine Mother who did it". So this lady, even when she was in the temple, was not really in the temple, but was in the Law Court. It is what you are within yourself that determines whether you are leading a spiritual life or a worldly life, and not the place you are in. That gives the secret of living a Yogic life in and through the world.

Everything can become Yogic if you spiritualize your life, and the method of spiritualizing life has been expounded in the most glorious way in the most sacred scripture, the *Bhagavad Gita*. Yoga is union with the Divine and if you live your life in constant inner union with the Divine through a link of great devotion to Him, through a link of genuine love for the Supreme, then whatever you may do, wherever you may be, and in whatever manner you may be living, you are living a life of Yoga: for, you are living with God and you are at one with God in your inner life.

Such a life of at-oneness with God, such a life of conscious effort to be for ever united with Him in love and devotion, and an awareness that the whole of this life is meant for totally consummating or perfecting such union—that is Divine Life. It is a life of Yoga. If you are consciously trying all the time to reach out towards Him in spirit, to draw nearer and nearer to Him day by day, then you are living a life of Yoga, no matter what shape your external life might take.

This spirit, then, is the most important factor in living a Yogic life. This spirit is the most essential factor which makes a life spiritual. In the light of this, we have to consider what those factors are which we can include in our daily family life which will enable us to be united with God in the interior of our being.

The Four Main Aspects of an Individual's Life

Of course, we take it for granted that the first thing is to be conscious of one's purpose in life. Ever be conscious of why you are living. Ever be conscious of what purpose you are to fulfil in life. That is the most important thing. Know that the whole meaning of life is the utilizing of its every moment to attain the supreme purpose.

You are already aware of the spiritual goal in life, knowing that in God alone true peace and happiness can be had, that in God alone all the imperfections of this mortal existence can be overcome, and that in God alone all sorrow can be transcended and the state of eternal life, immortality, freedom and fearlessness can be had. Knowing this, there has already been created in you a great urge and aspiration to live the spiritual life so as to have the Supreme Attainment here and now—in this very body. To such a person as you, when living a busy family life, difficulties come in the way; and the greatest is that so many activities clutter up your day-to-day life that there seems to be no time for the essential exercise of the spirit in the way of devotion, in the way of prayer and worship. This is one great obstacle, but it is not a very serious one, nor is it the main one.

The main obstacle is constituted by the numerous duties of your worldly life, of your secular life, which you have to fulfil. Why? Because the whole of life's set-up is economic and one has to work to earn one's livelihood. Gone are the days of inherited properties and paternal wealth, and one has to work, and this is the dominant aspect of the secular life. The secondary aspect is the domestic life. It is from the home that one goes to the professional field, day after day, and it is to home again that one comes back after the day's work is done. The third aspect is that as a responsible member in a community, one has certain responsibilities of social life to attend to — such as club life, meeting friends, etc. Lastly, each one has one's own personal, individual life.

The personal, individual life is the basis. The individual aspect of your life is the most important to you. Next comes the family life or the domestic life, where there are the different relationships between husband and wife, parents and children, brothers and sisters, etc. Then comes the professional life. It is much less important than the individual life and the family life. In fact, it is the least important, though it is indispensable from the point of view of money. The professional life has to be gone through, but it does not have any serious significance for the true life of the individual — except in some extreme cases when the profession happens to be that of a hangman or a military man who has to destroy people, and then, serious ethical and spiritual problems are created. But, for the vast majority of people, the professional side does not have any special impact upon the spiritual and the ethical side of life.

Now, in the four aspects of an individual's life that we have enumerated, how are we to ensure that spiritual idealism is given the first position?

The Sanctity of Marriage

Householders should not forget even for a moment that marriage is a sacred thing. The sanctity of married life has to be realized in all its fullness and in all its seriousness. Marriage is a sacrament. It is not just the union of two bodies. That is the least important part of it. The husband and the wife should not think there is absolutely no love above their physical life. There is a love. Marriage is the bringing together by God (through some mysterious law which operates in this universe) of two souls in this vast, vast phenomenon called life—in this vast stream of existence where countless millions of souls are moving in their individual planes of spiritual evolution towards the Divine. Through the Grace of God, through the Divine Will, and through the operation of certain laws that govern this universal life, two souls are brought together. That is the meaning of marriage.

Through the coming together of these two souls, God means an important process to be worked out and that is the sharing of the spiritual impulse between the two. What they have earned, what they have learned, and their spiritual potential—the husband and the wife are to share. The husband is to enrich the spiritual life of the wife and the wife is to enrich the spiritual life of the husband and both are to go hand-in-hand toward the Supreme Attainment of the Divine Consciousness. That is the true, inner meaning of family life. Marriage is sacred. It is not to be treated lightly. It is not to be considered in a vulgar sense. Marriage is an alliance which is for something more than mere physical enjoyment, for something more than even the all-important purpose of the propagation of the race (though, to a limited extent, this is also a purpose of marriage). The offsprings of the husband and the wife are also to be spiritual beings, because they are other souls coming into this earth-plane to work out their own evolution. It is therefore, the sacred duty of the husband and the wife to provide an ideal home and the proper initial impulse to these souls that come as their children. The children are to be held in trusteeship for a while until they grow up and go out into the world. The growth and development of the children will be in accordance with their own spiritual nature, with their own spiritual evolution, with their own Karma which they have brought with them; yet, the mother and the father can give a great deal from their own lives to the initial spiritual unfoldment of their children until the children attain a stage when they can themselves mind their further spiritual evolution. If healthy spiritual ideas are implanted in the young minds from the early age, they are bound to sprout forth at a later stage and bring blessedness to the children.

And, as the children are to be brought up to respect the law of celibacy, of continence, until they are actually married, so the husband and the wife should adhere to the law of continence and celibacy; and for them, this law should operate in the form of a strict moderation of marital life. Marital life should be based upon self-control, not upon indulgence. Then, the wife should regard the husband as the only partner and *vice versa*. The wife should not have any other male and she should not think of any other man, but should be devoted to her husband; no thought of any other man should ever cross her mind. All the rest of humanity should be to her like children — she is the great Mother. The husband must have the vow which Rama had — the vow of the single spouse. That means that the thought of another woman will never enter his mind. To him, the only woman is his wife and their marriage ties are sacred. In this way the whole family set-up becomes sacred and holy and the interior life of the spirit goes on unhampered. There is nothing in the exterior life of the being to injure the spiritual life. There is nothing in the exterior life — either in the family life or in one's personal life—to hold back or obstruct the spiritual life.

And thus, both husband and wife go in perfect harmony, and their lives, on the dual wings of exterior activity and interior prayerfulness, go to the ultimate blessed state of supreme God-consciousness—Divine Realization. Blessedness becomes theirs. in and through their family life, wherever they are.

The Home—A Sacred Place

The home should be known to be a sacred place. The home is to be a sort of counterbalancing factor for all the bustle, for all the restless activity, of your daily professional life. The moment you leave home and go into your professional activity, your whole mind, your entire personality, is brought out. You are to be active. You are to give your attention to things of this world and, therefore, your recollectedness is lost. You are brought away from your centre so that your inner spiritual closeness to God is completely lost when you go into your professional activity—your day-to-day life. Now, when you come back home, the home life is meant to be an effective counterbalancing factor. In the home you are "Self-centred", you are recollected, you are in God. So the entire atmosphere of the home should be pervaded by a sense of God's presence. You should feel God in every nook and corner of your home. It should be a place where, the moment you enter, the mind, which in the morning was brought out forcibly due to the secular, professional activities, is once again brought back into its own. It finds rest and peace in God. God should be the centre of the home. You should not feel, "This house is mine. This home is mine"; but rather, "This is the abode of God, and here I am privileged to pause, and here I am privileged to work out my salvation, work out my liberation". This should be the attitude of both husband and wife, and it is in this attitude that the children should be raised.

The home atmosphere should not be made vulgar and the home should not be a place which is sort of a show-piece, where you just show off your opulence or show off your superior tastes to others or show off your pride of possessions—it should not be that. Neither should it be a place where a sensual type of entertainment is indulged in, with people throwing cocktail parties, with people getting half-drunk, with jazzy music, with noise and bustle and card-play. The sanctity of the home atmosphere, the sacredness and the holiness of the home atmosphere, is of paramount importance. The home should always be kept sacred. This is essential. If the spiritual atmosphere of the home also is destroyed, then how can you find your spiritual centre? If outside there is nothing to be found, and when you come home, it is worse than the outside, then how can you build a spiritual life? This way your spiritual life is destroyed by your own hand and this should not be.

However, this spiritualization of the home atmosphere should not be done in an eccentric fashion or in the manner of a fad or a fetish, marking you off as a superior person, way above your neighbours, but it should be graciously and simply accomplished with a spiritual naturalness adorned with humility and with thanks to God for the gift of this awareness. In the home, there should be nothing secular. In the home, everything should be spiritual. In the home, everything should be Yogic. There is enough of materialism, enough of forgetfulness and heedlessness of God all around you outside; so why should you add to it and let the home atmosphere also become vitiated? Keep God intact in the home. Let every atom in the atmosphere of the home be full of holiness, and do all that you can in order to maintain the atmosphere of the home. Keep it sacred. Keep it sanctified. Always feel the home to be a place where you can get very close to God.

Spiritual Guidance to Children

The training of the children comes next. It is a great and onerous responsibility of the parents. You are only the trustees of these souls and have no permanent connection with them—the children whom God has given to you—and you should try to do what you can in the little time they pass through your hands to touch them and make their lives more radiant for their having come to you. Therefore, the proper training of children is one of the most onerous duties, and if this is done in the attitude of being privileged to be the parent of His own children, then everything you do towards your children becomes part of your Karma Yoga, becomes part of your own spiritual unfoldment. For, by giving to them the spiritual impulse, the spiritual life, by your own ideal lives, you become the partaker of God's life, because you fulfil the great gospel of Karma Yoga, viz., selfless activity without attachment, with only love in your heart, in order to do some good to others. If you train them along the path which will take them to their eternal welfare, to true blessedness, then that is the highest bestowal that one person can confer upon another in this earth-plane.

Children are imitators. The great bestowal upon them, therefore, is the bestowal of the inspiration of your personal example. This is your great duty. The parents at home have to be ideal. Their speech, their actions in all situations, their behaviour with each other, their conduct, their behaviour in relation to their neighbours, their general behaviour—if these factors are ideal and based upon virtue and ethically perfect, then they do not have to give anything else to their children. The children get all their education just by basking under the radiance of the parental influence. This is the great Yoga of the home: to give to children the ideal atmosphere and the ideal example. It is worth more than anything else that can be given to children, such as good clothes, good education—which are all things which touch but the superficial aspects of these souls that are under your care.

There is no such thing as 'starting too early' for your children. They may start even from the time they are one-year old. Modern wives pride themselves on disciplining the children, and even when the children are three months old, their mothers exclaim: "Oh, she knows when to expect her food. She won't whimper before that hour. She knows everything—when to cry, when not to cry; when to accept feedings and when not to accept; and if it is given before time by some baby-sitter, she will refuse it. You see, she has been trained". When you pride yourself on the training of children as regards feeding habits, why not train them right from the start in the spiritual line also? You can train them even before they are born. Even when they are within you, you can send towards these children all holy thoughts, inspiring spiritual vibrations, spiritual ideas about God, about prayer, about love; then a part of that nature will be imbibed even by the unborn child. In this way, you can influence the children beneficially right from the very beginning.

Let the little child watch the family in prayer. In such prayer, the whole family should be gathered together, and if a guest is staying with the family, then the guest also should join in. There should be a separate hour set aside for such worship and devotion in the morning and again in the evening. The day should not commence without this one hour. The creation of this time is in your own hands. It is in retiring early to bed and not being glued to TV. This is one of the things I would like to say—that to a great extent the spiritual life of children is being destroyed by the carelessness of their parents. Parents never care what the children do as long as the latter do not bother them. That is all they want; they just do not want to be bothered with their children. If they do not want to be bothered with them, if they do not want to care for their children, if they do not want to shoulder the responsibility of training their children, why did they bring them forth at all? They should not have had any children. They should have controlled themselves. Let people marry and live like celibates. Let them not bring forth a human child. To bring forth a child and not to care for its development, particularly its ethical and spiritual development...there is no sin greater than this. For, such parents have betrayed a trust. Out of their own volition they have created a trust and betrayed it. This should not be done. The Law of Karma says retribution is unfailing.

In the modern house, what do you see? Most of the children develop their own propensities, not from the example of the father and the mother, but from what they see on the TV screen. This is warping their souls and it is addicting them to hang on to pictures that flicker upon the screen and to completely lose their individual personality. They then have no time for anything else, but are always fascinated by TV.

A Spiritual Daily Routine for the Householder

Each householder should have an ideal daily routine. The home life should not be left to itself, but taken care of. In addition to those unexpected things that come up every day—a visit of someone, a telephone call, an invitation to go out with someone—every one of you should have an accepted basic programme, a basic schedule for your daily life, which should include an hour of prayer in the morning and an hour of prayer in the evening. The prayer hour might include the reading of scriptural texts, the reading of sacred and inspiring spiritual books, a few minutes of quiet, indrawn medita-

tion, a few minutes of actually articulated prayer, inspiring prayer. The prayer can be spontaneous; it does not
necessarily have to come out of some book. Or it can be
both, as there are some very inspiring short prayers in
the Gospel and also in some other books. The children
should also be trained in this way.

There should also be some actual act of external
worship. After all, we are embodied creatures and we
wish to exercise our bodies also in devotion. When you
are in a state of worship, the body also should take on
the attitude of worship. You should light a candle, burn
a little incense, bow before the Deity, offer supplication,
ask Him to enlighten you, to fill your heart with virtue,
fill your heart with divine love, goodness and selflessness,
and then, bowing low and with genuflection, kneel, press
down with your forehead. In this way, you have to
humble yourself in the presence of God. Then, as the
body genuflects, prostrates and humbles itself, the influence of those little acts has a chastening effect upon
the mind. We cannot become completely heedless to
these reactions of the body upon the mind and the mind
upon the inner spirit. Therefore, each day, you should
have an hour when you have scope for the exercise of
all these several aspects of your being—for the exercise
of the body, the heart and the feelings in prayer; for the
exercise of the mind and the intellect in study, reflection
and enquiry; and for the exercise of the spirit in inner
contemplation, silence, indrawnness and meditation.

Each member of the family should have a private
altar. The mother should have her own nook or little
corner, where she has her own little prayer, little conversation with God, little asking for guidance, little intimate
communion with God. The husband, likewise, should
have a little altar for himself, and if this cannot be had,
at least he must have some time for himself, when he
communes with the Maker individually. And the children

should be trained right from the very beginning to have such separate little corners for themselves. Just as they have one corner for their toys, another for their books, a third for their pets, so they must have a corner for their own communion with the Most High, and if this habit is developed from childhood, then later on, they will be able to have their own independent spiritual life.

Dynamic Spirituality—Remembering God

Throughout the house you may have any number of external symbols which bring to you the thought of God. Perhaps tastefully framed mottoes: "ALL LIFE IS SACRED", "GOD IS HERE NOW", "BE GOOD, DO GOOD", "BE KIND, BE PURE", "SPEAK THE TRUTH", "NEVER HURT THE FEELINGS OF OTHERS", "SEE GOD IN ALL FACES", "TRUTH IS GOD", "GOD IS LOVE", etc. And pictures. Every day, when the householder starts from home for his work, he should have five minutes of prayer, when he should say: "Now, Oh Lord, from this Blessed Abode of Thine, where I am privileged to pass my days, I go out to worship Thee through my bodily activities, through my work. May all that I do today with body and mind be accepted by Thee as my worship, as my Karma Yoga, as my dynamic prayer". Only after uttering this little prayer should the householder leave his home.

When he approaches the office, he should do so with a worshipful attitude. Be you a steno-typist or a salesman or a drugstore assistant, be you a doctor or a lawyer or a school teacher, be you a carpenter or a mason, whatever you are, the place of work to which you go day after day to exercise your vocation or profession is to be to you a sacred temple of God and the work that you do should be the worship offered to the all-pervading Presence which is at home, which is within, which is everywhere, and which is also at the place of your work.

If you are a workshop man, at your bench you must be working with God. You must feel God working with you and, now and then, about once an hour, you should renew this spirit. It should not be monotonous and mechanical and it should not be dull. You must renew the spirit by: "Oh Lord, accept this work as my worship of Thee. All glory be to Thee. It is Thy Grace that makes me work. This work I offer to Thee as flowers offered at the altar".

If you work in a prison, or if you are a lawyer and have to work, as it were, "on the edge of a sword", then it is very, very difficult. It is extremely difficult to be a lawyer and not to utter a falsehood, to be a policeman and not to take bribes. In such work, people have to be pitied, because they are wasting this great thing called human life. They themselves are most unfortunate, because they become enmeshed in a set-up where, even though they do not desire to do so, they do things which are unethical, unrighteous. If one is a conscientious spiritual seeker, then these professions should be given up. Or else, you should walk with a great deal of caution and with great devotion to God, constantly praying to God to keep you on the straight path. Everything has to be offered to God in worship, and worship cannot be rotten, worship cannot be crooked, worship cannot be impure, and therefore, the one rule that should govern your life is that it should be honest, based upon truth. All your activities should be based upon truth, honesty and purity. Then those activities, when offered to God in worshipfulness, become Yoga. They become Yoga anywhere, in Paris, in London, in New York, in Vancouver. The time or the age in which you dwell—be it the twentieth century or the twenty-first century—matters little. The place where you dwell—whether it is in the West or the East—matters little. What is of importance is that you look at all work as worship and see that all your activities are guided by the principles of righteousness and truth and purity. Thus your whole life becomes pervaded by the spirit of Yoga—your personal life, your home life and your office or professional life.

During your lunch hour, try to snatch fifteen minutes for silent interior prayer and inward meditation. Get away by yourself, and if conditions are such that you cannot do so, then try to get behind a newspaper in a corner somewhere, and while pretending to read the paper, contemplate upon God for those moments. Or pretend to take a nap, close your eyes and go into prayerfulness—but do not *actually* take a nap! Forget the world, forget life, work, body, everything, for that time, being wholly intent upon God. This is a dynamic process. If you dip into your innermost being now and then, say twenty times a day, or once in every half an hour, for just one minute, that is enough. It is a great life-transforming process. It is dynamic spirituality and the transformation that will come upon you will in no wise be less than the spiritual transformation in a contemplative monk, for you are doing a task which is even greater than his, for he has all the proper facilities and, therefore, it is natural and easy for him to go into God. But with everything against you—when the whole atmosphere, your whole environment, all the factors that go to make up your life are totally material, externalized, and grossly secular—if, in the midst of all that, you have this thought of interiorness once in a while, then the token of your love for God is so earnest, so deeply genuine, that the return for it is tenfold, one hundredfold. Therefore, try to have little minutes of deep and intent God-thought periodically during the course of your busy day. Somehow or the other, connect everything with God. Whatever you do, do it for His love, and try to speak to Him in and through your activities.

If you are a waiter in a restaurant, when you are

serving someone, see God in the person who has given the order, and when taking the dish to him, take it worshipfully, as if you are taking an offering to the altar of God. For the time being, let the table of your customer become your altar. In that way, you have to connect your every activity with God-thought and let devotion fill the heart. (This is not to be mistaken for a mere emotion, or just sentimentality, but implies actually a steadfast state of genuine worshipfulness. Strength, and not weakness, is the criterion of true devotion.)

The Curse of Fashion

Along with all this, live a simple life. It is in the simple life that mind moves upon a straight path without wavering. Whereas, it is dispersed and scattered if life is made too complex and too much filled with an accumulation of objects. Have a simple life and do not be too concerned about your physical existence, about care of your body, about your beauty, your dress.

I will tell you a simple truth: fashion is a curse. Fashion is a curse and fashion is slavery. It is a slavery subtly imposed upon you by shrewd people who have products to sell. If you have some intelligence, you will know a very deep and significant fact: the manufacturers of dress and of all things fashionable will never keep any particular style or model constant for more than one year. They will surely bring in a change, a new model, a new fashion each year, attempting to persuade you that items which you have purchased the previous year are worthless. Do you see the absurdity of it? Slavery to fashion complicates one's life beyond measure. The simple life keeps the heart simple, the mind simple, and you are able to give your mind and heart to God. In a complicated life, the mind and the heart are dispersed and the essential interior life is lost.

The Value of Time

Realize the value of time. Utilize every minute, and with great niggardliness, try to salvage every minute and add it to your spiritual life. Do not have the habit of gossip—genteel gossip. It is one of the social qualifications—when two persons are together, they must have some gentle back-chat about a third person. If that is done, you are destroying your own life, you are wasting time. Life is time, and time is verily life. If you just fritter away precious minutes and hours in loose chatter and gossip and a little genteel scandal-mongering, it means you are robbing yourself of the most precious thing in life—the rare opportunity to attain God.

You should try to develop a little backbone. You should not be afraid to be different. You should not think: "If I am like this, if my house is run in a certain way, if the neighbours peep in, what will they think?" Why should you care what they will think? Let them think what they like. What do you care for: the opinion of God and the opinion of your own conscience or the opinion of others? Have a backbone. Have the courage to be unique in certain respects and dare to be out-of-the-ordinary. Do not think you should always conform. You must conform in the things that are necessary for the social well-being of all people; but in the interior life, you need not conform to anyone. Do that which you think is best in the eyes of God. You must have a certain degree of independent thinking and arrange your family life and your interior life in a way which you think is best and is in the light of the highest idealism.

This, in short, is the method by which you can bring the spiritual element into all of your life. It does not matter if you are of the West or of the East, if you are ancient or modern. Everyone, wherever he is, can touch his innermost being with this attitude of worshipfulness

and base his life on the principle of ever moving towards
God. In all that you do, move towards God. Let all actions be of such nature that will bring you nearer to God.

Some Concluding Remarks

Develop virtue as a rule in your life. Let virtue be
the criterion with which you judge all your thoughts, all
your actions, all your speech. Is it virtuous or not? That
should be the yardstick to guide you in your life. And the
principle should be to move towards God—ever and
ever.

Items which can go into the family schedule are
some moments of calm reflection and exchange of
thought between members of the family, some moments
of common spiritual reading, moments of hymns and
songs together. All families should have a daily custom
of singing together, hymns and sacred songs learned by
heart.

Always have the principle of offering food to God
first and then alone partaking of it—the saying of grace.

While doing her housework, the wife should dedicate everything that she does to God—washing the
dishes, mopping the floor, preparing meals, everything.
She should say, "O Lord, for Thy love, for Thy glory—
this is worship". And the hand should do its task with
love, so that you know the heart and the hand are both
dedicating to God.

Then, develop an ideal relationship with your neighbour. You must be a good neighbour and all the family
members should try to develop themselves into good
samaritans. If there is any distress, if there is any opportunity to help, even if help is not asked, if you feel that
a certain person is in difficulty, without revealing yourself, you should help. There are various ways, if you want
to exercise the spirit of charity and the ideal of the good
samaritan. You can do it, even today. These things

should always be uppermost in your life. So, you worship God and fulfil the ideal of Yoga, of compassion and goodness and selflessness, even through your dealings with your fellow-beings.

Let the week-ends for the family be periods of recreation as well as spiritual re-creation. Why should there be a craze to go somewhere on week-ends? Why should children want to get away? If the home atmosphere has become so ideal, so beautiful, so full of sweetness and happiness, then on week-ends, no one in the family will want to go anywhere at all. You will love every minute you live in the home, within the family, and you will not want to get away. When the family atmosphere is totally vitiated and there is no faith in God, there is no faith in His presence, when there is no devotion, when there is no love and charity, no understanding between husband and wife, between parents and children, then the children have no good example, and when this is the case, they become disobedient and careless. But if the home is ideal, with a harmonious atmosphere, with love for God as the centre of your family life, then not one of the family will want to get away from home; and the time spent at home will be solid week-ends full of spiritual gain where you put by for yourself wealth that no moth can eat away, no rust can cause to perish, and no thief can take from you. Even nuclear bombs cannot take away the spiritual wealth gained thus from living a Yogic life.

That, I think, sums up, more or less, the whole structure of a Yogic way of life in the home and in the family.

10. THE LAW OF KARMA AND REINCARNATION

Glorious Immortal Atman! The subject of "Karma and Reincarnation" is one that merits the careful consideration and the intelligent perusal of everyone, for herein lies an exposition of a law which governs our existence in this universe. People are often apt to make loose reference to this subject as "the Indian theory of Karma" or "the Hindu theory of reincarnation". This is a misnomer. It is not the evolution of a theory with which we are concerned, but the revelation of a law. It is interesting to note that this law is not the especial possession of the people of the East, but is at the very origin of all religions, and is commonly held by practically every religion of the world. Therefore, it is not a Hindu law in the same way that the law of gravity is not Newton's law. Newton had no claim upon the law—it did not belong to him—he was merely the one who observed its workings and declared it. Similarly, the principle of Archimedes is neither a Greek law nor a Greek invention. It did not commence working when Archimedes discovered it. It was eternally in operation, and in the same way, the Law of Karma and Reincarnation did not have a beginning in the East. It was eternally in existence. The law was operating already when some sage or seer at a particular time in the history of mankind realized it, or had it revealed to him in deep meditation, and then declared it to mankind.

Now, the working of this law was revealed in deep meditation to the Hindus long ago. One may ask: "Why should modern, advanced people of the twentieth century bother about this law? It may perhaps have been interesting to the Hindus centuries ago, but how can an ancient law have any practical bearing on the modern world?" First of all, it is not a Hindu law. The Hindus had nothing to do with it. It is God's law; God created the laws that govern the universe. Also, it is not an ancient, outmoded law which is no longer effective, but a universal law which is eternally effective. It is the law of God Himself.

Biologists discovered long ago that respiration was essential for physical life. Now, one cannot say that this fact is of no further interest, just because the fact was brought to light long ago. Man cannot dispense with respiration as long as he is a corporeal creature; breathing only will sustain his physical life and oxygen will be necessary. If oxygen is denied, he will die. The law remains effective and concerns him vitally.

The Law and Its Implications

The statement of this Law of Karma and Reincarnation is not a startling one, either. It does not require any special effort to be understood or accepted. Even now, this law is being recognized and accepted in deep conviction by great scientists and has been defined in terms which have been made familiar to everyone. According to their interpretation of the law, restricted to the plane of physical matter, every action has a corresponding reaction and every cause has an inevitable effect. Every chemist, every physicist, believes that this law operates in the external universe governing physical matter. This is the same law that was revealed to the seers of India long ago in the moral, ethical and spiritual planes. Just as in the world around us we see that every cause has its inevitable effect, and that every action brings about a certain reaction, so in the moral and ethical realm, every cause brings about a certain effect; every seed sown bears a particular fruit or yields a certain harvest. The simplest statement of the law of Karma is: "As you sow, so shall you reap". Interpreted by scientists and applied to physical matter, the law is: "Every cause has an effect, and every action has a corresponding reaction". To this we have to add that every cause brings about an effect which, in its nature, tends to be similar to the nature of the cause which produced it. This is a highly logical postulate. In India there is a saying that the behaviour of the individual accords with the mind and, conversely, the nature of the mind accords with the deeds he has done in the past.

This great law of Karma holds many practical implications for the life of the human being and a great many misconceptions have arisen about these implications. One of these misconceptions is that, since the law goes on operating in man's life, the necessity of guiding his own actions is obviated. Since whatever happens will happen in accordance with the law and is all inevitable, how can man act at all?

Now, as one sows, so shall he reap. The very statement of the law recognizes the agency of the human being. As it is man who sows in the field of action, so it is he who reaps the harvest of fresh seeds which carry him forward into further action. If man is not a free doer, then the very law of Karma becomes absurd. This is a very vital point which we have to understand. The Law of Karma does not make man just a puppet, helpless under the law.

The Hindus say that man suffers or enjoys under the law according to his Karma, and that neither suffering nor enjoyment can be escaped. How can this idea be reconciled with the idea that man has freedom? We have to understand the law in this way. There are dual factors working in each man's life. One is the experience that the individual has to undergo, the pains and pleasures that come to him, the misfortunes that he has to suffer, the losses that he has to endure. These *experiences* are inevitable; they cannot be escaped; one has to undergo them all. But there is another factor, and that pertains to *the actions the individual engages in*. These actions are based upon the will of the particular individual.

Whereas he has no choice in the experiences he undergoes, he has choice in the doing of deeds. To this extent, he is a free agent. He may not be entirely free because of the many restrictions raised on this earth-plane, viz., social restrictions, tradition, etiquette, etc. It is unnecessary to enter any metaphysics at all to prove that man is not a *totally* free agent and that the Law of Karma *also* is there. Man cannot do anything he wants, but he can exercise his will; and in this exercise, man has freedom. He had no freedom, no choice, no alternative regarding life's experiences, but he has choice, he has freedom to a certain extent regarding his will to act.

The Threefold Karma

The actions that operate in the life of every individual according to this law have been divided into three categories. By applying the scientific law of cause and effect to the first category, it is seen that in a person's life-time some activities have effect immediately, some have effect after a few years, but some perhaps have no effect at all in this life-time. What happens to an action whose effect has not been worked out in this life? The potencies of such actions—the potencies of re-activity, as it were, of unresolved causes—go on accumulating in each individual's storehouse of Karma. That is one category of seeds of Karma.

The second category is this. Out of the re-active stores, a certain supply is taken out to be worked out in the form of sweet and bitter experiences during a particular life-time. That supply forms the seed, as it were, of experiences in that particular incarnation. That supply determines man's birth and death—all that he weeps over, all that he suffers and enjoys. All that he experiences, in short, comes out of that part of the store of accumulated Karma. That is the second category.

And what is the third? In this earth-life, man goes on instigating action. He thinks in certain ways and he acts in certain ways and the activity of this particular earth-life is contributing towards the formation of fresh seed. Sometime in the future he has to reap the effect of this activity. To what category does this fresh Karma belong? Naturally, it belongs neither to the experiences of this life nor the accumulated store. It belongs to a fresh batch, and this is the third category. In it are the activities of the present and it is referred to as "that which is being done" (Kriyamana) and also as "that which is to come" (Agami), because that which is to come is actually the product of that which transpires in the present. Therefore, there is the threefold Karma: the accumulated store, the experiences chosen for this particular incarnation, and that which is created in this life.

The actions which are done in this life have two distinct effects. One is the effect which is on this earth-plane and this effect may be produced immediately or tomorrow, or next week, or in ten years, but the effect which this action produces on the mind is instantaneous. The mind immediately receives the impression of the nature of the action that is done. If a harsh and cruel act is committed, then the impression of harshness and cruelty is immediately etched upon the mind. Repeated impressions contribute towards the formation of distinct tendencies in the mind and they build up and impart to the mind a particular quality. The sum-total of all qualities thus acquired by the mind through impressions, through these tendencies developed by it, becomes the nature of the individual. It is often called the character of the individual. The outward effect of action is not the main concern of the spiritual being, but the impression that the action creates in the mind is of vital concern to him. Why? Because, these impressions form the natural bent of the mental being and they portend what harvest will later be reaped.

Now, the sower has to return to his field if he has to reap his harvest and, in the same way, man has to return once again to this field of activity, i.e., to the earth-plane, in order to reap the harvest of his threefold activity. Thus, the soul returns again and again to work out the effect of its activity. As long as the causes in Karma are there, there is a necessity, by law, for them to be worked out. When man finds the way in which to act so that he does not create fresh causes, then perhaps, after a series of lives, the storehouse of Karma would become depleted and thereafter, in one glorious incarnation, he would find himself without any Karma at all at his back. This does not usually happen, because man never allows the pile to be reduced—it is ever being added to—and that is the great folly of man.

Man—The Builder of His Destiny

Is this great law a curse or a blessing? It is mixed. Ultimately, it is a great blessedness. People have a tendency to look at it from only one particular angle, and that angle is, that as long as a human being is bound to the wheel of this law, there is no happiness for him and he is miserable and he weeps. In this view, Karma will always plague man and the Law of Karma, like the hammer of God, will descend upon his head and inflict perennial suffering upon him. But, is it not clear that this Law of Karma is not actually just a law of retribution or punishment? There is another view, a glorious view, to be taken of it. Just as man cannot escape the results of his activity which are bad (for this, he has to reap tears and suffering), in the same way, he cannot escape his reward. The whole world cannot rob him of his deserved reward. The good actions of a person will follow him anywhere and will overcome for him the greatest difficul-

ty and the greatest sorrow and give him the harvest of
joy.

If properly understood, the Law of Karma is a law
which gives infinite hope. It says that man's destiny is in
his own hands. It says that what he shall be depends
upon himself. He is the one to decide on the pattern of
the experiences to come. No force has any power over
him to coerce him into wrong action. He has to take care
of how he behaves, how he acts and what thoughts he
thinks. He is the master of his destiny. He is the architect of his fate. He has nothing to fear in this
universe, nothing except his own wrong actions and
thoughts. He has to say: "Who has the power to give me
any experience that I do not choose to select for myself?
No one on earth has the power to injure me, to bring
sorrow upon me, to inflict destruction or evil upon me".
Thus man takes infinite courage. He is determined to
guide his own life into a future containing bliss and
radiance. The Law of Karma gives him an inducement to
sow the right type of seeds, to fashion all his activity
along ideal lines.

It is this law which upholds the moral standard of
this universe. Had it not been for this law, there would
have been no inducement either to avoid evil or to
embrace good. Both these lines of action spring out of
this glorious law. Man knows that if he does not avoid
evil, he will sow weeds and thorns. He knows that he
should do good, because he will be the blessed enjoyer
of the fruits of those good deeds. According to this view,
the Law of Karma is not a doctrine of fatalism. On the
contrary, it is a doctrine of high orderliness, serving as
the basis of the moral order in the whole universe, and
the attitude instilled into man by this law is fearlessness.
It fills man with fearlessness and infinite courage and a
great urge to be ideal and good and lofty in all his
thoughts and activities. Man is thus revealed as the

builder—having in his own hands the materials out of which he can build whatever he chooses.

Breaking the Bondage of Karma

Thus the law ultimately implies that man can free himself from this wheel of birth and death by consciously avoiding all that brings him back into incarnation and by filling his life with ideal activities to refine his nature more highly, until ultimately a lofty stage is reached where the over-all goodness in his life bestows upon him the knowledge of his real Self; and once he attains to this knowledge, the Law of Karma comes to a halt. Bondage is broken. Why? Through their deep insight into the workings of the Law, the Hindus discovered that is was inoperative in the realm of the Soul. It is only in the realm of the mind and the body that this law operates.

Man lies within the jurisdiction of this law and remains bound to the wheel as long as he identifies himself with the mind and the body. The moment he breaks this attachment and detaches himself from this false identity, then he destroys this ignorance utterly and realizes his transcendence, his oneness with the pure spiritual Consciousness. The law cannot any longer touch that soul whose life has become illumined with the essential knowledge that he is neither body nor mind, but pure Consciousness. That is the way of stopping the Wheel of Karma.

One thing more I would like to tell you. This law is concerned not only with outward activity, but even with mental activity, for it is thought which is at the root of every action. Thus, every deliberate thought, of whatever kind, is actually included in man's Karma, no matter whether it is given any outward physical expression or not. This has to be understood. In the *Gita* we are given a very clear statement of the Law when we hear that as long as man continues acting as an egoistic individual, so long will he, casting aside one body, take up another body. It is like regular progression. We therefore say that it is like going to a school in which we progress from grade to grade until the learning process is complete and we graduate from that school. Ultimately, man must attain perfection and then only will he obtain freedom from this law and be liberated. Until that stage is reached, until he learns how to base his actions upon the Absolute and to adopt the pure ideal, he will have to take embodiment again and again.

The Law of Karma and God's Justice

There are two or three questions about the cosmic form of this law and about the individual operation of it which I will answer now. One is: "What is the relation between God and the experiences and actions of individuals upon this earth?" We have said that God does not create the experiences of the individual, but that his experiences are determined by the particular nature that he has acquired.

Now, all life is brought forth on the surface of this earth by the falling of rain, and so we may say, in one way (and rightly), that it is rain that causes all life. Now it also happens that when rain, the universal common factor as it were, falls and sets life into growth, the life that springs forth is not all of the same kind. Wheat sprouts up as wheat, corn sprouts up as corn, and grass sprouts up as grass—the rain did not have anything to do with it. Within each seed there is an inherent nature which sets a different pattern in growth, though the rain is common and impartial over the whole of the earth. In the same way, it is the seed within one's own nature, implicit in the thoughts that one thinks and the actions that one engages in, which determines the experiences one will have. According to the mind is the nature of the person determined at birth and, according to this nature are the fresh impressions of life to be received.

The second question I would like to answer is: "In the operation of the Law, is there justice?" Even though it seems that a doer of good deeds is not reaping happiness and that an evil-doer is very well off, one must know that there is not necessarily any causal connection between the type of life one leads and the type of experiences one undergoes. Effects are not *immediately* produced from causes; and the activity in which man is presently engaged may be considered as the fresh seeds he is sowing, whereas the experiences he is undergoing may be considered as the harvest of a previous sowing. There *seems* to be a contradiction, but actually there is no contradiction. A compassionate and holy person may give succour and refuge to a fleeing criminal and because he gave shelter to the fugitive, may himself be arrested and sentenced, notwithstanding all his protestations of innocence. People will inevitably jump to the conclusion that this man who acted like a true Christian, giving refuge to a fellow human being in distress out of compassion and charity, was yet made to suffer for his charity. It looks as though his sentence were the direct outcome of his sheltering the criminal. In fact, the police will tell you, the judiciary will tell you, and even death will tell you that because this man harboured a criminal he was condemned, but if we look below the surface, we will find that the juxtaposition of action and experience is only apparent and not real. The kind and compassionate action will be rewarded with blessedness in the future, and the sentence will serve as the reaction from some Karma brought forward from the past. The Law is very mysterious and we cannot immediately understand all its operations. Its simplest statement is: "As you sow, so shall you reap". Every cause has an effect; every action has a reaction which is of a like nature. This law is universal. This law operates in all human experiences. Therefore, live wisely in the alert awareness of this law and walk along the path of righteousness, the path of goodness. Lead an ideal life and reap a future of peace and bliss.

11. THE MYSTERIOUS MIND AND ITS CONTROL

Glorious Immortal Soul! A great deal has been written in the West lately about psychological theories and investigations. The subject we are going to discuss, therefore, may contain several ideas already familiar to most of you. Nevertheless, so important and invaluable are the things which have to be known and remembered about the mind that frequent repetitions are necessary. These are facts which have to be carefully considered and properly assimilated, not once, but many times. If they ever happen to be forgotten, you should be able to remind yourself by such repetitive thinking. The knowledge about the mysterious mind is ancient. From the dawn of civilization, these truths have been expounded by the Great Ones. From times immemorial, man has been reminded of his true supra-mental nature by the revelation of the wise sages and illumined seers.

We shall consider also certain aspects so entirely new that until recently very few, if any, of the modern-day psychologists were even aware of them. In the West, knowledge of the human mind has been acquired by what is known as the 'scientific method'. It has been more or less an inductive approach. The students have sought to study the behaviour of individuals, and from their behaviour, to infer certain facts relating to the mind, and then generalise it all. They proceeded from "outside to inside" as it were. In the East, the investigations have been on a different line altogether. Their method has been the method of intuition, and their approach has proceeded from "inside to outside". Their method, though inductive in nature, has been proved through the test of time to be beyond error, because their first premise was infallible—based as it was upon intuition.

The Mind as Seen from a Vantage Point

In the East, the scientists of the spirit rose beyond the mind through processes of Yoga, and totally separated themselves from the mind and all its associated functions, and from that point of vantage, untouched by the mind, and entirely free from the influence of its habitual patterns of thought, patiently studied its essential, inherent nature and its behaviour. They beheld it in the light of a tangible and higher spiritual experience upon which they were established, and from where the mind was seen to be a distinct object apart from the seer, a thing to be observed and studied. How many of the modern psychologists of the recent century or two can claim to have thus risen above the mind and gone beyond its irresistible influence and from that vantage point studied its behaviour as a master-witness and observer? The Yogic masters, scientists avowedly of the inner realm of man, did gain a supra-mental freedom and independence and were able, as it were, to "put the mind before them"; and then they carried on their study of its workings in an objective and masterful way.

When the observer is himself involved in the subject of his study, his results are bound to be incomplete and coloured, because he himself becomes a factor in that thing he tries to study. It is impossible to get a perfectly undistorted and distinct view of his subject unless and until he finds out how to study it in a totally objective way. So long as you have not developed a faculty other than this mind (in this case, the supra-mental faculty), so long as you have not disentangled yourself from the mind, you will be unable to conduct competent research in the realm of the mind. As the Indian expression has it: "You cannot see your own eyes". For this, a mirror has to be placed before your face. Similarly, for studying the mind, objectification of the mind is required. Long ago, there were great seers who managed to reach the supra-mental state in which suitable methods for such objectification could be adopted, and out of their deep studies came the great discoveries which have given man powers which hitherto he was unable to possess.

Mind is a Marvel

Stones, trees, grass and sand, which might have been existing in a given geographical area for centuries, can know absolutely nothing about their physical environment, but the moment an intelligent man enters into the area, he gathers innumerable facts pertaining to the same. He correlates these facts and in this way acquires useful knowledge. He may, for instance, ascertain the composition of the soil, the elevation of the land, the quarter in which the sun rises, the directions in which the water flows and the wind blows. Stones and boulders are immobile and insentient. Vegetation is entirely unconscious of itself and its environment, knowing nothing about the soil in which it grows, about the winds blowing above it, about the water soaking it. In man alone, there is some miraculous factor which gives him an immediate perception of his surroundings, and simultaneously gives him the ability to develop knowledge out of which new ideas are created for himself. This phenomenon is the mystery of human life. It is the mystery of the mind.

If you are in possession of this amazing mental faculty, wherever you go, knowledge opens its doors to you; whereas, deprived of this faculty, you are just like a pebble or a stone or a cabbage. When you go into sleep, and as soon as the mind is absorbed, you 'lose' all practical knowledge. The very moment the mind withdraws—it does not even have to leave you—that very instant you become like a block of stone or a piece of wood. This occurs every time you lapse into that state termed 'sleep'. The moment the mind starts its activity once again, the whole miraculous motion involved in life begins anew.

What precisely is this thing called mind whose function makes man the master of creation, and whose non-function annuls him and makes him a non-entity? What is this mysterious thing that makes so much difference to our being by its activity and its non-activity, by its projection and its withdrawal? In five minutes man is able to reduce a whole mass of perception and observation into well-marshalled facts of information and, through the process of rationalisation and co-ordination, he incorporates them into a comprehensive system of knowledge. By a no less astonishing process, man is able to walk and talk and execute various intricate movements, all impelled by the thoughts and ideas of the mind.

Man is all too unconscious and ignorant of this inner marvel of his own mind. Who gives thought to thought? Who turns the mind upon the mind and tries to know something about it? Rather, do you not take the mind for granted? If you do notice it at all, it is only when it starts going haywire; and then you are horrified. What greater tragedy can strike a home or a family than the loss of mind of one of its members? With the loss of the mind, a person no longer seems to be a person. Suddenly, then, you realize how utterly important the mind is, that its least upset causes life to go to pieces! A most dignified and notable gentleman, who drinks a little too much some evening, has his thought process befuddled and he makes a fool of himself even before his subordinates, juniors and friends, as well as before taunting observers. A person who is drugged and has his mind-functions arrested is in a state of living death. A total change is brought about in that personality in whom the mental function goes out of order. Such a person loses all the respect previously paid to his importance. He loses his importance — even his 'individuality'.

The faculty of the mind is the greatest gift that God has bestowed upon the individual soul. There is no gift greater than this. Human nature consists of the mind, but unfortunately, the mind can be the greatest single curse as well. This paradox is one of the great mysteries of life. Everyone knows from experience how the mind can plague man with its restless activity; nevertheless, the nature of that activity is the most specific difference between man and the sub-human species. This supreme faculty places man at the pinnacle of God's creation and is indispensable to his life in this framework of earthly existence.

Now, we see that happiness or unhappiness is totally a question of the state of mind. Passion, unlimited desires and uncontrolled impulses are the unmaking of an individual. They lower the state of mind, and total loss of peace, terrific agitation and intense restlessness are the result. All this is experienced as pain, sorrow and suffering. Such mental experiences as these make man miserable no matter what other benefits God may have bestowed upon him. You may have family, friends and many possessions, but if your mind is disordered or disorganized by ungovernable desires, it can create a hell out of even the best things which God has given you on earth. There is, therefore, a great and serious purpose in trying to understand the mind and in making proper use of it. The mind is designed as an instrument. Thought is the greatest power which you possess. Everyone has heard this, but what exactly is power? And what, exactly, is meant by "Thought is power"? Thought is, itself, your happiness and misery. Thought, itself, is your freedom and bondage. Thought, itself, is your heaven or your hell. Thought can either make you or ruin you. When the thought process is ultimately stopped, life comes to an end. Thus, thought is life.

Now, mind and thought are not two different things.

If a person is able to stop thought temporarily or permanently, then temporarily or permanently, mind ceases
to be for him. If this were ever to happen by itself, the
person would be ruined, but if it were done deliberately
and scientifically, then he would become the master of
the whole universe. He would control the whole universe,
for he would have heaven at his command. Total and
complete stoppage of all mental activity by complete
mastery over the mind immediately gives man the experience of his True Being. When the mind is totally
eradicated, then the experience of what you really are
becomes your very own. You rest and have your existence in your real Self.

Man's consciousness is never as it essentially is. The
mind clouds it over, chokes it, and acts as the barrier,
as the obstruction, to the play of Pure Consciousness
which is your true being. You should consider mind as
an instrument, for when its behaviour and its functions
are understood, you can use it as the greatest power that
God has given. When it is not properly understood, when
nothing about its control is known, then you are just a
plaything in the hands of the mind. You should recognize
yourself as the master of the mind; otherwise you will fall
into the error of regarding yourself as a thinking
machine. You are *not* a thinking machine. You are the
thinker—the independent director and controller of this
thinking machine called mind. If you do not realize this,
you become enslaved by the mind. As the mind is inclined, so are you propelled. You are not at peace. You
are tossed like a piece of cork on the surface of stormy
waters. Instead of using the mind, you become its cat's-
paw; you become helpless. This must not be.

Mind—The Barrier Between Man and God

It is universally acknowledged that the mind is the
only link between man and the body, and between personality and the external world. Right from childhood

man learns everything about the universe through the mind. Senses just feed in data to the mind. It is the mind which actually correlates the data and produces knowledge. It therefore provides the most important factor in man's life. The importance of this factor is recognized by the East, but in addition to this, the East has something more to say about the mind that has been unsaid by the Western psychologists. The East says that the mind is also the greatest barrier lying between man and the true source of his being. It is the barrier which for ever denies him access to the experience of infinitude. It is the limit within which the human being is confined and cramped into the dimensions of a narrow individualised personality. Struggling to expand and go beyond this limited range of consciousness, man is strongly opposed by his finite mind.

To understand, control and finally overcome the barrier of the mind is the most important business in the life of man. The mind has to be overcome. At the back of you there is that Consciousness of a perfect state of being where no sorrow touches and where there is no fear. There is that unchanging Reality which lies behind the fleeting experience of this phenomenal world, just as there is an immovable screen present behind the flitting, flickering figures of a cinema show—a screen which remains unchanged by the rapid shadow-play cast upon it and remains unaltered even when the play is finished. In the same way, behind all finite experience, there is that changeless, infinite substratum of indescribable pure Being. That is indestructible. That state of changeless imperishability is your true basis. That is your eternal abode. That is a state of freedom, fearlessness and joy— and that is blocked off from you by the barrier of the mind.

Now, exactly in what way does the mind deny man access to that limitless experience? This is a very impor-

tant question. Upon this question rests a most crucial
point: how can the mind be understood and how can it
be dealt with? This is a point which has been overlooked
in the West. It is in a very peculiar way that the mind
acts as a barrier and blocks off man's access to the
Supreme. It does not do this pernicious work by getting
behind you and preventing you from finding the access.
That is, it does not actually lie *between* you and the supernal experience. You are actually nearer to that Consciousness than the mind. That supernal experience is
represented by the innermost core of your being and the
mind is a barrier in the sense that it draws you outside
and ever keeps you away from that Centre. It ever en-
tices you to remain on the surface, in the shallows, for-
bidding you to go down into the depths of your
innermost being. Through its desires, its outgoing tendencies and its constant habit of objectification, the mind
draws you away from your Centre, channelling your being
into the multifarious names and forms that constitute the
external universe. This is the way the mind acts. It dis-
tracts you from your true conscious Centre and scatters
you amidst the externals.

Origin of Western Psychology

Western psychologists have studied the mind in
terms of characteristic action and behaviour. This approach is due to the way in which their attention was
first drawn towards the mind. Western psychologists were
primarily doctors. They started to work in the hospitals
where treatment of various ailments and diseases was
being studied and improved upon, but they found that
certain diseases could not be cured by all the medical
and therapeutic measures and, in this way they stumbled
across the fact that the causes behind many of the diseases were mental. From this discovery, they proceeded
to investigate the mental functions and found that there
were certain clear connections between the functions of

the mind and those of the body. Right from the start, the investigations of these Western psychologists centred around sick people—people whose illnesses defied medical treatment. We could say, therefore, without exaggeration that the study of the mind in the West originated in a sort of morbid psychology. The diseased mind was the focus of the psychologists' attention.

Out of their observations was evolved a great science, but in its development, the scientists were at a great disadvantage, for they were unable to study the mind as it was. They observed the diseased mind, rather than the mind of the perfectly healthy individual; they investigated the peculiar and the abnormal mind, rather than the mind of the representative person. In the East, on the other hand, the great Masters studied the universal man. The mind as an inner centre of life, and in its universal aspect, was the object of their study, and not mind in "this condition" or "that condition", ill or well. The Eastern Masters also considered both matter and spirit and carefully correlated their facts. They delved into themselves, and through introspection and meditation, uncovered amazing facts about this inner instrument we call the mind. Theirs was a pure subjective study. In meditation, the Eastern masters reached the very heart of their subject matter and there they had the Truth revealed to them. Thus they have authoritatively declared what has to be known about the mind. In this manner, the Eastern origin of this science was so totally different from the origin of Western psychology.

Characteristics of the Mind

The prime characteristic of the mind is externalization. The sages found that the flow of the mind was outward and not centred inward. That is the law of life: everything spreads outward from its centre. But there is a force which is trying to draw everything back towards their source and centre. When the externalizing force is overcome, man is able to release that re-integrating force, and in this way finds his Centre. When this is done, his search is over. Life is mastered.

The second characteristic of the mind is constancy of activity. Never for a single moment is the mind still.

The third characteristic is wideness in the range of its activity. Not only in one direction is it active, but in many directions. Now it is here, now it is there and now it is everywhere.

Thus, externalized, constantly active, and flitting from one thing to another, the mind is very difficult to control. To understand it requires much subtlety. It cannot be seen; it cannot be put into a test tube and analysed; it cannot be looked at under a microscope. Although man can do scarcely anything about the mind, the mind can do practically everything about the man! It is so subtle, so abstract, and so totally internal that man finds it very difficult to grasp it. One moment it can expand into the thought of the Pacific Ocean or outer space, and then it can diminish to the thought of a mustard seed or a pinpoint or an atom, and the next, with its centre seemingly within the confines of the human brain, as it were, the mind can think about everything up to infinity. With one leap, it can encompass the whole stellar, lunar and solar systems, and with the same capacity, it can think about something as small as a grain of sand. What a mysterious mind!

The mind assumes three recurring states or conditions in every human being. Your consciousness functions through one or the other of these states (referred to as 'Avastha' in Vedantic philosophy). It may be external or it may be internal and, if it is internal, it may be either partially withdrawn or totally withdrawn. The greater part of the time the mind is external and you call this state the "waking state". When you retire to sleep at night, the mind is partially withdrawn in relation to the external

universe, but is still vigorously active within. This you
vaguely know as the "dream state". Here the mind
creates a world similar to what you perceive and experience during the first-mentioned state, viz., your
waking consciousness.

When the mind goes beyond this dream consciousness, it sinks still deeper, and becomes totally withdrawn
and absorbed. This third state that you experience daily
is "sound sleep". Little is known about this state and you
hardly even think about it, but actually it is the most significant and vitally important state, for it holds the real
clue to your innermost true "Self" right at the very core
of your being. In this state of total withdrawal of the
mind — a state of sound, dreamless, deep sleep — you
come closest to your true, essential inner nature. In this
state, the mind is closest to its source and centre, but at
the same time it is so totally obliterated that even its innermost and primal "I" thought stands suspended in its
function. The barest indication of its latent presence is
the unmistakable feeling of "I rested well" or "I slept
soundly" of the individual upon emerging into waking
consciousness.

The Primal Root Thought

Why does the mind not abide in its centre? What
causes it to emerge again into external consciousness?
The first answer is that by its very nature the mind tends
to be externalized. Secondly, it is prevented from abiding
in its centre by the irresistible momentum of the primal
root thought "I". This root thought "I" forms the very
basis of your limited, false separatist individual personality and it is this root thought which mysteriously induces you into the error of identifying yourself with the
body, the senses, the mind and its moods, and with
names and forms.

What is the nature of this root form that the mind
takes? It is a universal common denominator and is the

basic nature of all normal individuality. It is a root common to the mind of everyone upon the surface of the
earth. It does not have to be thought in English. Its form
appears in all languages. In the spiritual sense, it is the
arch-enemy of inner evolution. All the vagaries of the
mind spring from it. It is the thought "I". How many
times daily does this thought come into your mind! It is
the first thought that comes into your mind upon waking.
Imagine yourself suddenly awaking from deep sleep in
the dead of night—even before you open your eyes, the
first thought that comes to you is "I". This "I" thought
then brings to you the whole universe. You may realize
that it is the dead of night, that you are resting on a
couch two and one-half feet above the floor. Time and
space, which is the very stuff of this universe, emerges
out of this "I" thought. After all this, your identity
mysteriously comes. You know who you are—your name,
your age, your false, limited personality. This is the pernicious work of the mind. The basic pillar, the "I"
thought, of your psychological personality arises first and
the entire structure of the finite individual being is then
propped up on it.

Out of this structure comes the thought "mine".
While still lying on the bed, you may start to feel, "My
back is stiff", "My feet are chilled", "My neck is sore",
"There is a draft". Now you want comfort and warmth.
Whether you like it or not, from "I" and "mine", the
basic selfishness then arises. This is not to be interpreted
in the moral or theological sense. This "selfishness" is
the natural outcome of the mind function and is the
basic nature of all normal individuality. Everyone wants
something for oneself. This is as old as the world and
human society functions upon this basic factor, unflatter-
ing though this be. You may say, "I am unselfish", but
the deep fact is that you act unselfishly because that
means something to *you*. It brings something to you

which you like and which is pleasing to you. As in everything that the human being does, there is a deep inner
motive even behind "unselfishness". In this motive, in
this selfishness, lies the centre of the personality, the
centre of life. Thus, the subtle basis of man's being is selfishness.

In action, the ever-revolving wheel of the mind has
in it two spokes, as it were. These two spokes are attraction and repulsion, like and dislike. What is it that man
likes? He likes those things that are pleasant, comfortable and convenient. He dislikes those things that are
painful, uncomfortable and unpleasant. The hub of this
wheel is the ego.

As this revolving wheel flashes upon the ego, as the
reflections of likable and unlikable things are perceived
through the senses, desires are engendered in the mind:
desires to contact and obtain things which are pleasant
and likeable and desires to escape and avoid those things
which are unpleasant and not likable. When you analyse
the life of any human being, you find two categories of
activity making up the entire business of living, since all
activity is either that occurring while one strives to obtain
what one likes, or that occurring while one struggles to
avoid what one does not like. Annoyance or anger is felt
when such an attempt is being made and the attempt is
thwarted or obstructed by someone or something. Intense
restlessness and agitation manifest when a desire is felt,
but is not fulfilled. Then, when a desire is felt and fulfilled—but the fulfilment turns out to be something other
than the original concept one had of it—what then? Disappointment is experienced; painful disillusionment
comes. Even when the desire is fully fulfilled, as expected, there commences anxiety in the mind—anxiety to
preserve the thing or the experience thus obtained,
anxiety that it may soon end, as end it must and does,
for all things are finite and therefore soon change, perish

and pass. What is still worse, if in one's feverish quest of an object one sees others already in possession of it and 'enjoying' it, then jealousy, hatred and envy torment and destroy the peace of mind.

All of these attitudes come out of the prime thought "I" and its chief successor "mine". They all succeed one another at such an incredible speed that the whole of man's life is constantly filled with the internal clatter and clamour of ever-flitting, altering moods, thoughts, and sentiments of this mysterious thing known as the mind. "I" and "mine", like and dislike, desire, restlessness, and then anger, disappointment, selfish elation, attachment, jealousy and hatred ever afflict the mind and keep it in a ferment. This is the common course that the mind follows. Why? Because the mind has lost itself in attending to things *outside* of itself. Having gone out, by its very nature, it becomes attached and bound up with outside things and thus involves itself in endless external activity. Terrible attachment and bondage is the fate of the non-discriminating mind and the unenlightened reason of the common man.

What happens then is very significant. The moment an experience is obtained by the mind going through the senses towards a desired object, a most significant thing happens, and this brings you to the study of another startling phase of your mind; a most important phase, indeed. It is that the mind immediately registers the experience thus obtained by its sense-contact with the external object. A subtle inner impression is made upon the mind. This impression is well-nigh indelible.

Operation of Subtle Impressions

Just as a seed is sown in the soil, so the impression of every experience is made on the mind. These impressions of experiences are "alive". They have in them the direct power to recreate the entire experiences which caused them in the first instance. (In fact, each impression seeks a repetition of the corresponding original experience.)

Now, desire always tends to gain strength whenever it is fulfilled. That is the very nature of desire. Thus, as the impression of a particular experience, of a particular desire-fulfilment, becomes more and more deeply confirmed by each successive fulfilment of the same desire, that impression begins to develop into a definite tendency in the mind. Desire is never satiated by its fulfilment.

Predilections of the mind are just waiting to be stimulated. As soon as the desired object is seen once again outside, or is heard about, or is even thought about, immediately the desire is aroused. It manifests itself and goads the mind to go outward. When these thought-waves flow in the mind, the imagination is called into play to show up how sweet and desirable the object is and how alluring its attractions are. The moment the imagination becomes thus engaged, these thoughts manifest as a strong craving. Such thoughts, with the imagination playing upon them, bind man. His total identification with the various moods of the mind makes him a slave of the desires operating therein. Thus, when an urge is felt, you are pushed by it. Even the will aspect of the ego is bound up with the desire nature of the mind. It is thus brought to bear upon the whole matter, and the individual is pushed into action, taken into action, in order to satisfy his desire; the desire, being fulfilled, the vicious circle is once again completed. Once again that experience has been obtained, and the impression etched upon the mind has been made still deeper.

This is the circle in which the human being is caught. He is like a toy, a puppet, a plaything of the mind which refuses all restraint. The mind wants to be full of desire and agitation and does not want to be controlled. Unless it is watched and disciplined daily, man will live his life like a puppet and end his life in slavery.

The vast majority of human beings are just pushed and shoved about by every little desire and impulse of the mind. They have no freedom. Individual freedom is just a myth. Freedom of the press, freedom of speech, and the *Habeas Corpus Act* they may have, but unless and until they have gained control over their minds and their desires and their impulses, all men actually live in slavery, and their freedom is in name only.

When man has an understanding of the activity of the mind (how the "I" thought is the very root thought of the mind) and finds out how it moves, then he will be able to get a hold over it. Here is one of the most interesting things about the mind; because the "I" thought is completely in the grip of the mind, man is unable to get into the core of his being where the centre of his consciousness lies. That ineffable experience of freedom is denied to man by the mind precisely in this aforementioned way.

How to Transcend the Mind

Now, the problem has been clearly stated. What is the solution? The solution lies in the complete reversal of this process. First you must try to control the externalization of the mind by overcoming desire. Very easy to say—but, how can desire be overcome? This is not too easy. Right thinking and discriminative reasoning hold a key to this solution. Various methods have been given. The great thing is to know yourself to be distinct and different from the desires. YOU are entirely separate and apart from all desire and thought. YOU are Consciousness, a being deeper than, and fully beyond, mind and all its countless modes. This is the secret key. You are not the mind. Know yourself to be independent of the mind. This is very difficult to realize because the mind is so persistent and your present feeling of identity with it is so complete. The subtle "I" thought is so elusive and slippery as to defy a steady analysis and it escapes calm observation, but when you have managed through persistent and repeated attempts to grasp it and dissect it, when you know yourself to be distinct and apart from it, then you are given a glorious vantage point from which you can view the mind. Formerly, when you were indisciplined and indulgent, you were helpless; but now when you stand aside and apart from the mind and the "I" thought, you are the master. You can observe it as the Witness-Consciousness apart from it.

You must be able to thus perceive all the modes of your entire personality. You are the silent, unattached Witness-Consciousness within. You are not the senses; you are not the mind; you are not the thought, emotion or sentiment. You are beyond even the intellect, which is deluded and overcome by this illusion of false identification. Thus, what you have to work up to, ultimately, is that you are not even this "I" thought which is dearest to you, and to which you are clinging. Even this "I" thought is merely a mode of the mind, like any other thought. The true "I" (the real YOU within) is a supramental factor. You are a pure Being distinct from this "I" idea which the mind habitually thinks. Transcend the mind. You are pure Consciousness and your true identity is "Conscious Being". You are the true "Thinker" of the "I" thought and you make use of the mind to express yourself. This Consciousness is the basis of your Being whence the "I" thought is derived. In your present state of delusion, this is not perceived. Your perception is clouded. The moment the "I" thought is conceived by the mind, the mind is already afflicted by the most pernicious of diseases. This disease, according to the *Vedas*, is the superimposition of yourself upon the physical body. You imply that you are this—the eyes, ears, nose, tongue, hands, feet, head, etc. Is it not enough that you are caught within the limitation and bondage of this individual body that holds you? Why make it infinitely worse by identifying yourself with every single feature of it? The body is actually a prison-house, and when I say that it is made infinitely worse, I mean that it is the mind that does this work, and not YOU, for your affliction is the mind, with its "I am this body" notion. This mind will not give you rest. It is only when you can shatter this wrong idea that you will know that you are not this body, that you are not this mind.

To make the outgoing stream of thought in-going is the great science of the mind that has to be learned. Begin by non-co-operating with the mind. Whenever the mind builds up a want and wants to do a thing, assert your independence and say, "No, I will not do it", and whenever the mind refuses to do something, say, "You shall do it". Always tell yourself: "I am the master of this house (body-mind). I will not be dominated and commanded by the desire-ridden mind. I shall do the dictating. I will assert my mastery and make the mind listen to me and obey me".

Mind, as thought, is not overpowering. Mind, as "I", is also not overpowering, because it has no dynamism in it; it is just a habitual mode of the mind. But, when desires are evolved out of the "I" and "mine" thoughts, and when imagination is brought into play the mischief starts. It is letting the imagination play upon your thoughts that gives them a dynamism of their own. The more a thought is dwelt upon, the more quickly it grows into the dynamic form of a desire. Therefore, the moment that a thought appears, stamp it out. The Hindus say that great forest fires can be averted if you stamp upon the tiny sparks right at the beginning.

Supposing the thought does not reach the condition of a desire, still you must try to remember that it is not YOU. Do not couple yourself with it. Do not get involved in it. Do not identify yourself with it. Know yourself to be apart from the thought and do not fulfil it. Disconnect yourself from the thought and stand aside.

Even though the mind seems to be capable of thinking a hundred different thoughts at a time, the precise scientific truth about it is that the mind can think only a single thought at a given moment. This is a mysterious characteristic of the mental stuff. Due to its finite nature, the mind can think only serially. The mind thinks with such rapidity that it seems as though thoughts are simultaneous, yet only one thought is ever entertained in the mind at one time.

. From this fact it has been suggested that if you consciously raise certain thoughts independently, then no other thought can occupy the field of the mind at that time. Create your own thoughts masterfully and you will be free from the plague of loose and miscellaneous thinking. You will no longer be a prey to vain imaginings. Control the mind. Create right and noble thoughts; then no other unworthy or negative thought can persist.

The Raja Yogic Technique of Selective Thinking

Patanjali, the expounder of the most complete science of mind-control, has said that if you want to get rid of any particular thought, then you should instantly raise a counter-thought of the opposite nature. If, for instance, you have a certain negative thought of fear, then introduce a positive thought of courage. If you have a negative thought of hatred and hostility, create immediately in your mind a positive thought of love, friendship and brotherhood. Fill yourself with the feeling of cordiality. If you are overcome by a thought of prejudice and intolerance, raise thoughts and feelings of sympathy, understanding and oneness. This can be done at any specific instant, with reference to any specific negative thought. This practice can also be undertaken as a complete course of psychological self-transformation with the technique systematically practised day by day. It is an invaluable inner discipline for your ethical unfoldment and progress. It can help you even in your spiritual awakening.

If you are easily subject to anger thoughts, then deliberately fill the mind with thoughts of patience, love and kindness. Also, set apart some time daily and, in silence, reflect upon the glory of kindness and compassion and forgiveness. Meditate upon it. Think carefully of the disadvantage and undesirability of anger. Reflect positively upon the great advantages and desirability — physical, mental, social and ethical — of a sweet and even temper. Meditate upon the sublime personality and life of Jesus Christ, Mahatma Gandhi, Saint Francis or Abraham Lincoln. After persistent practice, anger thoughts begin to drop away entirely. They are unable to remain in the mind, because the mental stuff has been altered.

If you do not fill the mind consciously with deliberately chosen thoughts, then it will always fill itself with its own wayward thoughts, and that will be allowing the mind to grow wild, as it were, into its own self-willed nature. Selective thinking is the key to the problem of mind control. Discriminative thinking is the essence of mind control.

When you take up the task of disciplining and training the mind, you become selective in your thoughts. Then you feed the mind with good and pure thoughts, right and proper thoughts, positive and pleasant thoughts of your own choice. Keep certain thought-pictures frequently before the mind's inner vision. You will be inspired. These thought-pictures will elevate you. They will build up a new personality within you. These thought-pictures can be written down and placed before you on the outside as well — on the wall, on your table, in the home, at the office, in your pocket, inside your wallet. Through outer sense as well as inner mental vision, through the eye as well as through thought, mind is remade and cast upon a new mould. It is truly a process of mental re-creation. It is a psychological re-birth. This could well be, and actually is, the precursor and fore-runner to 'becoming reborn in Spirit', patiently explained by Jesus to the earnest and enquiring Nicodemus.

Practise this selective and discriminative thought-technique in a systematic way. You will soon be able to renew the nature of your mind totally. You will begin to see that you are not the mind. You will realize that you are the inner artist who is to mould the mind-stuff into a beautiful form of your choice. You have to work upon it even as a sculptor works upon his material—a great master chiselling away at the marble to bring out of it a wondrous beauty. Remember, so long as you think yourself to be one with the mind, the true power of thought is denied to you. Therefore, assert your independence. This is the key to mind-control.

Hatha Yoga—An Aid to Mind-control

In addition to these positive methods of overcoming the mind, you may also know that the mind is played upon by the three inner vibratory states, or movements, called (in Yogic terminology) Gunas—meaning qualities. They are Sattva, Rajas and Tamas. Sattva implies purity and light. Rajas implies passion and activity. Tamas implies inertia, darkness and grossness. Purity tends to steady the mind and make it go inward, whereas passion and impurity throw the mind into a state of unsteadiness and turmoil and take it outward, away from its centre. The mind which is rendered Sattvic is beautifully balanced. Purity of life, in all its departments, is thus a great requisite for the refinement of the nature and the heightening of the being.

To enhance the steadiness of the mind, the practice of certain Yogic postures is useful and beneficial, because there is an inter-connection between the body and the mind. Hatha Yoga is here recommended as a supplementary technique, and the practice of a few of the preliminary exercises, for half an hour every morning and every evening, helps to change the vibratory state of the mind. It takes it onward from passion to purity. By learning to keep the body steady and poised, the mind becomes subdued, and a beautiful harmony is created within. These Yogic postures and simple breathing techniques can be practised by all as auxiliaries to augment the effect of other efforts at mind-control.

The central fact to be remembered is that the mind is an instrument. It has been made to be used by you. It was not made to use you. It is to be kept under your control. You are the master. If you feel this fact, power is aroused in you. This fact is truth. Truth is all-power and positive. Always keep yourself, therefore, as the unaffected, detached Witness-Consciousness. Look upon the mind as something distinct from you and soon you will be able to grasp it and chasten it. As you do this, gradually, success will come.

Difficult though it undoubtedly is to develop a new habit, once the foregoing secret is known, the whole process becomes greatly simplified. The right technique is not so much to struggle against the habit which is to be broken, but to start building the new habit that is to replace the old. When this work is started, the old habit cannot stand. This is the "trick" (if you will have it that way), and amazingly and without any effort, the old habit just disappears. Every habit can be broken and the whole mind can be totally renewed.

At a certain stage in this renewal, you find yourself in a very curious and interesting position. You seem to have two minds—a higher mind and a lower mind—a pure mind and an obstinate, unregenerate mind. The very arrival at this position implies an overcoming of the negative thoughts of one's personality and then alone does one come to the stage of contemplation.

If this scientific method is properly used, and the right emphasis is given to the total eradication of all the negative aspects of the individual personality, life becomes based upon virtue and self-control. Proceeding on in this way, according to Raja Yoga, the lofty inner state is then reached in which all thoughts become arrested and the lower mind ceases to function. Your Pure Consciousness, your glorious Inner nature, full of bliss and peace, begins to manifest. As the silent Witness-Consciousness, you begin to experience Truth. You realize your true Self. This is Self-knowledge, the knowledge of the Truth within. This Knowledge makes you free.

12. THE ONLY SOURCE OF TRUE HAPPINESS

Happiness seems to have been the quest of man on earth ever since creation began, but this quest does not yet seem to have ended. Happiness is the quest of the whole world, but at the same time the despair of all of us. There does not seem to be any finding of it. Happiness seems to lie far in the future, on the distant horizon as it were, where, like the horizon, it recedes out of sight the very moment you think it attainable. After several thousand years of known history, modern man seems to be as far away from the actual experience of happiness as his remote ancestors. Yet, there is no doubt that during this time tremendous efforts have been made to attain it. Throughout the centuries man has striven, often tirelessly, to create countless devices to fill his external life with pleasures. But all these devices have failed to serve the exact purpose. For, if man is asked the question, "Are you really happy?", hardly anyone will give a forthright and direct answer, "Yes, I am!". Almost everyone will begin, instead, with "Er,...Oh, I think so..." or "Perhaps..." or "May be not quite..." or "I can't exactly say...". Anything but a definite affirmative!

If people have been searching for happiness for centuries and have not found it still, does it mean that there is no happiness to be found? Does it mean that happiness is merely a figment of the imagination, something which does not exist in fact, but arises like a phantom from ideas of our own making? Either it must be concluded that happiness is inaccessible to man or that man has made some fundamental error in his assessment of happiness. Some may say that the method that man has adopted in his quest for happiness has been imperfect. If one sets out to do a thing, but in the wrong way, the goal will not be reached. Some may say that the place where man has been searching for happiness has been the wrong one. Supposing a thing is in one room while the search for it is carried on in another, the object of the search will not be found even though it definitely exists. Whatever the reason may be—and this we will try to investigate—happiness does seem to have eluded mankind. It is one of the most elusive of things! Man cannot quite avail himself of it, even when it seems to be right at his finger-tips. Why, exactly, is this?

All the wonderful and tremendous activity on earth indicates that there is some specific, universal want that man is trying to satisfy. This want, we have seen, is the desire for happiness. This desire may be pursued either in a positive way or in a negative way. One may seek to enjoy those things which he conceives in his mind as productive of happiness; or he may try to get rid of all those things which appear to be contrary to his happiness. No one wants pain, sorrow or misery. All want to avoid these afflictions, because they are the very antitheses of happiness. By getting rid of pain and sorrow, people mean to attain to that state in which happiness is clearly perceived.

Happiness Is an Experience

This much is certain. Man knows what he wants. But he does not know the true nature of what he wants and why his happiness eludes him. That there is a surpassing supreme happiness which can be obtained in this human life is the great declaration of the *Upanishads*, the *Vedas*, and the *Bhagavad Gita*. "Know thou that the Reality is indescribable bliss and the highest conceivable happiness. There *is* that happiness which is so intense that the intellect cannot even comprehend it and the senses (which ordinarily experience happiness) cannot even grasp it or convey it—it is so intense and so transcendental!": that

is the happiness which is the goal of man. Fullness and
perfection pertain to the highest happiness. It has nothing
to do with the imperfect, for imperfection implies a mixture, and in a mixture of factors, there is no uniformity
of experience. If salt and sugar are mixed together and
the mixture is placed upon the tongue, one cannot taste
a uniform sweetness because of the two elements inherent in the mixture. One will taste sweetness, but at
the same time he will make a wry face, for the taste of
salt also will fill his mouth. A mixture by its very nature
cannot impart purity or perfection to an experience. The
great thing is to find surpassing happiness. He who attains that goal passes beyond all grief and sorrow. This
assertion that happiness is an experience available to the
human being is not stated merely as a theory. It is as-
serted authoritatively as a substantial, self-experienced
fact by those who have actually attained to that supernal
experience.

Where is the source of this happiness? Before man
can set out in quest of this source, he has to know what
he is seeking. The correct conception and the right idea
of happiness should be clear to him. Unfortunately, few
men demonstrate the use of their intelligence by defining
clearly what it is they wish to obtain. The whole world
is madly going after something of which it has no clear
conception in mind. All this effort becomes practically
futile, for it is not backed up by intelligence. The first
thing to realize is that happiness is an *experience*. It is not
an object. Also, it is not an acquisition. Rather, it is an
awareness of an internal state that is already an essential
and, therefore, an irrevocable part of your very being.
One cannot just go to a place and bring it away as
though it were something to be had. Happiness is a condition of the being. Once it is clearly understood that it
is not a thing, then the filling of your life with things will
be regarded as a great delusion. Things in this world are

not sources of true happiness. At most, they are capable of keeping out (in some doubtful measure) certain known, universal inconveniences and miseries of the human being. This is their only intrinsic value and utility. They have been created by man, and man himself is imperfect. He himself is subject to misery, sorrow, suffering, grief and pain. Things created by such an imperfect being cannot partake of the nature of perfection. We know that it is in perfection that a uniform experience can be had, uncontradicted by anything external. Mixed experiences obtained from man-made things cater to the physical part of the being, providing sensual satisfaction perhaps, or removing discomfort, but imperfect things cannot give us happiness.

Possession of Objects Means No Happiness

Now the question may arise in your mind: "What about all those beautiful things, those pleasant things, those tasty things, those colourful things, those melodious things filling the world? Do they not give happiness?" Certainly these things do give definite experiences. But, can these experiences be called *happiness*? That is the point we have to decide now.

The experience derived from all these things depends for its validity upon our coming into contact with them. Without coming into contact with them no experience can be obtained. Surrounding yourself with a plethora of the most beautiful objects and then closing your eyes will demonstrate this point. You will not be able to obtain any experience from their physical presence in your room. Why? Because the sense of sight has not made any contact with them. They are things to be seen, and if the sense of sight does not contact them, no experience can be had. Again, let the most wonderful music be played. Plug your ears. Now it is impossible for you to enjoy the pleasure of the sound, because no contact has been made between your ear and music. Similar-

ly, unless the tongue contacts the food you eat, you do
not obtain pleasure from the most exquisite banquet of
delicious dishes spread out on the table before you.
Hearing, seeing, touching, smelling and tasting — all
depend upon the contact of the instrumental sense with
the corresponding object.

Physical experiences are of the nature of sensations.
As such, they are limited by the capacity of the senses
to entertain thought of external objects and to carry the
sensations to the mind. Beyond a certain limit which
marks the sense capacities, things become disgusting and
detestable. Moreover, by the very fact that all these
things afford experiences dependent upon sense contacts
followed by the conveyance of sensations to the mind,
the actual state of the mind is clearly seen to be a condition affecting one's experience of pleasure. In certain
states of mind, one is in no mood for enjoyment. Supposing, for instance, one has received a telegram that his
eldest son has just been killed in an air crash. Then the
presentation of all manner of pleasurable things will not
be able to arouse in him the slightest indication that
there is any pleasure that can be derived from them. No!
He will be incapable of obtaining any pleasure because
the factor which is within him, and which is essential to
his happiness, has been overcome by his state of mind.
Not all the things of the world could then give to him
the experience of pleasure.

It is not surprising, therefore, that opulence and
misery oftentimes go together. Some people who have
everything from which sense pleasures can be derived
nevertheless live in misery. They have no peace of mind.
They are dejected or in despair. They even contemplate
ending their lives. Why? The answer is that there is no
invariable causal connection between objects in plenty
and the derivation of the experience called happiness.
The contrary is also apparent. There are some people

possessing very little, but who are filled with happiness. They are always laughing, always singing, even while they work. How is this? If external objects are indispensable to the experience of happiness, how is it that there are people without possessions—clad in rags perhaps or sorely in need of a shoe repair—who are at the same time filled with happiness? If the prerequisite for happiness were the presence of objects, then their absence should rob these people of all joy.

Thus it is that the absence of objects is yet found to be compatible with the experience of joy, just as the presence of objects is found to be compatible with the experience of misery. Clearly it is seen that there is no causal connection between the objects of this universe and the experience of happiness.

Happiness—A Lost Treasure

How do people, who have all the things that are ordinarily envied, act when they get a few days free from their work? They go on a trip to the mountains or to the national parks or perhaps to Hawaii. Though they own everything usually conceived of as sources of happiness, yet when they are given a little freedom, they in fact try to get away from what they already have. Who ponders over the significance of these things? Who sees their implication? To the thoughtful person, it is clearly revealed that objects of the universe do not have the subtle power to give man the experience of happiness. The thoughtful person sees that happiness is not the *getting* of anything. What then is the special significance of the expression "The quest for happiness" or "The search for happiness"? Why do we use the words *quest* and *search?* Seeking or searching implies that something has been lost. If a thing was, and then is not, we may immediately go in search of it. When the lost thing is found, we have simply recovered it. Life, therefore, is not so much a struggle to *discover* the source of happiness as an effort to *recover* lost happiness. In its aspect as a quest, life is an attempt to recover that which has been lost.

This brings us to a more subtle point and a higher implication. If happiness is a state which you once had and now have lost, then by regaining the missing factor, you could recover that state for your experience of happiness. Wherein does this factor lie? The very clear and definite answer is: this factor lies *within* you. It does not lie *outside* of you. Then, in what relationship does it stand? Is it a part of you or is it close to you? Or is it in the relationship of identity with you? You yourself are that happiness. Happiness is your essential nature. Happiness is your innermost nature. You can never actually lose it, because it is identical with you.

The present temporary state of absence of happiness and a search therefore is a state of forgetfulness, a state not of actual loss. This has been explained in various ways in philosophy. When I was a youngster, in the Third Grade I think, we had in our English textbook a very humorous little lesson called "Grandpa's Spectacles". We are introduced to a tumult in the drawing room of a house in which Grandpa has lost his spectacles and has set a whole brood of grandchildren on the search for it. Jean and Peter and Joe and John...and the hunt is on. They look underneath the sofa and lift up the rug and climb up to the mantelpiece and peer behind Grandpa's pillows. After the search has gone on for some time and Grandpa is getting more and more impatient, little Tommy, who has been searching everywhere and is in despair of finding them, cries out suddenly, "Please, Grandpa, remember where you put them before you went to sleep?" And then, when he looks up at Grandpa, behold! there they are right up on Grandpa's forehead. There they have been all along. They were never lost. There seemed to have been a loss, because Grandpa was unaware of the spectacles on his own forehead pushed up absent-mindedly after finishing his newspaper.

In your quest for happiness, your position is precisely the same. The very nature of your being is indescribable, perennial, unalloyed happiness. The absence of happiness is not so much the loss of the thing as such, but the loss of your awareness of its presence within. The source of true happiness lies right within you. The source of true happiness is your Self. Until man realizes his own true nature and taps it at its very source, is he to be totally deprived of happiness? By no means! Just as you are, you may avail yourself of any number of means of getting some experience of happiness. What are these means? There is a very simple way. You may get rid of all those factors that rob you of your happiness. This effort is largely negative, because you do not do anything positive to obtain happiness. You assume that happiness is there, but is not being experienced. Then you wonder what is preventing that experience and proceed to remove the obstructions—and there it is! If a light is there and somehow has been covered over, then you have to uncover it and let it shine. If a quantity of gold is buried at a spot, to obtain that gold you have only to remove the intervening earth and stones and pebbles. Then you find the gold and get it. What are those factors that all too effectively rob us of our happiness? They are of our own making. They are due to the original error of man which lies in the thought that happiness is to be found in objects, and out of this deluded thought has arisen all those factors out of which man has created his own fallacies.

Desire and want, which arise from this prime delusion, destroy all peace of mind. In a mind devoid of peace, how can there be happiness? Happiness depends upon peace of mind. It is in that calm tranquil state of mind that happiness arises, for essentially true happiness is your inward spiritual state. Fortunately or unfortunately, the only media through which it can be expressed are the intellect and the mind. If these two media are thrown into such a state of agitation that they cannot serve as proper channels for the welling up of this inner happiness, then their condition becomes unfit and unfavourable. It is only when there is peace and serenity in the mind and intellect that the inner happiness makes itself felt. The robber of your peace and serenity is the sense of want and desire which arises out of your prime error that happiness depends upon objects. That is the error in which you start your life. In childhood one is taught that to have a good time means going places, or doing things, or getting objects, and so children grow up in this delusion. The adult that is produced is at the mercy of things which are outside of himself. Even a grain of proper understanding of this world, as it really is, instilled into young people would grant a rich harvest in terms of happiness and joy.

The Limited Utility of Sense Objects

Try to evaluate objects as they really are. To lead a proper existence here on earth, one has to assign a limited value to objects. Certain objects are indispensable for the maintenance of life. To that end they should be utilised. But, let them not assume an undue prominence in your life. For, instead of serving as sustenance, they may become the veritable tyrant sapping life of all true contentment and satisfaction. Your happiness may then become mortgaged to these objects. These objects may then come to have a stranglehold upon you and tend to dominate you and enslave you. A proper understanding and a right evaluation of objects as they are, and for what they are worth, is of prime concern to the human individual. "Thus far, and no further!" you must say, when objects try to invade the interior kingdom of your life.

Time-tested Aids to Happiness

As far as possible, you must always try to simplify your life. Simplicity of life is the true secret of happiness. Unhampered experience of the joy which lies within comes out of simplicity. Therefore, your life should never be complicated with too many things. Due to too many things, due to too many desires, modern man unfortunately has missed this joy. You have seen the bright posters printed by Pan-American Air Lines, TWA, etc. The "paradise" which they feature, for a holiday, is not in metropolitan, highly urbanized America, but in the South Sea Islands. Why? Not because they have drive-in theatres, barbecue hamburger stands or race tracks — none of these things are there. Such places rarely offer the ordinary conveniences, yet one readily admits the idea that there is a "paradise" there, because one knows of the natural simplicity of those places. The Hawaiian native always sings and dances. He is comparatively carefree and filled with the happiness of simplicity and contentment. We envy him and even try to imitate him, at least for the time being, by leaving all distractions and going away to his place. In simplicity, man has the key to happiness.

Unwillingly it is that modern man allows his life to become so complicated. He knows that simplicity is the secret of happiness. "But I can't help it!": saying thus, he weeps. He tries to forget even the wonderful paradise. He takes tranquillizers. He goes into a saloon or a bar. He does something — anything — to make him forget the total inadequacy of his present condition.

Have the capacity to derive joy out of whatever situation you may find yourself in. Assert: "The situation has not the power to alter my experience. My experience is alterable only to the degree to which I allow it to be altered. If I say 'No', then I can have the same peace and happiness within no matter how the situation changes. It can change every hour, yet I can be changeless". So much blessedness will come if you have simplicity and contentment. You will find, first of all, that you are free from debts. This nightmare of instalments, of credit plans, that comes month after month, year after year, will be gone. Some people do not have any freedom. They just slave away for those various companies to which they owe instalments. Right to the end of their lives they go on paying instalments on the house, on the car, on the radio, on the TV, on the refrigerator, on the washing machine, and on heaven knows how many gadgets that have all been invented!

A simple and a contented life depends more upon God-made things than upon man-made objects. There are hundreds of things that can fill you with happiness if only you have the eyes to see. When you get up in the morning, you can step out of your room and look at the dawn and be happy. When the sun rises, still more happiness. When you hear the birds warbling, even more happiness. When you feel the cool breeze blowing—well! there is no end to happiness. Know the technique for deriving happiness from these simple things—from the dawn, the sunrise, the birds, the laughter of children, the beautiful·blue sky, the white clouds slowly sailing like majestic ships, little dancing flowers. They can inspire you if only you know how to derive joy. If you discover this secret, there will be no end to your happiness.

Also, learn to experience joy from the happiness of others. Instead of becoming envious, become filled with joy whenever you see others happy. Feel happy by beholding the happiness of others. Train yourself to derive happiness out of bringing happiness into the lives of others. Learn the technique of getting joy by making others joyful. Your happiness will multiply a thousandfold. At the present moment, it is circumscribed

by the experiences undergone by yourself alone. But if
you begin to get joy from all others, then you will be
happy perpetually. Everyone's happiness will become a
part of your happiness and will go to multiply it and add
to it.

Try to derive joy out of the beauty of all things, not
just from those things which you possess. In this way you
will develop an impersonal capacity for happiness.
Without touching a cent in your pocket, you will realize
an illimitable treasure of happiness which lies strewn all
around you and everywhere about you. When we realize
the many things that God has given for which we have
reason to be happy, the whole day will not be long
enough for us to be thanking Him. Untold treasure He
has given. Just consider your own body, your own self.
You have two sound eyes. Supposing someone says, "All
right. Give me one of your eyes and I will give you twenty thousand dollars". Which person in a sane condition
of mind would comply with such a request? Supposing
you were offered one hundred thousand dollars for your
tongue—would you give it? So, that means that you have
things that are worth millions and millions of dollars!
And yet there is mopping and fretting for a few things
which we do not have, not realizing the untold worth of
the precious things which we already have. There are
some people who are unfortunately deprived of these
things. Compared to them, how fortunate you are! If you
simply reflect on how *much* God has given you, your
whole vision of life will become changed. Know these little secrets. They are little, but they are very important.
They can mean the whole difference between darkness
and light.

Learn to accept the experiences that come through
life. There is no use fretting and fuming and making
yourself miserable over them. You perhaps may just add
more misery to the misery which these experiences bring.

Have calm and wise resignation. There is one Supreme Intelligence that is guiding the lives of men here and these experiences that come from that Source, learn to accept like human beings. Endure the little troubles that come through life. If there is a little sorrow, endure it and learn to take away its sting. Thus you may enrich your life out of those very experiences which you find painful and unpleasant.

Be friendly to all. Towards your superiors, have an attitude of complaisance. Do not be full of fear and timidity and nervousness in their presence. That can also rob you of your joy. Be serene. With your own equals, be friendly. Feel oneness with all. Towards those who are inferior to you in status, in health, in strength, in beauty, have an attitude of kindness, love and compassion. To those who are troublesome, wicked, unpleasant and nasty, be indifferent. Do not work yourself up into a state of irritation or annoyance or unfriendliness or hatred. Just ignore the wicked. These four attitudes will provide you with a means of not being put out—complaisance towards superiors; friendliness and brotherhood towards your equals; kindness and compassion towards those who are inferior to you; and a perfect indifference to all those who are inimical to you, who are troublesome, nasty, evil or wicked. All these four categories of people you are bound to encounter in life.

Above all, do not give way to anger. Anger, more than any other single factor in this world, destroys happiness. It can totally wreck the entire happiness of a home. If one member of the household has a temper and gives vent to his anger, he can destroy the happiness of all members of the home—even the neighbours may be affected!

Maintain a rational restraint over the senses. The urge toward carnal enjoyment is a natural part of the human being, but it pertains only to the mental-physical part of your nature. We have to recognize this as such. However, it is the prerogative of every individual being endowed with high intelligence to hold a rein over the senses. That way the senses cannot destroy happiness. If they are allowed to hold a sway over you, then you cannot have any happiness. This is the Law of the Universe.

Base your life upon virtue, truth and purity. If purity is always your guiding rule, guilt complexes and neuroses will go and psychiatrists will be unnecessary for you. Happiness fills those who base their lives upon virtue. Virtue is a direct emanation from the Divine, just as happiness is a quality of the Divine. Although it may be difficult in the beginning, yet, how many headaches would you save yourself if you would base your life upon virtue and truth! If you tell a lie, to support it, you have to tell a chain of lies. Sticking to truth takes away from you all anxiety and a thousand pin-pricks. A life of truth and purity is a life devoid of many of the factors that contribute to the misery and unhappiness of the modern world.

Even more important, keep close to that great Inner Source of all happiness, all joy, all bliss! Call It by whatever name you choose—I do not want to give It a name. Make That the centre of your being. That is the Eternal Thing that supports your life. That is your alpha and omega, your all-in-all, your supporting substratum and your destination and goal. Keep close to It by developing love. Love the Supreme! Always remember the Supreme! Great ones who have become absorbed forever in the Supreme Blessed State of happiness and bliss have told us one great secret which provides us with an unfailing method of attaining happiness. That secret is the Divine Name. They said, "Practise the Divine Name. The Name of the Supreme and the Supreme are not two; they are one. If you have the Divine Name within you, you have the Supreme within you". This is a great spiritual truth.

This is a great fact. If you remember this fact and try to make the Divine Name your own, if you always repeat the Divine Name, always invoke the Divine Name, always fill yourself with the current of the Divine Name, then happiness and blessedness will be present with you always.

Happiness, in the truest sense of the term, is that changeless experience right within you. It is that awareness which, being present, enables you to derive sweetness out of all other things; and which, being absent, deprives you of all the sweetness in anything. That is the most important fact.

It works like the figure "1" in mathematics. If "1" is there, you may add to it any number of zeroes; each zero progressively increases the value of the number enormously; the zeroes then gain great significance. But if "1" is not there, all the zeroes are just ciphers without any value of their own whatsoever. Similarly, all things gain the capacity of giving happiness only in the presence of the ONE BEING. Make Him the centre of your life. Make Him the most important and paramount thing in your life. Then you will never be taken away from your happiness even for a single second. No one will be able to take you away from It, for you are yourself in that Happiness. When a fish is taken out of a little bowl and released into the ocean, it swims about anywhere and always remains in the vast ocean. So, from the tiny bowl of deluded life where we have paid this undue attention to external objects, let us lift ourselves out and enter into that vast Truth. In God lies happiness, and within me He is, and He and I are one.

Within lies the perennial Fount of Eternal Happiness. May you live your life in this Truth. Then I will assure you that your life will become a stream of happiness. May your life thus flow forth not as a vale of tears but as a perennial stream of infinite happiness. This is my prayer: may God give you the strength and the inspiration to blossom out into that simplicity and contentment, that shining and radiant virtue, that serene state of detachment, that friendliness with all beings, out of which this great gift that is waiting to be bestowed upon you will become your own. May your life become radiant with joy.

13. THE TRUTH ABOUT YOGA

This is a world of passing names and forms. In it all things change and soon reach their dissolution. One Thing, however, abides changelessly amidst all change. It is the Great Reality, the imperishable, the indestructible, changeless Being whom you call God. This Great Being, this Universal Spirit, is the eternal source, substratum and the goal ultimate of all existence. He is existence eternal, knowledge absolute, infinite bliss, immeasurable and perennial peace. To attain Him is to become fearless and free and immortal. By attaining Him you transcend death; you pass beyond all sorrow, pain and suffering. You reach a state of indescribable joy, ineffable peace and a supreme exalted consciousness of bliss and beatitude. This is as tangibly and substantially possible as plucking a ripe fruit and tasting and enjoying it.

Yoga is the means by which the human soul attains the Supreme Being and experiences the infinite bliss which is all-perfect, unalloyed and absolute. Yoga is the approach to Divinity. This is the simplest meaning of the term Yoga. It is the ascent unto Truth, or the movement towards the eternal, absolute Reality. The subject of Yoga is very important. This science has been evolved by the ancient seers and sages of the holy land of India and bestowed upon mankind for all time. A proper understanding of this universal heritage would, indeed, be a very great step towards the understanding of yourself and the world. A true evaluation of this great science would enable you to live your life in a more satisfying manner.

The Wisdom of the East

At the present juncture in this momentous Twen-

tieth Century, the concept of one world is gaining ground
in the minds of all thoughtful men. The necessity for the
exchange and interchange of cultural values and scientific
knowledge, and many other aspects of human life, is
being felt more and more. The achievements of the different human races and nations are becoming the common property of the whole world. People everywhere are
becoming more and more conscious of the oneness of
humanity.

It is evident that the Occident has evolved many
wonderful things in the external field of man's life,
whereas the East, and India especially, has evolved
wonderful things in the field of man's interior life. By
pooling both things together, there would be mutual
benefits for the East as well as for the West. If we of
the East were to take of the benefits that the Occident
has to bestow due to its progress and advancement in the
external, material sciences and you, of the West, were to
receive of the great wealth and wisdom of the East and
to borrow the practical methods for the perfection of
your interior life, a new balance would be brought about
in the world. In this context, the topic of Yoga is of real
importance. It is even more important at this time to
state clearly what this great science consists of, because
there abound so many misconceptions about it, varying in
degree from the absurd to the fantastic. I shall, therefore,
try to give as clear-cut and unmistakable a view as possible of what Yoga is and dilate upon what significance
it holds for every person in this great and eventful Twentieth Century.

What Yoga Is Not

First and foremost, Yoga is not mere acrobatics.
There are some peculiar notions about Yoga, as though
it were primarily concerned with the manipulation of the
body into various queer positions: standing on the head,
twisting the spine, or assuming of the odd poses

demonstrated in the illustrated texts on Yoga. These techniques are employed for one type of Yoga practice, but they do not form an integral part of the most essential type. It is possible that without hearing of these physical poses, or knowing anything about them, one could yet be a perfect Yogi. The practice of the poses is not an indispensable part of Yoga. At best, the poses serve as an auxiliary or a minor aid to Yoga proper.

Secondly, Yoga is not the performance of magical feats. I mention this especially because, unfortunately, there are many misconceptions in the West due to certain pretensions made by some fake Yogis or pseudo-Yogis of the East. I am not ashamed to admit what is a fact. During the past fifty years, many great Swamis and Yogis have come to the West, but also some charlatans and fakes. Without any right or claims to this great science, they have posed as Yogis in order to gain for themselves a comfortable living or to serve some other selfish interest. They have terribly disillusioned many sincere seekers in the West. In the past they have come and they are present even now. Unfortunately, anything that is good always gets corrupted by perverted people. This has happened all over the world at all times in history. There is some selfish motive behind the deliberate mystification of things pertaining to Yoga. The consequent distortion of this true science has caused much disillusionment. It will not be out of place for me to tell you in frank and clear terms that not all that has been put across as Yoga by Hindus is really Yoga. Yoga is not magic, nor is it the performance of any extraordinary or unusual feat.

Yoga is not Fakirism — as is believed by most tourists and travellers in the East, especially news people, who always prefer the fantastic and the sensational to the sensible and the normal. These people have managed to bring back to the West the idea that Yoga is some form of self-torture: such as lying on a bed of nails, burying oneself underground, chewing and swallowing pieces of glass, drinking acid, swallowing nails or piercing oneself with pins and needles. These are the pictures they present of the "Yogi of India". They may portray a man with matted hair and naked body who lies on a bed of nails or who is suspended, perhaps, from a tree branch, head down and feet up. This has nothing to do with Yoga, and real Yogis have nothing to do with all this.

Yoga is not any weird ceremonial or peculiar rite. It is not hedonism. It is not paganism. It is not palmistry. It is not fortune-telling. It is not prophesying. It is not astrology. It is not thought-reading. Nor is it the dispensing of charms to ward off evil spirits. None of these is Yoga. If people call themselves Yogis and then explain their Yoga by doing any of these things, they are just misusing the name of "Yoga", the label of "Yoga". Yoga is the pure science of realizing your divine nature, the pure science of unfolding the perfection that is inherent in you, the pure science of achieving the true purpose of life. Yoga is not auto-hypnotism or self-hypnosis. It is not going into a hypnotic trance by the repetition of certain incantations or by the monotonous performance of certain gestures, though this is the view held by some of the so-called enlightened and intelligent people who have studied the science. Such a view shows a woeful and deplorable lack of understanding of the real import of Yoga.

Yoga is not experiences like those obtained by taking lysergic acid or mescalin or peyote (of Mexican origin) or divine mushrooms. These experiences are not Yoga, nor are they even *like* the experiences resulting from the practice of Yoga.

Yoga is not occultism or mystery-mongering. Although some of the Yogic techniques have been kept a secret, there is a good and valid reason for this. Just as you keep a child away from an intricate piece of machinery, just as you keep an intricate piece of machinery out of the reach of a child, some of the techniques of Yoga have been kept in secret—but this is not secrecy for the sake of secrecy. It is in order to ward off those who are not yet fit to go into those aspects of the science which require care and close attention. When these very people have attained the necessary fitness, they are immediately taken into the inner knowledge of the secret techniques. Thus, Yoga is not mystery-mongering or secrecy.

Lastly, Yoga is not a religious cult. Because Yoga was evolved in the East, it does have certain Eastern concepts behind it. This is true. But these concepts form only the metaphysical background to Yoga proper. They do not have anything to do with the actual evolution of the science of Yoga proper. The highly evolved and practical techniques of Yoga may be applied by all races, nations, castes, creeds, churches and sects. Your affiliations are of little account, because this body of practical techniques stands out distinct and entirely separate from all those metaphysical concepts in the background. It is true that Yoga was evolved by the Hindus as they refined certain concepts of religious significance, but this one result of their researches—Yoga—is of universal value. It is in this way that you should clearly distinguish Yoga from the metaphysics from which it stems. The concepts are peculiarly Hindu and Eastern, but Yoga, separable from its philosophical and historical background, is beyond theoretical concepts; and therefore cannot be correctly referred to as Hinduism.

Sorrow and Suffering—The Genesis of Yoga

Now, having tried to tell you what Yoga is not—not acrobatics, not magic, not torture, not weird rites or ceremonials, not hedonism or paganism, not occultism or mystery-mongering, not auto-hypnosis or LSD and mescalin experiences—I shall tell you what Yoga is. Yoga is essentially a spiritual matter concerning a spiritual method. It is an intensely practical approach towards the realization of the Supreme Reality, the very Centre of your lives—God. Yoga is the heritage of all humanity.

Briefly, I shall now touch upon the genesis of Yoga. Observing man's life on earth, you will have to admit that life is not all ice-cream and chocolate milk-shakes and drive-ins. It is birth, growth, pain, suffering, sorrow, loss and gain, honour and dishonour, fulfilment and disappointment, struggle, affliction, disease and, ultimately, decay of the human frame and death of the body. These things are absolutely inexorable and inevitable.

Man is full of defects, full of weaknesses. His mind is filled with like and dislike. Some he calls his very own, others he calls not his own, and thereby opposes the interests of the one group to the interests of the other. Enmity, malice and spite arise. Friction, riots and quarrels break out. This problem—that of sorrow, suffering, disease and disappointment, decay, dissolution and death—is the great problem that brought about the lofty science of Yoga. Yoga provides an unfailing and effective solution for all ills for all time.

Yoga traces its origin to the necessity felt by man to rid himself of all sorrow and suffering and to free himself for ever from the bondage brought about by finite existence and to attain final victory over all fear, over death itself. To this great problem, Yoga comes as the practical solution. It provides the lost link between man and the Infinite Source of his being. Yoga plainly states that man is essentially of the nature of bliss, perfection, peace and freedom. Everlastingly he is one with That. The loss of his awareness of that oneness with the infinite, all-perfect Source of his being is the very cause of his involvement in this earth-process called life. To regain the true awareness and to realize once again his everlasting oneness with the Divine is actually the practice of Yoga. The means of overcoming the defects and imperfections of this earth-life and thus of experiencing union with the Supreme constitute its structure. Yoga shows how to overcome the imperfections of the lower nature and how to gain complete mastery over the mind and the senses. Man is essentially all-perfect. He is not the mind and the senses. Man is not these passion-filled sense urges. He is not this desire-ridden mind, being pulled here and there, torn apart by a hundred thoughts. Essentially he is an all-perfect being, an emanation from the Divine Essence.

A Science Built upon Practical Experience

What Divinity is, that, essentially, man also is. Man partakes of the same nature, and is enabled to regain his awareness of that divine nature by subjecting himself to the process of Yoga. By availing himself of certain well-tried practical techniques, one is raised in consciousness from the physical level to the vast transcendental spiritual level. This higher level becomes one with the Consciousness of God. It is Divine Consciousness, God Consciousness, Cosmic Consciousness. This is the attainment that is bestowed upon the Yogis who have tried again and again, a hundred thousand times, the various practical methods which culminate in this glorious experience. Seers and mystics throughout the centuries have proved the validity of these techniques right to the very last factor. The science does not depend merely upon belief, but upon experience gained from the practical application of its principles. The actual living realization has been attained and the glorious experience declared with the authority of many who have mastered themselves. Such masters there are, even today, in all parts of India.

Outside of India too, there are perfected men and women whose souls have been illumined by this divine experience. But India's view of the purpose of life points

directly towards the attainment of this very experience —
God-realization. Therefore, there are fewer God-il-
lumined souls outside of India. They may be few, but
there still are some holy souls with high spiritual experiences in America, in Europe, and in the Far East.
Not wishing recognition, they often live in obscurity.
They are all Yogis, nevertheless. Whether you apply the
term "Yoga" to their practices or not, their mode of life,
their attainment, is Yogic according to the Sanskrit
meaning of the term — a state of union with the Divine
or an experience of oneness with the Great Reality. This
is the real meaning of Yoga. Yoga stands for the experience of Truth or the Consciousness of Reality or
union with the Divine.

There are secondary meanings of the term "Yoga".
All the techniques which eventually bestow upon the
practitioner the experience of Divine Consciousness may
also be designated by the one word "Yoga". These
various techniques, for the sake of an explicit classifica-
tion, have been divided into four or five different practical approaches, each of which culminates in the
experience of the One Great Truth. Certain definite,
scientifically evolved and intelligently formulated techniques enable man to divest himself of all the impurities
imposed upon him by the nature of his body, mind and
senses, and to concentrate his thoughts entirely upon the
Supreme. According to this definition, Yoga means to
direct your mind towards God, to come on to a deep
level of interior worship of the Divine and, finally, to
realize your oneness with the Divine Consciousness. So,
there is also a simple meaning to the term Yoga and it
implies any effort that the soul may make in its effort to
attain God.

It may be something you have found in text hooks
on Yoga or it may be something which you have started
to do without any prompting from any external source;

if you find that a certain thing helps you in going towards God, and is in accordance with your individual need and temperament, then that thing is a part of your Yoga, whether or not it has been expounded in a Yoga text or explained to you by a Hindu teacher. In Yoga, there is scope for infinite expansion. It is not a rigid science where changes and adjustments are forbidden. The basic techniques remain essentially unaltered, but the details of the practices may be modified to suit the practitioner, depending upon whether he is a Hindu or a Westerner, a man or a woman. Also, a certain technique which may be suitable to you in one form at a particular period in your spiritual life may be modified and altered to suit you in another stage of your spiritual life.

An example of modification is to be found in one of the simplest forms of Yoga. This is the practice of the utterance of the Divine Name. By constant repetition of the Name of God, you keep the thought of God in your mind always. By this remembrance of Him, you begin to feel His presence, and it helps to keep your mind free from all unworthy thoughts. You establish your mind in peace and calmness and lead your inner life in silence.

Now, the Name of God may be repeated in an audible manner. Your mind becomes concentrated if you hear your own repetition. Later on, as you evolve and begin to get the ability to concentrate the mind spontaneously, you may dispense with the audible type of repetition and carry on your chanting inaudibly, mentally. Thus you apply this single technique of repetition of the Divine Name in a particular way when you first begin, and at a later stage, in order to suit your new level of consciousness and convenience, you modify it and apply it in a different way.

Yoga is the practical method for the unfoldment of the inherent divine perfection that is within you. You are Spirit devoid of name and form. The mind is simply the medium for your expression. Yoga leads you into an awareness of your real nature. By means of Yoga, you qualify yourself for the realization of your eternal oneness with the Supreme.

A Universal Technique for All Time

While this science was being evolved, the great seers were not so much concerned with the requirements of particular groups such as the Hindus or the Easterners; rather, they undertook a consideration of *man on earth* as he was constituted. It was apparent to them that the physical body and the mind served certain purposes: the body as an instrument of the mind and the mind as a channel for the expression of the soul. They observed that most unfortunately man was enslaved by the body, gripped by the senses, and caught up and tyrannized by the cravings of the mind. This was the picture of the earthly man—sense-bound and desire-ridden, the glory of his spirit entirely eclipsed—and this picture they sought to change by their practice of Yoga.

Yoga uses a technique by which you overcome the bondage of the body through restraining your senses, mastering your mind and controlling your thoughts and desires. Going beyond them, you reach the inner depth of your being where you know yourself to be what you really and truly are: an all-perfect and Divine being. Yoga was not given to man of any particular place or religion. It was given to all humanity. When people ask me about the suitability of Yoga for the modern mind, I feel that the question is pointless, for there is no such thing as the modern mind in relation to Yoga. Yoga deals with the perennial man. It deals with your Divine Essence encased within mind and matter, just as it has been since the dawn of creation and will be as long as the world lasts. There is no question of modern and ancient. You may call yourself modern now, but two thousand years from now, people will look back on 1960 and say, "Oh, those ancients of a bygone era!" So, 'modern' is just a relative term, whereas Yoga is a science not only for the past, but for the present and the distant future as well. As long as man exists on earth, he will always be plagued by the problem of pain, suffering, disease, birth and death, and Yoga will always be the solution to this great problem.

The application of Yoga is universal. It may be applied within the framework of the religious life, yet it transcends religion. It is supra-religious. Yoga is far removed from any dogma or doctrine. its basis, in so far as its concepts are concerned, is entirely universal. The extent of its applicability is coterminous with the whole of humanity for all time.

Now that we know that the central problem of life is man's bondage to mind and matter, what exactly does Yoga try to do? In brief, it tries to free you from your bondage and give you once again an awareness of your eternal Divine Nature. Yogis have found that the greatest hindrance and obstacle to this awareness is that thought in your mind which makes you say to yourself, "I am this body, this finite human being. I am subject to pain and sorrow. I am related to this and that. I am in need of this and that. I am suffering from hunger and thirst". To obtain pleasure and to avoid pain, the mind keeps man in a constant state of identification with this part of him that passes. Mind is completely externalized. It goes out through the senses to the sense objects. It beholds only the external universe. It does not withdraw itself from the senses and go inward to behold the true innermost nature deep within.

Mind is the hindrance. The channels for the outward motion of the mind may be found in the senses. Ultimately, it is the mind which is the supreme sense and the prime instrument. Now, it is bound to objects outside. If you were to make it go within, by careful introspection, you would be able to overcome all the defects and weaknesses of your human nature which are withholding from you that experience of the bliss and peace inherent in your divine nature.

Training of the Mind in Yoga

There is a fourfold expression of the mind. First, it is expressed as rationality or the power of reasoning. Second, it is expressed as emotion or love. Third, it is expressed as activity or dynamism. And fourth, it is expressed as reflection or contemplativeness. All four aspects of the mental being have to be disciplined and trained to go inward so that your resources are completely channelled and directed towards the Great Goal— God.

The power of reasoning should not be dissipated in the panorama of appearances called the world. This power should generate within you an understanding of the Supreme Essence which lies within, the very source of all intelligence, the shining light which makes your own intelligence luminous. Without It, you can neither think nor know. There are many wonderful techniques in Yoga for the diversion of all your thoughts towards the Great Reality, of all your emotions towards God, of all your dynamism towards the Great Goal, of all your reasoning powers towards the Absolute Truth. The channelling of these fourfold trends of your mind and nature towards the One Supreme Goal leads you beyond all sorrow, and makes you free for ever from the thraldom of bondage to the mind and the senses, and bestows upon you the luminous experience of Self-realization. You are made deathless.

Yoga is the science of getting your mind absorbed in God. You direct all your love to the Supreme Source of your being. You dedicate all your activities to the Great Goal which is your ultimate destiny. You concentrate all your thoughts in such a way that they can be withdrawn from this multifarious universe and made to merge into that great and glorious thought of God.

Directing all your intellectual abilities towards the realization of the Truth is known as the Yoga of the Intellect. In this branch of Yoga, you practise a supreme exercise by trying to grasp the Reality intellectually, by actual rationality. Developing all your capacity to love God is known as the Yoga of Devotion or the Yoga of Love. Dedicating all your activities in life to God is yet another branch of the science of Yoga, in which you integrate, on an unselfish basis, all the various phases of your life's activities. Lastly, in Raja Yoga, you are made more and more conscious of God as the centre of your being, and you are employed in a very special process in which your thought is made to merge in Him entirely. There are many heartening signs that this Yoga is being seriously considered by many seekers in the West as the most suitable method for them to solve the perplexing problems of their civilization.

Now you clearly see the relationship between Yoga and yourself. Yoga makes available to you the scientific method for approaching God. Actually, anything that you do in this approach is really Yoga, whether or not it is branded as such. There is a very surprising inference in this statement, for then, all the great Christian saints and mystics who have sincerely tried to love God and worship Him and contemplate upon Him and realize their oneness with Him would be Yogis. Saint Augustine was a great Bhakti Yogi and Jnana Yogi combined. Saint John of the Cross and Saint Teresa of Avila were both great Raja Yogis. They were contemplative mystics who attained the Knowledge of the Truth through concentration and meditation.

If all these people have followed Yoga, then what is

the speciality or the peculiarity of Yoga as it is practised in India?

Spiritual Research of the Indian Sages

First, as to the peculiarity of Yoga, there is none as it is practised in India. The same techniques are practised there as elsewhere. However, as to the speciality of Yoga, there is this—in India is to be found the clearest conception of the process involved in concentration and meditation. The Indian sages made deep and thorough spiritual research to learn all that was involved in the process that takes man from his lower condition to the ultimate glorious condition that he is to attain. They made it their special concern to study the process in such detail that every bit of the human anatomy was revealed to them on the ascent unto Divinity. Every bit was perfectly analysed and known. From their study they found what obstacles were present in the way of the practical seeker. They discovered why these obstacles came and which factors inherent in human nature were the source of these obstacles; and they found out the way to remove these obstacles at their very source. For this purpose they formulated wonderful techniques, tried them out and proved them effective. They explained how these techniques worked and how they were to be applied. Their knowledge of the internal mechanism was amazing. Their knowledge of the structure of the human being was unparalleled. This, then, is the speciality of Yoga in India.

A heart specialist is referred to as a cardiologist and a brain specialist is referred to as a neurologist. These specialists have gone so deeply into their sciences that they have acquired from their studies a knowledge of all the available facts. Similarly, the Indian Masters made it their life-work to plumb into the very depths of man's being, and thus to analyse every bit of the process of transforming and spiritualizing and divinizing the nature of man. There is nothing left untouched. They knew everything about the mind, the body and the senses, and about the various forces that act upon the body, senses, and mind such as the food you eat, the company you keep, the habits you develop. Therefore, we have in Yoga a science evolved to such perfection that we find therein the very quintessence of the wisdom and the practical knowledge acquired by man through the many centuries he has lived. Though here and there this knowledge is partially held among other people, in Yoga it is complete and perfect. Through Yoga, this perfect knowledge has been bequeathed to the whole of humanity.

The Over-all Pattern of Yoga Life

I shall now sum up briefly the over-all pattern of Yoga life. First of all, Yoga recognizes the true purpose of human life. It gives you the answer to the question: "Why have I come here and what is my task in life?" Then it opens your eyes to the true nature of the universe. It tells you not to be deluded by these passing objects which are perishable and therefore temporary. Objects do not give an unalloyed experience of pleasure or bliss. Yoga shows you the objects of this world as they really are, not as they appear to be, and warns you not to be duped and deceived by their external glamour, not to be thus lured and enslaved by them. It advises you to develop dispassion, for if you are passionately attached to objects, sorrow will be the harvest which you will have to reap.

There is an imperishable Reality which is all-perfect, which is of the nature of supreme bliss and immeasurable peace, and That alone will satisfy the great hunger which is in you for true happiness, for true freedom from all bondage, for freedom from all fear and from even the death process itself. Yoga points out to you the Goal and advises you to develop an intense aspiration to attain it. It shows you how to walk through this life as a serene and balanced being, unswayed by the pull of objects, not as an enslaved being easily unbalanced by the power of objects and thus plunged into agitation and fear.

Thus, one is armed to walk through life calmly, unattached. Or, if there is any attachment at all, it is only to the Supreme Goal, to the way of life which takes one towards it. One can be attached to virtue, to goodness, to purity, to truth. These attachments will purify the lower nature, expand the consciousness and bring you closer to an awareness of the Divine Essence. Be attached to God. Avoid the tragic blunder of attaching yourself to material and perishable things. Develop the dispassion and discrimination that comprehend all things in their essential nature. Cultivate keen aspiration.

These practices lead to the right unfoldment of the Yogic pattern of life. The science of Yoga makes a study of man himself and declares that he is a triune being: first, with a gross and bestial nature; secondly, endowed with reason, but full of impurity and many doubtful tendencies; and thirdly, with a divine nature which lies deep within, all-pure and all-perfect. Absolute unblemished perfection is in you. In this Essence is peace, bliss, freedom, light and wisdom.

The foremost feature in the Yogic pattern of life is the process of purifying the lower nature. The many impurities of the body-mind nature are the real enemies of man. His enemies do not lie outside. Atom bombs and machine guns are not the real dangers. The real enemies are carnal desire, anger, avarice or greed, deluded attachment to things, arrogance or pride, and envy and jealousy. These are the six great enemies, the six impurities of human nature.

By rational effort, these blemishes can be overcome completely. By the use of his intelligence, man can master himself and radiate all the higher qualities of goodness and virtue that lie within. He is not merely a bestial being with blemishes, but a radiant personality with qualities that are very close to God-nature. Compassion, love, truthfulness, purity and selflessness are virtues you have to develop. Out of this practice comes a recognition of life's true purpose.

The Different Yoga Systems

There are various systems of Yoga which I will very briefly describe. In the intellectual system, one gets an understanding of God by listening to the exposition of the nature of Reality, by reflecting upon It again and again, and through the power of reasoning and the intellect ultimately penetrating into It in the depths of meditation.

In the emotional system, one has a clear conception of God as a very dear, personal object—as one's own father or mother or beloved friend, or as the glorious king and master who is revered, worshipped and loved. Then a link is set up whereby pure affection and love is directed towards Him. This may be according to the pattern of links which human beings have. One may link himself with Him as His son, or as His daughter, or as His child; or one may think of himself as the parent and love the Lord as the divine child, perhaps as the child Jesus. Or, one may love the Lord as the humble servant of the Lord, thus dedicating all life's activities to His service. Or again, one may conceive of the Lord as his own friend. These are human relationships which are familiar to all; there is nothing abnormal or strange in them. Thus, the diversion and channelling of one's love-nature towards God is peculiarly suited and adapted to the person of emotional temperament. This is a very sweet path. One grows into this relationship easily by constantly thinking about Him, praying to Him, worshipping Him, feeling Him so close that you naturally walk with Him, talk with Him, live, move and have your being in Him. You will thus become totally integrated.

In the system of dynamic Yoga, the primary act is the shedding of the ego. Humility and selflessness are virtues which prepare the being to serve as an instrument of the Divine. For this, the personal ego has to stand aside completely. Then all creatures upon this earth may be seen as visible manifestations of God, as moving temples in which the Divine is enshrined. The service of others becomes the natural occupation of man, and in this way, every act is conceived of not as a secular act, but as an act of worship. One who is engaged in the transmutation of his dynamism into divine realisation does his worship everywhere. The teacher in the school, the doctor in the hospital, the farmer in the field, the businessman in the stock exchange, can all engage in activity which is transmuted into pure worship by the inner attitude which is brought about to bear upon it. Even the so-called professional activity that is apparently secular can become the means of practising Yoga.

The fourth system is that of integrating your thought and absorbing it in God through concentration and meditation. This is a very beautiful path also. Thought is the movement of the mind-stuff. The movement of the mind is affected by the movement of the vital life-force within which is termed Prana and also by the movement of the body. The body, the psychic energy and thought— all three are inter-related. In this highly systematic Yoga, there is total subdual and control of the body, brought about by keeping it in a fixed and steady posture. There is subdual and control of the inner psychic energy through the techniques of breath-control. Ultimately, there is the culminating process in which the scattered rays of the mind are withdrawn and concentrated upon the idea of God. There are so many exercises given for concentration that there is bound to be one to suit every taste. In this way, one is raised above the level of the mind and taken into a state of superconsciousness in which the experience of the realization of oneness with God is bestowed upon him and he is released for ever from the bondage of the body and from death. Supreme liberation is obtained in that way.

Purity—the All-important Foundation

All the techniques of Yoga require perfect ethical and moral purity. Purity is the foundation of Yogic life. One cannot be a bad man and then try to practise Yoga. One cannot allow himself to be impure, insincere, untruthful, deceitful, and harmful to others and, at the same time, try to practise Yoga. There cannot be any spiritual realization when interior circumstances are imperfect. There cannot be any religious practice or true interior life when moral goodness is not deeply implanted in the being. One has to be rooted in goodness, in purity, in truth and in selflessness. Half of the process of Yoga is in thus getting perfectly established in ideal moral conduct. When this basis has been established, then the application of the techniques of Yoga is like the striking of a dry match upon the match-box—immediately there is a flame. Without the basis, it is like trying to ignite a wet match by striking it upon a cake of soap—nothing happens.

If one is not prepared to change one's nature from passion to purity, from untruth to truth, from hardness and rudeness to kindness, then the idea of the Yogic pattern of life is still very far-fetched. This does not mean that until one is absolutely perfect in all moral and ethical respects he may never enter into Yogic practice. Man is born to practise Yoga. He is born to worship God. That is the only purpose of his life. All other tasks are just secondary, and have a meaning only in relation to this central task. Therefore, whether one's ethical conduct is perfect or not, one has to start trying to live out this purpose.

In the beginning of one's spiritual life, stress has to be laid on the all-important task of achieving perfect moral goodness and ethical purity. All other aspects of Yoga have only a secondary place in the beginning. Later on, when this task is being properly carried out, the emphasis shifts more and more to the conduct of the purely interior life. In a very simple way the Lord Jesus brought home this truth. He said: "When you draw near to the altar to offer worship unto Me, first remember that if any of your brothers has offended you and you have not forgiven him, go now and forgive him. Otherwise your worship cannot be accepted". And he also said, "Even if you have been offended not seven times, but seventy-seven times, go on forgiving the offender, for you cannot approach God nor find the love of God in your heart, if your heart is not also filled with the love of man, with the feeling of oneness with all beings".

In this way, one is made fit to enter into the House of Worship. God is Himself all-mercy and love, and if man does not grow into that nature, how will he be able to draw near to that nature? As you become godly, so you will have to approach God; then God will surely interfused with your God-nature. No barrier of an imperfect human nature will then be raised between God and you. The divine life will be sustained by the highest standards of moral and ethical perfection. It will be furthered by self-restraint and self-control, and it will be ultimately fructified through deep and intense meditation.

In all phases of the Yogic life, the supreme factor is the Grace of God. Call it what you will. It is the Grace of the Supreme Essence, the Source of all existence, in which alone man realizes his true nature and his deathless divinity. All the practices are purposeful when they make man move towards God and merge into oneness with Him.

Thus, in short: be good, do good, be kind, be compassionate; serve all, love all, see the Lord in all; be humble, be simple; purify, concentrate, meditate, realize; attain the Supreme Bliss.

14. MEDITATION AND PRAYER

The great subject of meditation, which we have the good fortune to consider now, is one which provides the ultimate solution to the greatest problem which has faced and challenged mankind ever since the dawn of Creation—the problem of life as well as of death.

Meditation solves the problem that menaces the individual making. him look upon life as fraught with bitterness, pain and suffering. It transforms life once again into a meaningful and a deeply significant and wonderful gift from the Supreme to the human soul. The key to this transformed view of life and the transformation in the very experience of life is, in a single word, meditation. The problem of death is solved, for meditation bestows on you an awareness of your true nature, the realization of your real Self which is deathless and immortal. Thus it takes you beyond all fear of death and frees you from terror.

Value of Meditation

In meditation, you are raised into an experience where you can laugh at death, where you can treat it as a mere trifle. You are given the realization of your ever-changeless existence. You are birthless, deathless, changeless, without beginning or end. You are given the solid experience of that realization right here and now—not in some after-life, not in the beyond. Even while you are in this body, you are thus liberated from the terror and the fear of death. You know that if something perishes, it is of the earth, earthy, but it affects you not. You are the deathless Spirit indwelling the body, remaining absolutely untouched even when the body is dissolved. You know that you are glorious and independent of the body and the mind. You realize that to you, there is no need of this body, that it is the same to you whether you are within the body or without the body. That is the triumph attained through meditation.

All scriptures, from the most ancient times, have forcefully, emphatically and unmistakably stated that anything achieved by man—individual as well as cosmic, terrestrial as well as heavenly—has been achieved through meditation. The sublime *Vedas* of India have declared in sonorous and authoritative terms that through meditation the Creator obtained the power to create; that through meditation, the Great One supports the earth. It is said that after the Creator meditated for aeons, creations streamed forth from His Being through the mere act of His will which became indomitable through the force generated in meditation.

In the human being, meditation works in a wonderful way. By gathering the mind from its scattered and dispersed state (in which state it goes all over the world) to an absolute pinpoint, by totally arresting its outgoing and centrifugal tendencies, by withdrawing its rays and making them converge upon one point, by making the mind atomic, as it were, the human being is able to release from within an infinite power which lies there in the very depths of his innermost being in a state of hidden potency.

Intellect and Intuition

Outwardly, due to the limitations of your physical frame, you are finite. Your powers also are limited. Your intellect is bound by the necessity of basing all conceptual activity upon name and form, for without name and form mind cannot conceive of any idea. Therefore, the very function of your intellect is possible only within the framework of name and form.

Whenever thought comes, it takes the support of

either a name or a shape or form for its very sustenance. Deep within, beyond the limiting factors of the body and the mind, you have your unlimited Self. It is that Supreme Consciousness that struggles to express itself, but cannot. Why? The channels of expression are limited. The truth of your Self, your innermost infinite Essence, is contained within these finite channels and is thwarted in its effort to find effective unhampered expression for itself. Meditation releases your Inner Being from this bondage.

Through meditation you find the dynamic force that breaks the bonds of the intellect and you transcend the intellect and go beyond it. Meditation leads you to that unique spiritual faculty lying deep within each human soul, the faculty of intuition, which is also called the occult third eye, or the eye of wisdom. That faculty alone is the rightful and legitimate instrument of the soul. In error you make use of the mind and the intellect which are, at most, the instruments of the "I" within you. This "I" or the individual ego, this little personality, this name, this form, this individual being, confined by the numerous limiting factors of nationality, race, caste, creed, height and colour, this erroneous "I", is transient and false. The real "I" within is the true Self which shines radiant beyond the veil of error.

The true Consciousness, becoming associated with this veiling power, with this erroneous perception, and vitiated by that association, identifies itself with the temporary name and form and knows itself as something which it really is not. To this false identity, the intellect and the body have become channels of expression. They may be adequate as instruments to this little "I", but for You, they are all too inadequate. The Supreme Being which has brought You into existence has given You an instrument for expressing Your Reality—an instrument *par excellence* and that inner 'instrument' is intuition.

To awaken and develop intuition and to release the vast infinite power that lies within you is the purpose of meditation. In its ultimate stages, that is what it achieves.

Life Is Meant for Meditation

Is it to be taken, then, that until our meditation has reached that ultimate stage of perfection, where it is able to open the intuition — the centre of true Consciousness — all our effort is futile or that, until that stage is reached, meditation is just toil and effort with no gainful return or reward? The answer is an emphatic "NO!" The exact opposite is the case. Meditation brings you a reward the very day you start it. Immediately you begin to feel the blessedness of meditation and you get a great return in terms of greater tranquillity, composure, clarity of mind, balance and peacefulness. All these results come from the very start of proper meditation. That is the greatness of this process.

Great souls, especially the mystics and the saints, have been so very enthusiastic about meditation and so very partial to it, that some of them have even declared that man was created in order to meditate. The function of meditation is recognized as the sole and proper function of the intellect. All other aspects of life have value only if they try to equip you for the process of meditation. These great people see life not as a vale of tears, not as a forest full of thorns and brambles, but as a great highway leading to the greatest blessedness. They regard human life as a great gift bestowed by God, and say that life is meant for the experience of infinite bliss and peace which is not of this earth, which cannot be described, which human mind cannot comprehend, which passeth all understanding. To this end, therefore, man is asked to meditate alone that he can fulfil his life and justify the receipt of this great gift from God.

Meditation and meditation alone (no other process has been discovered since Creation) has the power to reach up to the ultimate God-experience. St. Teresa of Avila, a mystic of great spiritual eminence, called it the Royal Highway to Heaven. She meant by 'Heaven' the experience of God, not some region created in outer space beyond the clouds. St. John of the Cross said that meditation was the Key to Blessedness, the Key to Immortality. St. Francis de Sales, a great devotee and a great lover of God, said that one of the processes by which he exercised his love for God was inner meditation. He deemed it the Portal which led to the Mansion of Blessedness. Meditation is the pivot and the central process of all Yoga.

Thus the process has been described by all the mystics — mystics of the East as well as of the West — and even now the followers of the Taoist philosophy in the Far East (in China and Japan) swear by meditation. They affirm this to be the only process which can take man beyond this limited empirical existence and make him deathless. Its origin is to be found in India. The name which has been given to it in India is Dhyana and that name was corrupted when it travelled outside the land into the Far East. Now, on the West Coast of America, it has become very fashionable as Zen Meditation, which is actually a redundant expression. The sad fact is that the great majority of the modern American Zen-fanciers have totally missed the true significance of this tremendous way of Dhyana.

Meditation is a subject of the most vital importance to everyone who wants happiness and peace, who wants to find strength within, who wants a truly integrated, radiant and magnetic personality. On every level of your life, meditation brings rewards in terms of your true spiritual nature, in terms of the spiritual experience which it bestows upon you.

The Process of Meditation
Now, let us consider the definition of meditation ac-

cording to those who have mastered this science and have expounded its principles. Pre-eminently, meditation is a process of the mind. It is a mental-cum-intellectual process and, therefore, it is entirely interior in its realistic form and takes place in the silence of your inner being. Patanjali, a great Eastern sage and exponent of the great science of mind-control, has given the world one of the most thorough and scientific works on the subject of meditation. He defines meditation as "continuous unbroken concentration" or "the unbroken flow of the mind concentrated upon a single subject". This means that meditation has a certain target, as it were, upon which the concentrated mind is brought to bear. The concentrated mind is kept in this state, and the flow or continuity of thought is kept unbroken. It may be compared to the flow of oil from one vessel to another. This is meditation.

The process of meditation implies, inevitably, concentration of the mind. Concentration is self-explanatory. It means bringing the mind to a centre, making the mind one-pointed, and directing it towards something interior, something either concrete or abstract. During the early stages of this discipline, the mind may be concentrated upon something exterior, too. Such a process is a technique of mind training.

In this more external phase in the process of meditation, you know that the mind is already outward and you train the mind by concentrating it and fixing it upon some object, some enjoyment, some experience, perhaps even a person or a memory, so that the outgoing mind, already dispersed among a hundred things, becomes indrawn. Later, the chief components in this great process of meditation come to be:

a) the withdrawal of the scattered rays of the mind from the many distracting things in the external world;

b) the concentrating or the fixing of the mind, thus' withdrawn, upon one point; and

c) the holding of the fixed mind in continuous concentration in which no extraneous thought is allowed to intrude.

So, it is the keeping out of all thoughts contrary to the one which you are holding. Gradually, by degrees, it is made more and more intense, and your meditation becomes deeper and deeper.

This is the simple process: withdraw the mind which is scattered outside, concentrate it upon one point or idea, keep it continuously concentrated, and at the same time, exclude all contrary thoughts and dive, plunge within like the diver who goes deep into the ocean for the precious pearls. Pearls do not float about on the surface.

Character — The Gateway to Meditation

This process itself is very simple; it is the preparation for the process which is complex. If you want to shake hands with the President in the White House, it is very simple. Nothing to it! But, although the ultimate process is simple enough, yet all the red tape and all the hurdles that you have to face and surmount in order to get yourself into a position in which you stand before him and merely have to raise your hand and clasp his, all this preparation may take many months. You have to have all your credentials and the date of the interview fixed by the President's Office; then you have to book a seat on the plane or train, reserve your accommodation in Washington, and then, even if you do actually enter the White House, you may find that there are others who have come before you and a long wait may ensue before you may actually see the President.

In the same way, if you want to go into the Holy of holies by the simple process of plunging into deep meditation, the preparation for it may well take much of your time, energy and effort. You may have to seek out and talk to a dozen different teachers on the subject of meditation; discuss different methods with other seekers who are practising meditation; carry on research of your own in books and lessons; and experiment and learn by trial and error. The process of meditation itself is simple, but the preparation that leads you into it is lengthy and complex.

First and foremost, the mind is in a state of grossness. Gross minds cannot still the thoughts; it is only the fine mind that can concentrate, and it is only the pure mind which is fine. The impure mind is gross. The stuff of the mind, which is called "Chitta" in Yogic terminology, is gross when the nature of the being is not fully purified. What does this mean? Does it imply that a cleansing, like a soap-and-water scrubbing, is required? It means that there are blemishes in the human nature and these blemishes have to be eliminated.

This is a scientific fact. In order to meditate, certain conditions have to be eradicated. These blemishes — the impurities of human nature — may be anything from harshness, irritability, a little petty envy to greed, passion, hatred, lustfulness, anger, arrogance, haughtiness, delusion or covetousness. All these blemishes make the nature extremely gross, coarse and base. They are totally unspiritual and they make the mind unstable and cause it to oscillate. They, therefore, have to be totally eliminated and this is the ground-work, the spade work, the preparation, which is no simple task. This discipline, though apparently just an ethical one, yet has a direct bearing upon the scientific technique of Yoga. This constitutes the basic foundation upon which the structure of Yoga is raised.

The great science of Yoga, which leads you to meditation, is based upon a pattern of perfect moral rec-

titude and the life ethical. It refers constantly to a life
of perfect goodness, to an example of perfect character,
to a course of perfect conduct and the highest virtue.
Virtue is the sheet-anchor of all great attainments, all
worthwhile attainments that do not vanish into thin air,
that do not last only upon this earth-plane, but are enduring and for ever. The total removal of all blemishes
is the very basis and foundation of all higher achievements, and if meditation is to be successful, the mind has
to be pure, and if the mind is to be pure, you must grow
in goodness, grow in virtue, and eliminate hatred and
harshness from your nature altogether.

You must be kind to others—kind in thought, word
and deed. Your speech must be sweet and your actions
compassionate. In fact, you must become godly in your
nature. This is essential because it is only a divine being
that can experience the Divine. You have to reflect the
nature of God. When God looks at you, He must feel
the reflection of His divine nature in you. That nature
should grow, unfold and bloom forth like a divine flower
upon the soil of human nature. It is this growing forth
into a life of virtue that is hard, for habitual traits in
human nature die hard. However assiduously you may try
to root them out, again and again you will find them
cropping up in some form or the other.

Lust, greed and covetousness have to be patiently
and earnestly rooted out of your nature. The great
Master of meditation, Patanjali, has said that the most effective way of growing into the divine nature is not so
much by picking out your little weaknesses, like a
monkey picking off lice (which is a waste of your time
and energy), as by filling yourself with virtue.

Therefore grow in goodness the positive way, the
forceful way. Be more and more truthful, exercise compassion, at every step create opportunities to demonstrate
fellow-feeling, selflessness and the spirit of service. You

thus grow in virtue by cultivating it positively and practising it actively. If you develop a tremendous passion for
goodness, the negative side cannot remain. If you bring
in the light, darkness cannot stand before it. Even so, if
you thus fill yourself with perfection, you will crowd out
all blemishes. Go all out an grow in this way into an
ideal being.

This has a direct connection with meditation. One of
the very great aids in meditation is to develop yourself
into a pure and perfect being. The two processes are
mutually inter-acting. In order to reach the highest stage
in meditation you have to become a perfect being, and
in order to grow into perfection, meditation is the
greatest help to overcome all the weaknesses and defects
in your nature by augmenting your will-power, by giving
you clarity of thought, by sharpening your intellect, and
thus increasing your power of discrimination. You are
better able to discern what is proper and what is im-
proper and you are better equipped to analyse yourself,
because the mind becomes integrated due to concentration and meditation. It becomes subtle and sharp.

The Power of the One-track Mind

It is the concentrated mind which can work efficiently and powerfully. All outstanding achievements have
been won in every field by means of the power of concentrated thought. Master statesmen, master military
strategists, master engineers, master scientists, inventors
and surgeons have all achieved success through the
power of concentrated thought. They have had what is
called a 'one-track mind'. They made themselves so.
They deliberately cultivated the one-track mentality.
What was Einstein if not a man of meditation? He was
able to probe into the innermost secrets of the vast
universe in meditation and there the truths came tum-
bling to him. They were revealed to him. His intuition

got sparked and this led to the discovery of the cosmic secrets which he then formulated in amazing equations.

All the concentrated thought of these great men was external. The process which they consciously subjected themselves to was not an internal one. They focussed upon the external universe belonging to the phenomenal existence of the fleeting world of vanishing names and forms. The greatest astronomers and physicists pondered deeply upon things external to themselves and their meditations were set upon the world without rather than directed towards the Reality within. Therefore, while they won admirable achievements on this phenomenal plane, they failed to reach the ultimate and eternal Reality. Their efforts were nonetheless stupendous, praiseworthy and laudable. They are clear demonstrations to the average man, who never concentrates his thought, who does not know what it is to still the mind and ponder in silence, who does not know that meditation has the power to reveal great truths which lie hidden from the surface view of the phenomenal universe. This power is unknown to the vast majority of people upon this earth. It is something with which they have not even a nodding acquaintance.

The Laws of Thought

Meditation succeeds in a marvellous way in revealing the great truths of life through the operation of the laws of thought. The first law of thought is: anything which is held in the mind persistently and intensely dwelt upon for a protracted period of time soon becomes concretized into fact. It becomes as actual as a concrete fact. This is one of the great laws upon which the knowledge of the power of thought is based. The other law, which is not restricted to the mental and intellectual level, but goes deeper and beyond and is much higher, is a spiritual law. This law is: such deeply concentrated thought persisted in to its ultimate conclusion suddenly 'takes a leap' beyond the intellect and mind and enters the realm of intuition. This is the law of transcendence. When the mind is totally concentrated and deeply absorbed in this process of meditation, it transcends itself and you are plunged into the experience of Pure Consciousness. It is similar to the electric current switched on to an arc lamp. When the current reaches one terminal of the arc, it faces a gap separating the two terminals and then, suddenly, with a flash it springs out, bridging the gap in an instant and bursts into the incandescence of a dazzling light.

It is in just such an inner experience — at once thrilling and sublime — that you 'leap across ' the great void separating the relative from the Absolute, that you transcend all relativity and phenomena and attain to the Experience Absolute. It is a triumphant leap from the trifling bonds of confined human consciousness into the exalted vastness of the boundless and infinite Divine Consciousness, a supra-mental, superconscious experience in which meditation, the meditator and the object meditated upon, all three, fuse into undifferentiated oneness, merge into an indescribable experience of ineffable peace, limitless joy and dazzling light.

This great process of meditation is ultimately the one that links you with God and bestows upon you immortality; and concentration is the most important factor in meditation. What is it in your daily life that will be of the greatest help to you in developing concentration? In whatever pursuit one may be engaged, how does one begin to develop the ability to concentrate? You may be dishwashing, writing your accounts, preparing formula for the baby, penning a letter, licking stamps for an envelope, dusting or wiping a table-top — no matter what you may be doing — do it with meticulous care and *attention*. Give it your *full* attention. Do not try to think of half a dozen things at the same time. That is an art which may be very useful sometimes—especially if you have to wait at a downtown lunch-counter—but not for meditation. If you try to think of half a dozen things at the same time, you may become a very accomplished waiter or reservations clerk at an airport or travel agency, but such habitual miscellaneous and multifarious thinking will not help in acquiring meditation.

Therefore, try to be specific and definite in thinking and acting. Develop the habit of fixed attention. The more you practise, the more quickly you will grow into the habit of attentiveness. Your practice should not be haphazard or sporadic, but it should be regular; and you should have some exercise for the development of keen attention to be practised daily, throughout the entire year. If you persist in such practice, you will soon begin to find that you are developing the power of attention in a miraculous way and that whenever you fix your attention upon anything, there it stays.

Meditation is a matter of continuously fixing your attention upon something interior. Success in meditation depends upon the power of concentration. Concentration depends upon the ability to pay attention. Attention comes by practice and practice becomes regular through habit. If you practise regularly, you will be able to meditate and such practice is possible only if you are genuinely and sincerely interested in the entire thing.

The Role of Body, Mind and Prana in Meditation

Body, Mind and Prana are all interconnected. There is, therefore, another great help for you to be found in the practice of sitting steadily in one position without moving the body, and holding that position in tranquillity. In the preliminary stages of Raja Yoga discipline, you find that the basis of your life of Yoga has to be established on an absolutely pure, ethical and moral life. Then you are ready to start sitting steadily every day. At some special time each day you should retire into a quiet corner and sit there steadily poised for your practice. You may sit on a chair, if you prefer such a position, keeping the spine erect, relaxing your body totally, locking your fingers, resting them on your knees, and try to remain in that state.

When the body is thus held motionless, the mind will at first try to jump about in a hundred different directions. It will run about most uncontrollably, but do not be perturbed. Just allow it to run. Stand apart from it; remain alert within and observe its antics.

After a time, you will begin to find that there is one factor missing in this jumping about—that is YOU. You have become a spectator. The mind may continue to keep at this process very vigorously, but when you do not show any interest in it, it will wander in ever-narrowing circles, and ultimately, like a bird having flown from the top of the mast of a ship sailing at sea, it comes back to its perch. It returns to rest. The mind does not jump about and cannot indulge in miscellaneous thinking without the I-consciousness co-operating actively with it.

Therefore, do not identify yourself with the whirl of thoughts. If you remain apart and 'Self-centred' and do not get involved, the habitual effervescence of the mind gradually dies down. Some day, after sitting in sessions of silence for a couple of weeks or more, you suddenly begin to find that the mind is quieter. It is not jumping about any more. This is a great joy. You may begin to try taking advantage of that quiescence and evoke in your mind some pleasing thought upon which you feel inclined to fix the mind—perhaps the mental picture of a beautiful flower, or a wonderful melody you have heard, or the sound of the birds in the early morning, or a sunrise, a glorious sunset or a colourful rainbow. It should be something very pleasing so as to keep the mind attracted and held by it. Let the mind then dwell upon it—such is the training in the beginning.

As you continue with your meditation, you will find that the steady pose and the gradual quietening of the mind makes your breath very, very fine. Your breathing also becomes very rhythmical. This steadiness of the body and fineness of the breath immediately give you an experience of absolute serenity which will be entirely new to you. For the first time you will know what it is to be absolutely quiet, devoid of any worry thought, or of any type of negative thinking at all. In short, truly tranquil, without any tranquillizer! Mind is thus held in a state of true serenity, absorbed in a state of placid calm.

These instructions give you the secret of mental tranquillity. First the body should be steady, then the breath should be light and regular, because the body, breath and mind are closely interconnected. They are, as it were, the three sides of a triangle and they are all centred in the personality. Thus, when the mind is absolutely tranquil, you will find that the breath is also tranquil and the body is still. Whenever your attention is arrested and you are caught intently absorbed in something, you will find that the close attention which your mind pays to that particular thing slows down all your physical and respiratory processes. In the same way, whenever your breath is regular, you will find that inner harmony and poise prevail in your mind as well.

Breathing Exercise for Mental Tranquillity

I have explained this at length to students of Yoga to impress upon them the close co-ordination of body, breath and mind. This gives them a deeper understanding into the rationale of Yogic breathing exercises. Now, in these exercises, you have to concentrate on the breath. You may try one called Alternate Breathing. This is one of the simple techniques, alternate in the sense that you breathe in through one nostril, exhale through the other, then inhale once again through the second nostril and exhale through the first nostril. This completes one round.

Thus, for this Alternate Breathing, you close your right nostril with your right thumb and inhale through the left nostril. When the inhalation is complete, you close the left nostril with your ring and middle fingers, simultaneously releasing the right nostril by raising the thumb, then exhale completely, slowly, smoothly and gradually through the right nostril.

You will find that in the process of breathing in this way, the world around you disappears. You are not aware of this body even, but are totally concentrated on the breath. There is no idea of the time that is elapsing either. When absorbed in this exercise, half an hour may pass and you will hardly be aware of the passage of time. What is the reason? Because this is an extremely vital process. Breathing is life's central process on the physical level; it is the process that sustains all life, and when you begin to concentrate upon it, your whole mind becomes deeply absorbed. This is, therefore, the core of the very valuable means you may employ to get tranquillity and steadiness of mind.

To precede this exercise, and in the initial stages of the breathing discipline, the practice is very simple. You just sit in a relaxed and steady position, calmly breathing in and out through both nostrils. There are no complications. You just practise this deep, rhythmic breathing for ten or twelve days, or for a couple of weeks, morning and evening. You will soon find that your mind becomes more and more tranquil and steady. Things which upset you and irritated you before will no longer be able to do so, and whenever there is anything that you want to do, you will feel that the mind is already in a calmer state for concentrating and centering it upon the thing that you wish to do. Then, later on, you may start the Alternate Breathing exercise.

At the beginning of your practice of Alternate Breathing, just breathe in through the left nostril, breathe out through the right nostril, then take back through the right, and breathe out again through the left. Try this, say, six times, i.e., six complete rounds in the morning and six complete rounds in the evening when your stomach is not too full—not after your lunch or your dinner, but an hour before eating. After you have practised this for a month or so, then gradually insert at the end of each inhalation a short period for the retention of the breath inhaled. When you are in a state in which the breath is retained, you find that the mind is steady and calm. Take advantage of it, try to fix your mind and concentrate on some idea or symbol. You will find that under these circumstances your concentration is wonderful, for when the breath is arrested, the mind does not move and thoughts come under your control.

When you have reached the final stage in the breathing exercises, i.e., alternate breathing with retention of breath, keep at it and gradually try to increase the period of retention. This is an exercise that may be practised regularly by all people. Two or three hints about these exercises are:

(i) The retention of breath should at all times in your practice be comfortable and easy;

(ii) You should never feel as though you were suffocating or as though your retention were forced;

(iii) When you are about to exhale, you should be able to feel that you could retain the breath a few seconds longer if you wished;

(iv) The exhalation should always be smooth, unhurried and non-violent. Neither should it ever be forced. If it is forced and hurried, it means that you have over-retained the breath beyond your capacity and your lungs can no longer hold it. When you take care of the retention of breath, you feel that the exhalation is very smooth and beautiful. Just do it to a nicety.

Start holding the breath when you feel, "Yes, the

lungs are full, but I am not going to pack them or press them". As you retain the breath, develop for yourself a sort of rhythmic count by which you can regulate the period of retention. The counts may be gradually increased. If you do this systematically, you will soon find that the mind, in an amazingly short time, becomes progressively steadier.

When there is steadiness of mind and you know how to control the thoughts, stability is found to become the normal condition of the mind-stuff. It is not so much the acting mind that you are trying to perfect, but the mind *as it is,* the very mind-stuff. When the mind-stuff is thus acted upon — put into a state of stability and steadiness — a certain quality which is to be found in the mind which is of the nature of Light, which is of the nature of balance and harmony, is increased. This is called the quality of Sattva and it is a peculiar psycho-spiritual quality within. When that quality increases in the mind-stuff, the whole mind tends to become harmonized, balanced and steady, and then that balance soon characterizes your whole personality. With the quality of Sattva predominating in your character, you become a balanced person. You are no longer afraid. At the end of a day's work, you still feel that your mind is tranquil and serene. No one is ever able to put you "out of kilter". This is the natural result of the practice of the process of breathing, steady posture, concentration and meditation.

Meditation — Temporal and Spiritual

Now, before dealing with this subject, we have to note a distinction. We have been told that any process of concentrated thought is meditation. Meditation is a process used by all people. I have pointed out that scientists, for instance, are meditators; that inventors, statesmen, great military strategists like Napoleon, are all meditators. Great strategists, like Napoleon, sketched out their campaigns to the minutest detail, beforehand. Vast structures, like the Empire State Building, were erected by engineers who laid their plans, likewise, after concentration and meditation. Every nail that was necessary, every ounce of material, every angle and joint, was clearly indicated in the blueprint. As such, the process of meditation by itself is a purely scientific technique, but in its application in Yoga, it is entirely spiritual and not material or temporal.

Thus, when *I* speak to you about meditation, I mean meditation upon the Supreme Perfection which lies within, upon that Illimitable Bliss which is the Ocean of Peace, the Beauty of beauties, the Light of lights. It is That with which we are concerned; we are not concerned with this world. If this meditation gives us gains in terms of earthly achievements — greater intelligence, greater power of concentration, greater personal magnetism, greater success in life, greater fortune — let it give. We shall welcome these things; let them come as byproducts. If they do not come, we do not care, for what we want is the Supreme, the Highest, the Greatest, the Grandest, the Thing to realize which we have been born as human beings. We have to meditate on that Reality. We have to plunge into God, absorb ourselves totally in God, and let the mind become entirely saturated and merged with God.

The process of meditation is, to us, like becoming saturated. It is just like taking a white cloth and dipping it in a vat full of coloured dye. Once it is dyed, then it will never again have its colour changed. Meditation is like that. It is dyeing our entire being, our entire personality in the colour of Divinity. It is the directing of all our human nature, all our physical nature, all our thoughts and feelings, into God-nature. That is the supreme meditation for which God has given us this body, this intellect, this life, this opportunity. He has also given us His servants (saints and God-men) to remind us that meditation is one of the most precious gifts bestowed upon us. It lies undiscovered at your side until someone comes and cries, "There it is!", and then you realize, "Oh, I had it with me all the while, but I never realized!"

You have this opportunity of a human birth given by the Supreme in order to meditate and realize Him. Let not a single day pass without meditation. No matter how many obstacles there may be, no matter how unfavourable the environment may be, just do not think about any obstacle or unfavourable environment. Try to create time every morning and evening to go inward into silence, and draw nearer to Him in prayerfulness. If you have love for Him, there is no obstacle that can stand in your way, that you cannot overcome. You can take time from eternity and create time. You can even make twenty-five hours out of twenty-four.

Let me tell you the secret. As you develop the habit of meditating, you will find that you have more time than before, because you are now given the ability to do efficiently those very tasks which befuddled you previously. Even if you are a business executive, activities which previously took you ten hours to do, you will be able to do now in nine hours, eight hours or seven hours, or even less, for after all, in this process, you are perfecting the instrument of the mind and making it one-pointed. You are also given the ability to grasp things instantaneously. The mind is no longer scattered — such a mind can do all things efficiently.

In the beginning perhaps, becoming established in this habit of meditation takes a little time and you may find that no time is left for extra pursuits. Give up those extra pursuits without hesitation. Soon however, you will begin to find that this meditation which at first took so much of your valuable time, now gives you more time in return—and at compound interest! This is something that you have to experience.

All of us who are striving for God should always remember that success in meditation depends upon the degree to which we develop our love for Him. The more we love God, the more our attention is attracted towards Him. The more we feel this attraction, the more we enjoy our meditation. Very soon the hard task of concentrating the mind becomes sweet, and once the sweetness has been tapped, never again will a reminder be required from anyone to meditate. We ourselves will be unwiiling to come away from it too soon.

Aids to Successful Meditation

From the great mystics I shall give you some valuable suggestions for success on the path of meditation. They are:

(a) Constant recollection;

(b) Continuous prayerfulness;

(c) Repetition of the Divine Name.

If you develop the habit of constantly recollecting the Supreme Being, you will soon find that the mind is always filled with that thought. Hold on to it in an intense way. When you go to sit for meditation, the mind will have already developed the nature of going toward that thought and then instinctively, immediately, the mind will begin to flow in that direction. To develop the habit of constant recollection, the saints have given us some valuable hints. Constant recollection can be three-fold in nature. It can partake of your external nature, i.e., through certain external factors, you may be enlivened by the thought of your Supreme Goal; or it can partake of the nature of the imagination, inwardly; or, by making use of the faculty of discrimination, it can partake of the nature of the intellect.

External factors may be like the pictures of God you

find on the wall, holy icons, religious objects like crucifixes, candles, medallions, or religious and spiritual books. Further, you may associate all things in and about your house, and even outside, like the flowers, the birds, the spreading trees, the forests, the clear skies and the clouds with your Ideal; thus you always feel yourself to be bearing an attitude towards Him; you always feel that you are in His presence and that He is always walking with you or talking to you.

You may feel yourself to be His own son or daughter, His companion or friend, or you may feel yourself to be His servant. You may be taking orders from Him, carrying on a conversation with Him, if necessary. Anything that you do, refer to Him—be it the sublime, the prosaic, the humorous, or the difficult and the problematical. Whatever you are going through day after day, moment by moment, refer to Him. If there is a joke share it with Him. If there is a difficulty, ask Him, "Now, what shall I do?" If you feel fear, say to Him, "Now You are my courage!"; and if you feel weak, then say to Him, "O Lord, strengthen me!"; and if you have made a mistake say, "O Lord, forgive me!" So always be in contact with Him. By making this connection in spiritual imagination, you build up your relationship with Him, you evolve with Him. Imagination can be a help in constant recollection.

If you are not of a very emotional nature, if you cannot imagine the closeness of such emotional relationships, and at the same time if you do not like the purely external method, then bring your intellect into this process. If you are philosophical by temperament, your intellect will tell you that He is the all-pervading essence. He is everywhere. He is the innermost core of your consciousness. He is the essence of your existence. It is because He exists that you exist. Through an intellectual process, you fashion certain mental concepts. All things in this universe have a cause; the chair has a carpenter, the shoe has a cobbler, the textile has a cloth factory, and the substance, which is all around you in the universe, also has a Maker. The universe may be viewed as the effect evolved out of some great cause. When you look at the cosmos, your intelligence tells you that there must be some prime cause. Thus, by these intellectual processes, you may try to feel Him.

Look at the grandeur of the universe. How much grander must be the cause behind this, the All-pervading Essence! He is immutable. He is omnipresent. Through intellectual conceptions such as these, try to feel His presence always. Try to think of Him as the grand cause of all causes, as the indivisible essence pervading and sustaining everything. Try to see Him as the innermost core of your consciousness which has made your life possible. He is the life of your life. He is the essence of your existence, the very basis of your being. If you practise His presence thus, always and everywhere, then the moment you sit for meditation, that which was being done in a diffused way, becomes intense. Grow into this habit.

These methods for continual recollection which I have given you are from the Western mystics. The Eastern Masters add one more method. They advise constant repetition of the Divine Name—either verbal, semi-verbal or purely mental. This practice also keeps you in the thought of God. It may be either the repetition of the Name or some short formula, some short prayer. It should be short and brief—that is the essence of it. You may say, "Lord, I adore Thee! Lord, I adore Thee!" or "Hail, O Glory! Glory be to Thee!" or "Praise to the Lord! Praise to the Lord!" or "I love You! I love You! I love You!" or "Thou seest me. Thou seest me. Thou seest me!" or "I am always in Your presence!"

Go on with your repetition that way. Choose some

words by which you may call upon Him. "Be by me, O
Lord! Be by me, O Lord! Ever be by me." You can have
different sets of words for morning, afternoon and evening; or you can change them by alternating them in se-
quence. Go on using them constantly so that you keep
an unbroken current of God-thought or God-feeling
within you all day, at every hour of the day. It is this that
makes for real success. The interior life of meditation is
supported by this practice of constant recollection of the
Supreme Being. It is a deep spiritual process.

A great saint, a European mystic, said, "He prays
very little who prays when he is on his knees", which
means that if your interior life is just confined to those
moments when you are actually on your knees, while the
rest of the time your mind is like a wild monkey chasing
after everything on the surface of the earth, then you
pray very little. Your prayer cannot then be effective at
all, because all the rest of the time the nature of your
mind will be totally contrary to the meditative life, and
so meditation cannot be done. Try to make the mind
habituated to constant recollection of God. The real degree of effectiveness of your contact with the Inner
Reality, of your closeness to God in meditation, is in
proportion to the degree of continual dwelling upon God
that has been achieved through recollection throughout
the entire day.

We have taken this human birth in order to
meditate. Meditation is the only important thing. It is the
only way to attain true balance, true stability of mind, a
truly integrated and positive personality. It is the only
way to achieve real peace and real happiness. It is the
only way. I do not like to be dogmatic or to be strong
in my speech, but here I am absolutely dogmatic and certain that it is the only way of achieving true peace and
real happiness. If you leave meditation and try other
ways, you will realize bitterly in the end that life has

been wasted, and then it will be too late. Then you will
regret, "Oh, I might have started it right at that time".
Do not make that mistake. Do not make that blunder.
In all the variegated activities of your life, keep on with
the great process—the central process of human life. It
is the only way to happiness and the only way to true and
lasting peace—meditation.

We have then said that this process should be supported by your entire life. And the one great factor that
is of the utmost support to meditation is purity of life.
By that one term I mean everything: perfect moral conduct, fulfilment of the pattern of ethical life, growing in
virtue, growing in goodness—in short, becoming (in so
far as you can) like God in your nature. It is a pure mind
alone that can meditate, but do not postpone meditation
that gives you the power to overcome all evil, to eradicate all blemishes. It is the power that releases the innate
purity in you. It gives you purity. It gives you the power
of will to take hold of yourself, master the senses and
desires, and grow in perfect purity. Attention has to be
cultivated by daily practice. Attention increases concentration and concentration is the only means of
developing in meditation.

Develop your love for God. Where love is, there the
mind and heart are; therefore, develop love for God.

Last, but not the least, if you go home now and have
a period of meditation before you retire to sleep, and
then afterwards keep up the practice, never giving it up
even for a single day, whether you are ill or well,
depressed or irritated (whatever happens, it does not
matter), if you cling to this great treasure, this wealth of
wealths, and always meditate daily, then I assure you that
even the most difficult problem that life poses for you—
the greatest, sharpest blow of bereavement that you may
have to experience—the greatest test or trial or temptation—everything—can be overcome by the power of

meditation. By the power of meditation you put yourself into direct contact with God. He is the Power of powers. He is the greatest power, the greatest force and the essence of all goodness. He will help you to overcome everything; through that Power, everything can be overcome. Ultimately, death itself can be overcome. Let meditation take you to the Supreme Goal, the conquest of death and the achievement of everlasting life, the supreme triumph in God. That is my humble prayer to you all.

Meditation—A Panacea for All Ills

St. Peter of Alcantara, one of the medieval sages, has said that it is morally impossible for him who neglects meditation (mental prayer) to live without sin. He who neglects mental prayer does not need a devil to carry him to hell; he takes himself there by his own hand. It must be stated, without reservation, that no other means has the unique efficacy of meditation and that, as a consequence, its daily practice can in no wise be substituted for. The common practice of all saints and the important ecclesiastical documents demonstrate how highly one should esteem meditation.

Meditation is the process of the total spiritualization of your entire being. It is the technique of living in peace and happiness and prosperity. When the mind is full of purity, it attracts prosperity by its very nature. It is the fortification of the mind against the onslaughts of vice and immorality. Meditation is of very great value for all the 'isms of life. No matter what 'ism you belong to, individual or social, you need for your progress a harmonious development of the body, mind and soul. This is achieved at one stroke in this integral process of meditation.

Meditation not only connects and integrates the material and the spiritual aspects of life, the outer and the inner, but also increases the radiance of your being, integrating it with the Light of your higher Self or God within. Ultimately, it is the direct means to end all conflicts in the family and in society—those between husband and wife, between father and son, mother and son, between friends and friends, between sisters and brothers, between relatives and between co-workers, between subordinates and bosses, servants and masters, employers and employees. It fills one with peace and understanding.

What can it not do? It can do anything for you! Meditation is the surest means to put an end to all corruption in your life. It is the steady fire to burn away all sins. A sinner cannot remain a sinner in the radiant blaze of the fire of meditation. Meditation is the technique of living in the world of conflicts unaffected by them. It is the technique of living in the world unaffected by the binding influence of action. A life of liberation, even while living in the body, is the result. So I recommend, with deep earnestness, this process of meditation.

Let us all pray to God to give us the strength to prepare ourselves for meditation through a pure life, a good life, a life of selflessness and service, by increasing our devotion to God, by realizing the vanity of these fleeting and passing names and forms which we call this earth, this universe, by realizing the unparalleled glory, the worth and the precious value of God, the value of the Ultimate Source of our being, by cultivating attention, by cultivating concentration, by taking the help of the steady pose of the body and the regulation of the breath, by developing the habit of continual recollectedness, and by praying for the Grace of God.

Thus let us slowly reach higher and higher and higher into the realms of pure meditation and through the Grace of God drawn through prayer, let us soon achieve that stage of meditation which would take us into the highest transcendental realms of God-vision and crown our life with the glorious attainment of God-consciousness and immortality.

May the Grace of God be upon you all. May the blessings of all Masters and all saints ever follow you every step of the way as you walk resolutely upon this inner path of concentration and meditation. May their help ever be available to you all, and through the grace of God, may you fill your life with glory!

15. SAINTS AND SAGES

Blessed Immortal Atman! Glorious children of the Supreme! Beloved seekers! It is a great joy and a great blessedness for me to be with you all and bathe myself in the radiance of your holiness. It is said in India that the greatest blessedness a soul can have is to come in contact with those who love the Lord. Many things can be had—you can have riches and material things which may be very valuable, but this is not anything compared to having the company of the pure in heart, of people who love God, of people who aspire for Truth. This latter cannot be purchased. It comes to us only through His Grace. It is a bestowal that comes directly from God. It comes only when the Divine wishes to be gracious unto us. He has been very gracious to me in this way.

People speak of the modern age, the Godless age, the age of Godless-ism, of the material West, but I have, during the past one and one-half years moved only in the spiritual West. I have not encountered the materialistic West. For those who are in the environment of Godly people, it is a golden age. No matter what age you live in, to come into contact with those who love God, who cherish the aspiration to know the Truth, who have realized that life is not to be wasted away amidst passing changeful unreality, but that it is meant for the sublime task of realizing the Reality, to come into contact with such people, is to enter into the golden age. Such a person who courts the company of the holy is blessed indeed.

The Purifying Power of Holy Saints

Satsanga is a transformer. Satsanga is the company

of those who are at one with the Reality. "Sat" stands for the Supreme Truth or Reality. "Sanga" is association or company. "Satsanga" means being in close contact with the Supreme. The highest of holy company is to be with God in God-thought or divine contemplation, in meditation, in worship. You get close to the Reality with the aid of these processes.

The visible expression of Divinity upon earth is the great holy fraternity—the saints, the sages, holy people, devotees. God said, "Wherever My devotees abide, there is holy ground". It is all purified ground. Holy places, to which people go upon pilgrimage in order to bless themselves, derive their holiness from the presence of devotees there. They become holy places because devotees have been there and worshipped God and realized God—thus the places become holy. It is not so much that devotees went there because the places were holy, but the places became holy because the devotees went there. The holy people, the saints, are a purifying force in the world. The world becomes habitable, becomes a place worthy of being lived in, because of these saints. The saints stand for a great ideal. They shine radiantly for a certain experience.

It is an ancient spiritual tradition in India to regard the Holy Ganges as a sacred river, as a divine stream that purifies everyone who goes and bathes in it. How does the Ganges wash away sins? Someone said to Mother Ganges: "To get rid of the sins and impurities that one gathers upon oneself in a single span of earth-life, an individual soul has to do much penance, prayer, pilgrimage, spiritual practice and worship; whereas you, O Mother Ganges, constantly take upon yourself the countless evils and sins of millions upon millions of people, year in and year out. What is your secret, O Mother Ganges, that you are still regarded as the all-holy river?"

It is said that Mother Ganges replied: "If a million sinners come and take bath in me and make me impure, then, if one saint comes and takes a bath or dip in me, I am immediately purified. All the sins of the million vanish like that, for if a saint comes and takes a dip, his all-consuming purity is such that all the earlier impurities are washed away — they vanish". And the company of such people, contemplation of their lives, the thought of these saints, is a stream, as it were, in which to plunge and take a bath; and such a bath is thousandfold more purifying than a bath in Ganges herself; for, the Ganges stands to be purified by the saints.

Saints stand witness to eternal verities. It is easy to believe that this world exists, because we see it. All our experience is through some sense-perception of this world which is in our immediate presence, which demands recognition. We cannot say the world is not. The invisible, on the other hand, is just an idea to the vast majority until one begins to feel the stirrings of faith in the Eternal. And saints and sages, who have themselves, in their own wondrous life, contacted and realized the Infinite Reality of God, the Great Eternal — they become, as it were, the undeniable and irresistible witnesses to the presence of the Supreme.

If you are asked, "Why do you believe in God?", you can just say, "Because the saints exist", for they are God-filled. You see the son and you know there is a father. Even so, when you see the saints, you know there is that Source of Infinite Bliss and peace, for here in the saints, you visibly see that pristine peace. The saints are filled with that inner peace which is derived from no object. A renunciate saint, perhaps living in a mountain-cave or on the banks of a river, possessionless, absolutely devoid of all earthly wealth, beams with the radiance of joy, not of this earth, and nothing can take that joy away from him; and restless, peaceless, tormented people going to him may even find peace themselves. How the peace comes from him! For he has tapped the immeasurable Source of all peace, all bliss, through the experience of the Divine. The very existence of saints, therefore, becomes proof to the faithful of the existence of the world of the Supreme.

Conflicting Declarations of Creeds and Scriptures

The pathway to the Supreme is beset with many diffi-culties and it is confused with conflicting declarations. Especially in this modern age, man is confused about religion. He does not know what the truth is, or the right religion, or the correct belief, for diverse religions abound. There are different scriptures declaring the Ultimate Reality in different terms, one contradicting the other. There is mutual conflict. There is no agreement and each religion insists that its conception of the Truth is the only Ultimate Reality. Sometimes they do not stop at this, but go one step further saying, "All other conceptions will lead you to hell-fire and you will have to continue in that state, in the furnace of hell-fire and brimstone, for centuries and centuries. You who do not believe thus are all pagans and heathens".

The Mussalman will say, "He who believes in Allah, he is the only one who is saved. That is the only way in which the doors of heaven are open to you—the only way you can attain that land". And what is that land? It is the land of perennial spring, with streams and gardens, beautiful fruits and flowers everywhere, and well-fed turkeys, parrots and other birds playing about. This is a conception of heaven where all pleasure is immediately available. Whereas, the devout Christian praying in a church will have a heart filled with the burden of the whole world, wondering in what way he can save souls—going out of his way to save souls for Christ. And, he thinks that all those believing in his particular conception of God are the only people for whom one can hope; and

for all the rest, tears should be shed, for they are all
heathens and pagans, requiring their souls to be saved,
and if they are not saved by the Christians, they will be
eternally damned. So many times a Christian thinks it his
mission to save souls and the number of souls that he
saves goes to guarantee his own supreme salvation.

In each of these two religions, Mohammedanism and
Christianity, the followers think theirs is the only religion
and other people are just blind. In the same way, for instance, the Buddhists will say that save those who follow
the great path leading to Nirvana, all others are as
children, groping about in the dark.

Thus it is found that tenets differ, scriptures differ,
doctrines differ, conceptions of Divinity differ; and not
only do they differ, they are mutually exclusive and clash
with one another. In the same religion, different sects
have different ways of declaring the Truth, and each sect
is prepared to fight and say that all others are fools and
that they alone have the highest Truth. *And, they are all
sincere.* But they do not recognize the value of other
religions; rather they feel that the followers of these
other religions are blind with wrong thinking. Thus the
followers of each separate religion declare the absolute
ignorance of all the rest. An ordinary person who wants,
somehow, to make good use of his life and obtain the
Supreme Source, is confused and does not know what to
believe. A knowledge of all religions is easily available in
these days of jet travel, paperbacks and libraries; and the
more one learns, the more confused one becomes. However, the path of contradiction, confusion and anxiety is
not exactly peculiar to this age.

There is an old saying in India: "The ancient scriptures, like the *Upanishads* and the *Vedas,* differ in their
declarations. And scriptures like the *Bhagavad Gita* and
the *Mahabharata* also have divergent views on life and
matters pertaining to the Ultimate Reality and the duty

of man". If you go to the writings of the various sages,
Valmiki says one thing, Vasishtha says something different, as also does Buddha, and their opinions also differ.

One saint says: "Love of God is the only path that
can lead to the realization of God. Without love of the
Supreme and worship and prayer unto Him, all is useless.
Knowledge can never give salvation. It is the lover of
God who attains the supreme state of blessedness and
liberation through the Grace of God". And then comes
Shankaracharya who says, "There is no dream of liberation, of emancipation, without knowledge of God.
Knowledge is the ultimate fire that burns off all sin and
all past Karma and gives you liberation. Even in a
thousand births, with all worship, all the ringing of bells,
pilgrimages, charities and chanting, there is no hope of
liberation without the knowledge of God". Others say:
"By serving humanity, by feeling for others, by ceaseless
service alone can you attain salvation. Seeking salvation
for yourself is the height of selfishness. In that way you
can never break the bondage of earth-life".

The opinions of these sages and seers tend to differ.
Therefore, the true essence of duty, the true essence of
righteous living, is often hidden away in some inaccessible place. So we ask, "What is the way?". That way is
the one that has been trodden by the great ones.

Infallible Guidance from the Lives of Saints

So, if you go to the scriptures and they confuse you,
well, just look to the path which these great ones have
taken. See how these saints have lived, how these people
have tried to make themselves fit for the expression of
the Supreme. See how they have spoken, how they have
dealt with their fellow-men, how they have reacted to life
and its experiences. Behold! Channel your life upon the
pattern of the saints, and in this way, the great importance of the lives of saints for us is that they present to

us a blueprint of the life-perfect. Their lives offer to us a tangible scheme of living, a way of life, glorifying their own exemplary personalities, their own ideal personalities; and we find that now we are in safe hands if we can just follow in their footsteps. "Lives of great men oft remind us...they leave behind them footprints in the sands of time"—and these 'footprints', their ideal pattern of living, becomes to us the indicator of the path to Perfection.

So, let us follow in the footsteps of the great saints, steering clear of the great mass of underbrush, of theory and dogma and doctrines and various theological beliefs. Let us leave the theological beliefs safely in the hands of the theologists, because they are concerned with the things of this world. Rather, let us go to the heart of theology, into the essence of it, and try to walk the way in which the saints walked. If saints are to have any meaning for us in our lives, we must try to emulate them, we must try to live like them, we must try to feel like them, we must try to make their lives the standard, the measure, of our own conduct. In a given situation in which we do not know how to act, we should say to ourselves, "How would such-and-such a saint have reacted in this situation?" or "If St. Francis were in my place, how would he have reacted? If Jesus had faced this situation, what would he have done? If Ramakrishna and Buddha were in this situation, what would they have done?"

A high standard is a difficult thing to demand of yourself, but it is better to have a high standard and fail in reaching it, than not to have a standard at all or to have a low and petty standard. Saints, by the examples of their lives, show us what a man can attain if he wills enough.

Read the lives of great saints and you will see how they too started from scratch, how they also had humble beginnings, with all the weaknesses and defects of ordinary human beings. But, by being impressed with the love of an ideal, through their earnestness and sincerity and, above all, through their persistence in following that ideal, no matter how much they were assailed by the world and its experiences in this process, no matter how many obstacles confronted them, no matter how many problems faced them, they came out triumphant. Their problems and sufferings proved to be the very factors that thus polished their nature and completely removed all dross therefrom, making them shine like pure gold. Life came to them as a furnace that purifies the base ore and turns it into pure shining gold. In this way, the saints have shown us that any ordinary being can also do what they have done.

Thus their lives become to us a challenge and an inspiration. The details of their lives are thus sources of great wisdom and great courage. When reading their lives, we find that we have real wisdom at hand. Pondering over the lives of these great saints, courage comes to us in times of despair. Saints, therefore, are primarily examples on the way. God has given us saints so as to hold before us models of perfection, ideals into which we have to cast ourselves and become perfectly moulded like them. We also can reap the harvest of peace and blessedness by going the way they went, by following in their footsteps.

Is it not a very significant title which Thomas A. Kempis has given to his work—"Imitation of Christ"? Christ's life has to be imitated. We have to be as he was. We have to be as all the great ones, all the saints and mystics were. They are a perennial source of inspiration offering us the standards, the principles, upon which we should base our lives. These saints are a living embodiment of the scriptures. All the lofty teachings of the scriptures, the great truths of the scriptures, become visible and living in the lives, in the utterances, and in

the actions of saints and sages. A scripture as a book is
a mass of knowledge, but when we *see* the lives of saints,
we see the spiritual truths as a living force, as a living
truth. Through the saints, therefore, we obtain inspiration, great hope and courage. We get an indication of the
state of perfection to which we are to raise ourselves,
into which we have to grow, and we receive, easily available to us, a definite pattern of living, a definite way of
life and being.

In the twelfth chapter of the *Srimad Bhagavd Gita*,
Lord Krishna, concluding his short discourse to Arjuna,
upon the path of devotion, sums up in the last eight ver-
ses the ideal of one who is totally devoted to God, the
way in which such a one lives. It forms a blessed pattern
for us to follow.

The presence of these great saints, these mystics,
these men of God, teaches us this wonderful thing,
namely, a totally different sense of values. We find in
their lives that many a time their actions seem very
queer and completely out of context and out of harmony
with the rest of the world. They seem opposed to the
ways of the world, at least on the surface, but if you
delve beneath the surface, you will find that they have
the deepest rationality for their differing mode of conduct. The saints say, "You are after certain things which
are vital to you; therefore you are going after them in
your own way. We are after things which are very vital
and precious to us; and we are going after them in our
own way".

The vision of the saints is also something which is
totally different. The vision of a man of the world is always coloured by "I" and "mine"; he clings to things of
this earth. But the vision of the saints is always coloured
by the Bhav or feeling of "not mine". He feels that
everything he has belongs to the Lord, including his body
and mind.

The Transforming Influence of a Saint's Action

There was a saint living on the banks of the Ganges in the province of Bihar, a Vedantin, but devoted to Lord Rama. For many years he had been practising Yoga in a cave which he had dug out on the river bank and had attained to a very high spiritual state. He would be immersed in trance for several days and weeks and eat no food during that time. Due to this, he came to be known as the holy man whose food was air. Being a devotee of Lord Rama, he had many articles of worship (vessels, plates, pots, spoons, lamps and candlesticks) and devotees would come and lavish upon him their offerings (fruits, flowers, camphor and incense) and he would offer these to the Lord.

A thief broke into his little cave one night. Knowing that this man was a devotee of God, and believing he might have received much of value from his own devotees, the thief took with him a large sack. He had placed many valuable articles of the saint therein when the latter, who was in an inner cave, heard the intruder and came out to see who was there. Upon seeing the saint standing there, the thief fled, leaving the sack on the floor. The saint picked up the sack and followed the thief, and upon overtaking him, offered him the sack saying, "Here! this is yours. Why are you running away? You have taken a great deal of trouble to come and collect this material; so take the sack. I have also added a few things which you had missed". The thief was simply stunned. He did not know what to say. He took the sack and went away.

Many years later, the brilliant disciple of Sri Ramakrishna, the great Master of Vedanta who came and expounded the Vedantic message to the West, Swami Vivekananda, was on a pilgrimage in the Himalayan regions, visiting the holy shrines of Badrinath, Kedarnath, etc. And he found a holy man who was carrying on meditation and was shivering with the cold, not having sufficient clothing for warmth; and Swami Vivekananda stopped to chat with this man and wrapped about him a blanket which he was carrying.

Vivekananda spoke of his travels and of the many persons whom he had encountered. The man asked the Swami if he knew the saint who lived on air and the Swami said he had recently spent some days with him. The man then asked if Swami Vivekananda had heard about the thief taking away this saint's articles used for worship and how he, the saint, had run after the thief with the bag he had dropped and had added to that bag other articles which the thief had missed. Swami Vivekananda said that he had heard the story. The man then told the Swami that he was that thief, and from that one moment of contact with that great saint who lived on air, he had been purified to the degree that he went to work and earned his livelihood and had later on renounced the world in search of the Lord.

True Saintliness Is Egolessness

The principle which the saints enliven within themselves, the principle of seeing the Lord in all, beholding the Self in all, and of attaining to a state of absolute desireless non-possession—that is the way to liberation. The Supreme can be achieved only by making these truths live in reality within ourselves. And the forbearance of the saints! The very essence of saintliness is the total effacement of the ego. If you wish to briefly sum up the inner heart of saintliness, it is the total effacement of the ego. That is the perfect emptiness of which Christ spoke when he said, "Empty thyself and I shall fill thee"—a total emptying of ourselves of all "I"-ness and "mine"-ness and of all their offsprings, namely, desire, selfishness, attachment, anger, delusion and greed. From "I" springs "mine". If there is no "I", there is no "mine". "I" is the root thought that separates us from

God, and when "I" and "mine" come, there comes selfishness. The "I" wants to possess all things and countless
desires spring into life. And when a desire is blocked,
anger comes; and if the desire is fulfilled, more desire
comes and greed follows because desires are insatiable
and cannot be appeased. From desire springs greed—
greed to obtain and possess that which is desired. Out of
this possession comes clinging, infatuation and delusion.
Saints are devoid of "I".

My Master sings a Mantra: "Adapt, adjust, accom-
modate; bear insult, bear injury, highest Sadhana". So,
the highest Sadhana of all is to bear insult, to bear injury,
which means to become totally devoid of the ego principle, to become humble, to become like a child.

"Blessed are the meek. Blessed are the humble.
Blessed are the lowly in spirit." Why did Jesus say that?
He knew what he was speaking about. He did not simply
utter useless words. He himself was without ego. Therefore, when he spoke, he spoke words of light from the
truth of his being, and when he spoke those words, he
was humble, meek and lowly. Children also are like
that—in their very spontaneity, in their innocence, in
their egolessness. Children are humble. You cannot insult
a child. They are lowly, they are meek, because they are
transparent in their nature—innocent and pure. That is
the path that saints choose for their own lives.

We have the example of Ekanath, who was a very
great saint of Maharashtra—an embodiment of peace and
serenity and humility. He loved all, and naturally, people
worshipped him. People flocked to hear his words, even
though there were highly learned Pundits living in the
same place. Those Pundits could not tolerate this saint.
They considered him illiterate and resented his attracting
the crowd, with no one coming to seek their advice or
listen to them. They plotted to cause Ekanath to do
something which would cause the people to turn against

him, something which would cause him to lose his temper, to become angry and thus show the people another side of his nature.

So they hired a man, a real rascal, and told him to stand in a certain place where the saint would pass on his way from his bath in the holy river Godavari, carrying a container of water to worship at the shrine. They told this man to fill his mouth with water and when Ekanath passed, to spit it on him. To the Hindu, spittle is polluting; so one must wash even if only bringing the hand in contact with the mouth, and of course, if one were spat upon, he would need to take a bath before entering a shrine.

Ekanath went to the river the following morning to have his bath and fill the vessel with water, and as he was passing the city gate on his way to worship in the shrine, the hired rascal spat upon him. Ekanath looked at the man, bowed his head, walked back and took another bath. This happened not once, not twice, but one hundred and seven times! One hundred and seven times as Ekanath walked through the gate after his bath, this rascal spat upon him. Without a word uttered, without showing any anger, resentment or irritation, the saint just walked back and bathed afresh in the river. For the one hundred and eighth time, as Ekanath approached the gate at which the rascal stood, this man acted as though a thunderbolt had struck him. He trembled and threw himself in the dust at the feet of the saint and begged forgiveness. He said, "I thought I was dealing with a man, but find I am dealing with a god". This rascal became Ekanath's servant for the rest of his life.

There was a great king who had profound reverence for holy men and always had a number of them staying as guests in his palace. This practice annoyed his ministers who said to one another, "We serve the king. We give him advice and carry on his administration and are prepared to die for him in times of war; and these penniless vagabonds, with nothing to call their own, seem to be favourites of the king and he concerns himself more with their comfort than with ours". So they had a conference with the prime minister and told him that this practice must cease.

The prime minister went to the king about this matter, and the king said that he appreciated the feeling of his ministers, but that the prime minister should give an answer out of his own experience. So the king gave him a list of the holy men who were then staying at the palace, and he suggested that the prime minister should invite them and all the ministers to his home for a sumptuous banquet one evening and have them all as overnight guests. The prime minister carried out the instructions given to him by the king and the banquet went on into the small hours of the morning, with much dancing and music. The holy men had all been there to grace the occasion and to give discourses. The king told the prime minister to take a few servants in the early morning, about five or six o'clock, and just splash a little cold water upon each one of the guests to waken them. The prime minister did as instructed and had his servants rudely awaken the holy men first. They quickly wakened saying, "O Rama, Rama, Rama", "Om Hari Om". Every holy man wakened thus, uttering the Name of God.

The prime minister noted this and then followed his servants to the sleeping quarters of the ministers, who were also thus awakened. However, every one of them wakened with great cursing, swearing and indignation. At this moment the king appeared on the scene and said,"Now you see what is inside the holy men and what is inside the ministers and now you know why I value the holy men so highly and try to keep their company. To them there is nothing but God; they are filled with God. These ministers, in spite of all their earthly nobility...you have witnessed what is inside of them!" So, saints are filled with God and it is through such that God reveals Himself.

16. DIVINE LIFE

Blessed immortal seekers! Glorious rays of the Eternal Divine Light! Friends! I greet you in the name of my Master, the great Master, Swami Sivananda, and I greet you in Divine Life.

To such of you who are new to this type of gathering, who have come here for the first time today, I extend my warmest welcome and I express my love and greetings — especially to the people who are attending for the first time.

In this Divine Life gathering, we make it a special point to see that our meetings are thrown open to all groups. Ours is a group which embraces in itself every group that seeks God, and we identify ourselves with all seekers, absolutely, without any thought or reservation. It is quite immaterial whether they belong to any specific religion, faith or church or not. So, here are welcome Hindus, Christians, Jews, Buddhists, Parsis, even people who have not found anything yet but who are seeking something, seeking peace, happiness, seeking a nobler way of life, seeking upliftment of soul, the improvement of their total nature — this is a group which welcomes all such seekers. Therefore the absolutely non-denominational name "The Divine Life Group". We welcome all people who aspire for the Divine. We welcome all people who live to seek the Divine and who seek to live divinely, and therefore, in the name of Divine Life, my warmest and cordial greeting and welcome to you all once again.

What Is Divine Life?

Divine Life is life lived in the awareness of your

divine destiny. Divine Life is life lived in the full consciousness of your true divine nature, in the knowledge that you are not a body and a mind, but an eternal, all-pure and perfect spiritual being. That is the innermost central truth of your being; that is the true fact of your real nature. You are divine. You are spiritual. Therefore you are imperishable and ever-perfect. You partake of the nature of the eternal and inexhaustible source of your being, viz., God, even as every ray of the sun partakes of the sun's radiant and luminous nature. As is the source, so is the emanation. Therefore, as God is divine, ever-pure and perfect, whatever emanates from Him is also divine, ever-pure and ever-perfect, is also of the very nature of indescribable bliss and supreme peace. A life lived in the awareness of this true nature of yours is Divine Life. A life constantly lived in order to express this divine nature of yours through all your thoughts, sentiments and feelings, through all your spoken utterances and, more important than anything else, through all your actions, your practical life—such is Divine Life.

This Divine Life is the great need of the world today, not only of the individuals that live in the world, but of all nations and communities, all groups of people, all races and countries that are trying to evolve in today's world. For, in such an effort to express the higher nature that is within man, lies hope of the emergence of a better world from this war-torn and troubled times of ours, from this great and eventful age filled with so much wonderful achievement and advancement, but at the same time oppressed with so much of distrust, mutual suspicion, discontent, hatred and strife. Divine Life is, indeed, the great answer—individually and collectively—to this vexing problem of world discord and the great solution to this problem of a total breakaway from spiritual values.

This Divine Life is the one message of the great

Master Swami Sivananda; this Divine Life is the great way of life which he had been trying ceaselessly to spread throughout the modern world.

Divine Life is a life of divinity in practice. Divine Life is a life of our divine nature expressed in divine thoughts, divine work and divine action. It is, as it were, an expression of the spiritual man through the human man upon the plane of this physical world. This Divine Life should be lived both inwardly as an ascent into its all-full perfection, and also outwardly as beauty, as love, as goodness, as peace, as humility, as selflessness, as the spirit of service, for all these great qualities are part and parcel of the ever-perfect divine nature which lies within you and awaits to be unfolded and made manifest by your wise conscious effort.

The man of Divine Life seeks to live for a great ideal. The man of Divine Life is a peace-maker, for he beholds the essential spiritual oneness of all mankind. He knows that the one great divine essence knits all life into a great oneness and thus ever tries to see the whole world as a manifest expression of the Divine Essence, and thus deals with all with reverence and love. He sees God in man and thus seeks to live worshipfully. He seeks to give love as his worship to his immanent Divinity.

A person who practises this Divine Life, therefore, spreads love, mutual regard and respect. He works for goodwill and understanding and he ever seeks to bring greater spiritual harmony. The person living the Divine Life, wherever he goes, will make people feel the oneness of life and the spirit of brotherhood. The follower of Divine Life is a great example of selflessness and service. This is the outward aspect of the inward spiritual transformation which everyone seeks to bring about through Yoga, through practical religion, through prayer and worshipfulness, through the life spiritual.

Significance of the Human Birth

The Supreme Self illumines everything, but is over-looked in apparent appearances. When the great Atman is like the absolute void—nameless and formless—there is no creation. The world is not then, and there is no universe either. There is no matter and no motion, but only absolute, ineffable stillness. There is no matter and no motion, but only Pure Consciousness. And then the Pure Consciousness sets itself into motion as an act of the Absolute Will Divine. This motion brings into being subtle matter or Prakriti, as the Indian philosophy terms it. Then, from Prakriti, the universe comes into being. From the Atman or Supreme Spirit is light. From the Supreme is desire. From the Supreme is love. From the Supreme are all the elements from ether down to water. The Supreme sustains the physical world as physical proof. Even the broad sky above and the boundless ocean around remind you of the Supreme Absolute Spirit. From the Supreme Absolute come the countless universes; yet the Pure Consciousness remains absolutely unaffected. The sun's rays fall on the pure water of the Ganges, on the ocean, on streams, pools and ponds and on dirty puddles, but the sun is not at all affected in any way by this contact. Even so, the Absolute being is totally unaffected by the later evolutes, such as the countless universes. The world and the universes, however, continue to exist because of the divine motion set by the Pure Consciousness through the Absolute Will.

Motion or energy is not different from Pure Consciousness; it is only Pure Consciousness expressed or made manifest. Motion or energy cannot exist without matter to play upon; therefore the subtle matter or Prakriti was first created.

The subtle matter, the transcendental matter or Prakriti, was whirled into motion in its three qualities and it divided itself into various grosser entities. The grosser entities became still more grosser and found themselves as different universes. From the universes were created worlds. In the worlds, there evolved the various forms of life. The universal motion or consciousness found at last its expression in the human being, the last species to evolve upon the worlds. In the human being was created the mind. Mind thus became the most powerful agency of perception, discernment and understanding.

At first the human mind was gross—only instinctive, a little more efficient than that of the animal; but, as evolution progressed, it gradually started refining itself. When a higher stage of evolution was reached by the mind of man, there came the separate awareness of the lower mind and the higher mind. The lower mind identified itself with gross matter. The limited consciousness was thus identified, but the higher mind ever sought the eternal. It was dissatisfied with the limitation, bondage and imprisonment and thus started the quest of the discovery of the real nature of being. When that is realized, the cycle is completed, the consciousness which limited itself in the human form having become freed, having once again merged in its infinite, all-perfect, absolute, original source. This is the cycle. This is the true meaning of your human nature, of your human birth. Complete the cycle and culminate in spiritual glory. To lead the Divine Life is the secret of bringing about this achievement in a conscious way here and now.

This message becomes especially significant to you who are listening to me today, because today, the 2nd of October, is the birthday anniversary of one of the greatest of India's spiritual men of this century—one who embodied in himself such a divine life of ever seeking to reach and realize the Reality. And this man was the venerable Mahatma Gandhi. You all know the father of the Indian nation, the architect of Indian independence, the saintly man who developed the great theory and technique of non-violence — the technique of overcoming hatred through love. He was the twentieth century version of the great and benign Buddha of three thousand years ago. Mahatma Gandhi was a living embodiment of *Divine life and I wish to speak a few words upon how he exemplified this divine life in his own person; and that, I think, would indeed be a very fitting tribute to him on this day of his birth anniversary.

In India there are celebrations going on right at this moment in honour of Mahatma Gandhi's birthday, for the Mahatma is still regarded not merely as a politician, but as a worshipful sage who once again revived the ancient message of the great Indian sages — the message of Dharma. Dharma implies a life based upon ethics, a life based upon prayer, a life based upon a living faith in God, a life of truth. Thus, Mahatma Gandhi was the modern representative of the great sages who gave us our cultural idealism, and in his name, I wish to place before you a little thumb-nail sketch, as it were, of the great Gandhian pattern of life.

Mahatma Gandhi as a Spiritual Seeker

Mahatma Gandhi said at a certain stage of his life: "Those who think me to be a politician and those who think that my business is politics have really not understood me at all. They have totally missed the real being in me. I am a seeker or nothing at all. The truth about my life is my seeking, my quest for God. Politics is only an incidental part of my life".

Gandhi was ever seeking after the great Reality and this seeking started right in his little boyhood. He was a deeply devoted son of very religious and pious parents and he got the habit of repeating Ram Nam even when he was a little boy going to secondary school, and his

seeking developed and took the form of service of the
living God in the poor millions of India and, as India was
at that time going through a political phase, his service
took the form of political agitation for the welfare of his
people. To Mahatma Gandhi it was all a part and parcel
of his worship of God in and through man, in and
through the suffering people of India, in and through his
poor brethren, and thus it was a Sadhana to him.

Gandhi's life was based absolutely upon the ideal of
truth, purity and compassion and his was the path of service. In his life we see the ideals of self-discipline, of
ceaseless inward striving, of moderation, and a sublime
simplicity, the parallel of which the world has seldom
seen except perhaps in the life of Christ. Many have
called him the modern Christ. Many have called him the
modern St. Francis, the modern Buddha. He has been a
source of great inspiration to the whole of the modern
world and the world will hear much more about him in
the decades to come in this century.

The source of Mahatma Gandhi's great spiritual
force was not the great following he had, for he lived a
life dedicated to poverty and he had nothing which he
called his own. The source of his spiritual force was his
constant unbroken contact with God. How did he maintain such contact? Through daily prayer and the Divine
Name. Not a single day passed without his setting aside
all activity, without his turning away from all secular activity at the hour of twilight. When the sun had set,
Gandhi was found always in the middle of his little
prayer group, perhaps under a spreading Banyan tree, in
some peaceful spot, in the corner of some compound or
on a little wooden platform or stage, totally oblivious of
the rest of the world and totally merged in a wonderful
peace and sweetness of inward communion with God.

His prayer meetings were extraordinary. The vision
of universalism in his approach to God was something of

an object lesson to every one. His prayer contained portions of the Koran recited in Arabic, portions of the *Zendavesta* of the Parsis recited in their own Persian tongue, portions of Japanese prayer recited in the Japanese language, the Sanskrit hymns of the *Vedas,* portions from the Testament and the Lord's Prayer. Thus, practically every religion came to be represented in Mahatma Gandhi's daily evening prayer.

There was a period of silence and all sank into meditation. There was a group chant of the Divine Name, and then, coming out of his silence, meditation and communion, Mahatma Gandhi gave a short message of five or ten minutes to the people, and always it was filled with spirituality, vibrant with a living quality which came out of this ever-fresh contact that he maintained with the Supreme Being through such daily prayer.

Gandhi was essentially a man of prayer. He had his roots in faith and in daily prayer. He said, "Prayer is the real bread of my life. But for prayer, I would not find it possible even to live". The secret of all his great achievements, of the strenuous life which he led, was the Divine Name. The Divine Name was Gandhi's constant strength and support. He never parted from the Divine Name — the Name of Ram. To him, born as a Hindu, it was Ram, but essentially it was the Divine Name which was always on his lips and which was ever an under-current of his life, which few suspected and fewer knew; and only a few among those who knew understood its true significance.

All the activity of Mahatma Gandhi was activity centred in God by absolute detachment to the world and deep inward attachment to the Lord through love, worshipfulness, prayer and the spiritual link — the constantly repeated Divine Name. God was the ultimate value for Mahatma Gandhi in all his life. Not even political attainment, but God and God alone was the ultimate value in his life. He was the centre, He was the goal, He was the object of his quest, He was the object of all his life thus nobly lived. All this divine life of Mahatma Gandhi's was but a constant seeking, through activity, through service of his people, through service of the Divine Spirit that he knew and felt to indwell all people.

Spiritualize Your Activities

Spiritualize your activities. To live a divine life, offer all your actions—even reading, talking, playing tennis—to the Lord. Feel that the whole world is indwelt by Him. Feel that all your children are manifestations of the Lord. Serve humanity with such inward spiritual feeling. Then all your daily activities will be transformed into spiritual exercises. They will be transformed into Yoga.

Every day, side by side with your duties, you have to keep up this inward contact, this link with the Divine Source, through prayer, worship and silent meditation. This is your foremost duty. This should not be neglected on any account. Get up a little earlier in the morning and practice contemplation. Practise a few Yoga poses— do not neglect the body—and a few breathing exercises. Study sacred books. This inward silence and meditation is most important. Early morning, as the time for spiritual practice, is equally important. Silent meditation in the morning (even for a few minutes) and in the evening, at dusk, is very important. Be alert—do not neglect this.

Have a background of thought—thought of the Lord, thought of your divine ideal. Everyone has some background of thought or the other, but usually it is just worldly or sordid and material. A barrister or advocate has a background of thought filled with clients, courts, sections of the law, etc. The background of thought of a doctor is about his dispensary, injections, patients, medicines, fees. The background of thought of a grandmother is about her grandchildren and sons. The background of thought of a practitioner of Divine Life should be concerned with the glorious ideal of divine attainment, with God, with a life of goodness, with the Divine name. Cultivate divine qualities; eradicate negative ones. Change your mental attitude towards the world, towards everything. Waste not even a single moment of your precious time. Think and talk of the ideal, of the good life, of God, of Divine Life. Live for God. Spread the message of Divine Life to one and all you meet in the course of your daily activities. When you meet some friend, do not talk shop, rather ask what type of meditation is being done or the latest spiritual literature being studied—let this be your conversation. Let everything about you be noble and divine. Let everything about you be lofty. Give up idle gossiping. Abandon novel reading. Idle gossiping and novel reading will not give you mental peace. They disturb your mental equilibrium. They fill your mind with unnecessary, painful, worldly thoughts. Fill your mind, instead, with lofty divine thoughts. Let your inward being glow with divine radiance. Let purity permeate it. Remember always that this world is one of pain and old age and death and that your foremost duty is to complete the cycle, to realize God, to realize the Self, where alone you can find direct peace, eternal joy, eternal light.

Gird up your loins and apply yourself to the living of this Divine Life. Be a practical seeker. You will attain immortality. You will enjoy supreme peace, eternal joy. There is no doubt about it.

May God bless you all with health, long life, peace, prosperity, eternal bliss, success in all your undertakings, brilliant career, all-fullness and supreme divine blessedness, supreme felicity.

Elements of Divine Life in a Nutshell

I will close now with a little song in which the Master sums up the elements of divine living, of Divine Life and the virtues which one should cultivate in order to support Divine Life.

The elements of Divine Life are purity, selflessness, spirit of service, love (love of man and love of God), regular meditation, inward life, and ultimately, realization of the Absolute. Therefore, the Master sings about Divine Life:

"Serve, love, give, purify, meditate, realize,
Be good, do good, be kind, be compassionate.
Inquire 'Who am I?', know thy Self and be free.
Serve, love, give, purify, meditate, realize,
Be good, do good, be kind, be compassionate."

That is Divine Life in a nutshell for you. Herein we have a remedy, a wonderful panacea, a cure-all for this worldly bondage, for death and re-birth. But then, when you take medicine, you also have to keep some rules regarding your diet. And here is the diet—the "Song of Eighteen Ities":—

Serenity, regularity, absence of vanity,
Sincerity, simplicity, veracity,
Equanimity, fixity, non-irritability,
Adaptability, humility, tenacity,
Integrity, nobility, magnanimity,
Charity, generosity, purity.
Practise daily these Eighteen Ities,
You will soon attain immortality.
Brahman is the only real entity,
Mr. So-and-so is a false non-entity.
You will abide in infinity and eternity,
You will behold unity in diversity;
You cannot attain this in the university,
(You can attain this in the Forest Academy).

Practise these divine virtues. They will support you living of the Divine Life. They will support your interior spiritual life. For, without virtues, your life is dry; without virtues, your life is useless and cannot provide a proper field for the play of your divine nature. It is by conquering determinedly (and with full faith in God and in His power to help you) all the negative aspects of your life and making your whole personality a field for the play of all virtues that you afford full scope for the divine light to manifest in you and then to radiate through you. Live such a divine life. Make yourself an embodiment of these divine virtues. Completely conquer your lower nature and thus make yourself a perfect channel and instrument for the outflow and the radiance of the Divinity centred within you. Such is Divine Life.

May divinity infill you. May Divinity inspire you and guide all your actions. May your entire life be a wonderful and a radiant example of divine living. This is my request to you all. This is my earnest urge to you all. Live divinely, my beloved friends, live divinely. Live as you truly are, not as you have deluded yourself into thinking, by forgetfulness of your divine nature. Assert your divine nature and become wonderful flowers, beautiful flowers radiating divine beauty and divine fragrance, spiritual fragrance, in the garden of the Supreme.

May God bless you. May the Indweller inspire you. May Master Sivananda shower his blessings upon you. May all the sages of East and West, of the past as well as the present, ever back you up with their spiritual blessings and lead you on to the ultimate glorious goal of Realization — radiant realization of your glorious divine nature.

I once again thank you for having given me this wonderful opportunity of being amidst you and thus offering my worship through these few words to the God who is invisibly present amidst you, and to each one of you, my beloved fellow seekers. Ever be united. Ever be together — think together, seek together, work together and act together. Feel as one, and through such unity and fellowship, may untold blessings come for all those who come into your contact.

May you all become a great centre of divinity, a great centre of spiritual awakening to countless people, and may you become a great centre of concord, harmony, unity, and a great example of oneness and brotherhood, and may you spread the joy of divine living throughout the whole world in the years that stretch before you.

TWENTY SPIRITUAL INSTRUCTIONS

(Swami Sivananda)

1. Get up at 4 a.m. daily. Do Japa and meditation.
2. Take Sattvic Ahara. Do not overload the stomach.
3. Sit on Padma or Siddha Asana for Japa and Dhyana.
4. Have a separate meditation room under lock and key.
5. Do charity 1-10 of income, or ten paise per rupee.
6. Study systematically one chapter of the *Bhagavad Gita*.
7. Preserve Veerya (the vital force). Sleep separately.
8. Give up smoking, intoxicating drinks and Rajasic food.
9. Fast on Ekadasi days or live on milk and fruits only.
10. Observe Mouna for two hours daily and during meals also.
11. Speak truth at any cost. Speak little, sweetly.
12. Reduce your wants. Lead a happy, contented life.
13. Never hurt the feelings of others. Be kind to all.
14. Think of the mistakes you have done (self-analysis).
15. Do not depend upon servants. Have self-reliance.
16. Think of God as soon as you get up and when you go to bed.
17. Have always a Japa Mala around your neck or in your pocket.
18. Have the motto: 'Simple living and high thinking'.
19. Serve the Sadhus, Sannyasins and poor and sick persons.
20. Keep a daily spiritual diary. Stick to your routine.

GLOSSARY

The *astral body* is the repository for all the countless mental seed-impressions or Samskaras with which it leaves the physical body at death and travels on and enters another physical body.

Asanajaya is a Yogic term which means one is able to sit absolutely motionless and steady for a period of three hours without a break.

Samyama is the Yogic term for the simultaneous execution of the three processes of concentration, meditation and trance meditation (Samadhi).